The Limits of American Power

For bereaved, grieving and displaced families

– American, Egyptian, Israeli, Jordanian, Lebanese,

Palestinian and Syrian –

in the hope that they will demand accommodation

and peace, not retribution.

The Limits of American Power

Prosecuting a Middle East Peace

Douglas Sturkey

Visiting Fellow
The Australian National University, Canberra

Edward Elgar
Cheltenham, UK • Northampton, MA, USA

Published by
Edward Elgar Publishing Limited
Glensanda House
Montpellier Parade
Cheltenham
Glos GL50 1UA
UK

Edward Elgar Publishing, Inc.
William Pratt House
9 Dewey Court
Northampton
Massachusetts 01060
USA

A catalogue record for this book
is available from the British Library

Library of Congress Cataloguing in Publication Data

Sturkey, Douglas, 1935-
The limits of American power : prosecuting a Middle East peace / Douglas Sturkey.
p. cm.
Includes bibliographical references and index.
1. United States–Foreign relations–1989- 2. United States–Foreign relations–Middle East. 3. Middle East–Foreign relations–United States. 4. United States–Foreign relations–Israel. 5. Israel–Foreign relations–United States. 6. Arab–Israeli conflict. 7. Mediation, International. I. Title.
JZ1480.A55S88 2007
327.73056–dc22 2007000723

ISBN 978 1 84720 243 7

Printed and bound in Great Britain by MPG Books Ltd, Bodmin, Cornwall

Contents

Tables

Maps

The maps, reproduced by kind permission of the Foundation for Middle East Peace (Jan de Jong, cartographer), have been adapted by Hannah Gason, Research School of Pacific and Asian Studies, The Australian National University.

Acknowledgements

Many individuals and organisations have assisted me and responded in various ways to my needs and questioning and I am appreciative of their help. Responsibility for the views expressed in this book rests entirely with me, however.

I am especially grateful to Professors Amin Saikal (Director) and Stuart Harris (Visiting Fellow) of the Australian National University's Centre for Arab and Islamic Studies (The Middle East & Central Asia). The two have guided me through the research for and preparation of this book.

I would not have found it possible to conclude my research in the United States and the Middle East without the assistance of various organisations. The Middle East Institute in Washington DC generously hosted me for several months. The Institute for Political and International Studies, Tehran, and The Emirates Center for Strategic Studies and Research, Abu Dhabi, were also gracious and helpful hosts for briefer periods. My thanks go to their directors, Ambassador Roscoe Suddarth, Dr Seyed Kazem Sajjadpour and Dr Jamal S. Al-Suwaidi respectively.

Some of my former colleagues in the Australian foreign service kindly extended hospitality and/or advice about people that I might seek to interview. Their contributions were invaluable; and I am indebted to them and to those members of their staff who assisted me with the vagaries of making appointments in the Middle East – not all of which materialised despite their ministrations. To them, and others outside that circle, I express my gratitude, particularly to Michael Barritt-Eyles, Ross Burns, Michael Corbitt, David Cox, Ronni and Jack Fisher, Matthew Gray, Merilyn and Ian Hywel-Jones, Paul Keal, Rhodanthe and John Lipsett and their family, Betty Lowrie, Matthew May, Sarah Phillips, Marianne and John Tileman and the late Aileen Keating.

ISRAEL AND ENVIRONS

Introduction

The power of the United States of America has been employed since 1991 in order to achieve a settlement of the Arab–Israel dispute. It has, however, been applied intermittently and with less determination since 2001. There are a number of reasons for analysing the search for a settlement of the dispute as a study of the exercise of American power. Underpinning them is the fact that, since the dissolution of the Union of Soviet Socialist Republics in 1991, the United States has enjoyed international predominance, militarily, economically, culturally and technologically. 'Never since Rome has one country so nearly dominated the world', as Kenneth Waltz put it.[1] The US use of its authority to influence global developments was, and continues to be, a matter of considerable interest and discussion. There were many people in America and elsewhere in the early 1990s who hoped that with the collapse of bipolarity following the dissolution of the Soviet Union, the singular position of the United States would dispose other states toward accommodation with it. The possibility of the United States employing force in defence of its vital interests was not disputed, but its military and economic pre-eminence was, and is, so overwhelming that resort to force was presumed generally to be an activity of last resort. This gave rise to an expectation that the United States had a capacity in most situations to influence outcomes in its own favour without having to employ force.

Pursuit of the US goal was launched formally at Madrid in 1991 by President George H.W. Bush (1989–93) and carried forward by his successors, President Bill Clinton (1993–2001) and President George W. Bush (2001–present). Because of the similarity of the names of the father and son, it is important that some means of readily distinguishing between the two be established from the outset. Historically, a numerical system has been employed to identify persons elected to the papacy and monarchs who have adopted or inherited the name of a predecessor. That practice is followed here.

Bush I launched the peace initiative in the context of the success of the US in forging a widespread coalition to prosecute the Gulf War over Kuwait. There was an expectation that the leadership shown then, and in arranging the Madrid conference, could introduce a benign era of international cooperation into the Middle East.

That background informs, in part, the reason for the choice of the Arab–Israel dispute as an example of the projection of American power, but it is not the sole determinant. The dispute lay at the intersection of a number of important United States interests and its resolution was a significant objective in its own right. Second, it provided an early example of the projection of US political power after becoming the world's sole superpower. It might be assumed that, in the absence of a powerful rival, the United States was well-placed to achieve its objective. Third, it engaged the attention of Bush I and Clinton, and to a lesser extent Bush II, over an extended period. Fourth, the fact that the United States has been unsuccessful in effecting its desired outcome raises questions about the limits of American power. Fifth, while care must be exercised about generalising from a particular study, the possibility exists that it might reveal some lessons about the projection of power that could be applicable in other circumstances.

In order to secure its goal, a great power must convince 'others' to acquiesce in its wishes. It does so through the projection of its power, and is able to employ a variety of measures to attain its objective. It calculates its 'cost' in terms of resources, energy and reputation. If it is unable to achieve its desired outcome, a possible weakness may have been exposed. It might be assumed, therefore, that a decision by a democratic state, like the United States, to pursue a particular goal is the product of rational debate and policy making within the government, although in practice ideological objectives may determine the direction of foreign policy. For their part, the targeted 'others' must weigh the 'cost' to themselves of resisting the US efforts. This suggests that in the exercise of statecraft, presidents of the United States would manipulate its unparalleled resources in order to bring home to targeted 'others' that accommodating the US objective would be at best beneficial to their long-term interests, or at least a less expensive option for them than resistance to it.

If the limits of America's power are ever to be established, other than in the context of the use or threat of use of force, it can only be through an exhaustive analysis of the efficacy with which the United States employed the instruments of statecraft at its disposal. An analysis of how they have been employed permits a methodological assessment of their efficacy and a rational appreciation of the effectiveness of the projection of American power. It encourages inquiry into a state's commitment to attaining its professed objectives, providing a sounder basis for assessment than impression, intuition or conventional wisdom. Assumptions that the US Middle East policy is 'all about oil', or 'the influence of the pro-Israel lobby', or some variant of the two such as 'America exerts sufficient authority over Israel to satisfy Arab oil producers that it is doing *something* to address Palestinian grievances', might be challenged or sharpened by a close analysis of the use made of the US instruments of power. Has the best choice of instrument been made; have the chosen instruments been used effectively; if not, why not? What does this inquiry say about the motivation of American decision makers? The US interventions in the process of negotiation between Israel[2] and Jordan, Lebanon, Syria and the Palestinians are analysed in these terms. A study of the efficacy of the instruments chosen to address particular issues as they arose, and the effectiveness with which they were employed, enables a *post hoc* evaluation to be made. The evaluation could be useful in identifying how power might be projected more effectively in other situations.

The negotiation between Israel and the other four parties, under the aegis of the United States, has been well documented, including by some of the principal actors. While it is unnecessary here to rehearse the history in detail, sufficient narrative will be presented to illustrate changing circumstances and to show how three American presidents responded by deploying different instruments of power at the disposal of the US in order to achieve its objective. Philosophic questions about the rights of the parties principal and the rectitude of their causes are relevant to this study only insofar as they influenced the presidents in determining which instrument of power might best lead to the attainment of a negotiated comprehensive settlement of the dispute.

The negotiation structure devised by Bush I proved capable of producing positive results. For a brief period, from 1993 to 1996, it seemed as though the United States initiative in bringing the concerned parties into negotiation to effect a comprehensive settlement would be successful. Bush I had been able to build upon an unprecedented, though not universal, measure of regional participation during the Gulf War of 1991, and a climate of superpower cooperation, to bring the parties together at Madrid. As his successor, Clinton presided over the signing of the Declaration of Principles on Interim Self-Government Arrangements at the White House in September 1993. The signal achievement of a compact between Israel and the Palestinians dressed a communal sore that had been festering since at least the Arab Revolt of the 1930s. Signature of the Declaration offered the prospect of a peaceful settlement with other states that were party to the Arab–Israel dispute, and commanded the support of the United Nations (UN). A peace treaty was concluded between Israel and Jordan, and several agreements were signed between Israel and the Palestinians subsequent to their Declaration. Israel and Syria came close to agreement, and the Middle East and North Africa economic summits that were conducted in close association with the peace talks demonstrated briefly that Israel could be accepted as a legitimate player within the region.

But the Madrid process might reasonably be determined to have failed by the expiry of Clinton's presidency in early 2001. For reasons that will be discussed, the negotiation with Syria had been terminated in March 2000, and the *al-Aqsa intifada* which began in September of that year was jeopardising any possibility of fruitful negotiation between Israel and the Palestinians. Nevertheless, Clinton's legacy continued into the early period of Bush II's presidency. Clinton advanced parameters in December 2000 that may yet provide a basis for discourse on the compass of issues between Israel and the Palestinians, including the future of Jerusalem and the question of Palestinian refugees, on which some progress has been made in informal discussion. His framework has fostered unofficial negotiation in Geneva between some Israelis and Palestinians, and produced a 'model' agreement. An alternative framework was proposed through a roadmap crafted by the United States, the European Union (EU), Russia and the United Nations, launched officially by Bush II in 2003. Its intent was the creation of a sovereign Palestinian state alongside Israel by 2005. Israel seems more focussed on applying unilateral measures to assure its security than in pursuing a durable resolution of its contest with the Palestinians over their rival claims to land.

What the United States sought to achieve was a comprehensive and peaceful settlement of the Arab–Israel dispute. That could make a contribution toward the realisation of Clinton's global vision of an enlargement of the community of democratic nations in the world, an objective that was broadly to be shared by Bush II. *Why* the United States should wish to attain a peace settlement relates to its principal interests in the Middle East – support for Israel; access to oil at 'affordable' prices; a desire to halt the proliferation of weapons of mass destruction (WMD) that could threaten Israel's security and wider American interests; and the prosecution of counterterrorism in a region that has proven a fertile source of international terrorism. Linkages exist among these elements, and the Palestinian cause provides an anti-Israel rallying point. While a resolution of the question of Palestine would not remove all the tensions among regional states and between them and the United States, it would defuse the most probable incendiary issue at the heart of the Arab–Israel dispute and could lead to the legitimisation of Israel as a regional player. The United States and Israel thus share a common interest in a resolution of the dispute. *How* the United States objective might be pursued is a matter of power projection. A definition of power, including its ideational attribute, is located within a discussion about the means by which an inter-state vision might be realised. That discussion then proceeds to identify the instruments by which power may be employed by a state in the context of its diplomatic intercourse, and how the efficacy of their application might be determined. These matters are addressed in Chapter 1. Chapter 2 establishes how the Administration of Bush I used US power to persuade parties with a long history of antipathy toward Israel to enter into negotiation with it in the search for a comprehensive settlement of the Arab–Israel dispute.

The application of United States power, principally by Clinton, to produce a settlement of the dispute, is the subject of Chapters 3 to 7. Arranged in roughly sequential order, Chapter 3 analyses the US attempt to influence the negotiation between Israel and the Palestinians from 1991 to 1996; Chapter 4 focusses on Israel and Jordan, and the multilateral negotiations conducted within the Madrid framework; Chapter 5 looks at Israel and Syria; and Chapter 6 addresses the negotiations between Israel and the Palestinians from 1996 to 2001. The task is then transferred to Bush II, whose ambivalent contribution up to early 2006 is analysed in Chapter 7. Chapter 8 presents a *post hoc* evaluation of the application of American power to attain its goal, based on an analysis of the efficacy of the instruments of power identified in Chapter 1. The Conclusion draws upon the evaluation and analyses its implications for the projection of American power in other situations. It articulates principles that might be generally applicable to a more effective projection of American power, and points to matters remaining to be resolved between Israel and the Palestinians to which it might be directed if a negotiated settlement of their conflict is to be achieved with United States involvement.

NOTES

1 Waltz (2002) p.350; Reus-Smit (2003) p.423.

2 A comprehensive settlement of the Arab–Israel dispute was hoped to include a resolution of the Israel–Palestinian conflict at its core. The usage of 'Israeli–Palestinian' in most literature suggests competition between two *peoples*. The asymmetrical nature of the contest between a sovereign state and a people is recognised here by the phrase 'Israel–Palestinian'.

1. Power and diplomacy: the United States's 'unipolar moment'

The dissolution of the Soviet Union was seen by President Bush I as heralding 'a new world order' in which inter-state cooperation, under United States leadership, would replace the competition and confrontation that had characterised the bipolar era. He, and his two immediate successors, believed that United States pre-eminence would be used to fashion a post-Cold War inter-state society in accordance with its own vision. A resolution of the Arab–Israel dispute would contribute toward the realisation of that vision by addressing United States national interests and demonstrating that a 'public good' could be attained through the projection of power by means other than force. But what is power; and how may it be employed in the conduct of diplomatic relations among states to achieve an objective? This chapter will address these fundamental questions. Structurally, the chapter will consider what were the global objectives of the United States, articulated by Presidents Bush I, Clinton and Bush II; why the United States should have sought to resolve the Arab–Israel dispute; and how it tried to do so through the projection of its power. Discussion of the last of these elements will lead to a proposition about how the efficacy of the application of power may be determined.

AMERICA'S GLOBAL VISION

For almost half a century the contradictory ideologies of the United States and the Soviet Union provided the foundation for confrontation between the two states and/or their so-called 'proxies'. Other states polarised around the two superpowers and their ideologies. This bipolar system-wide theoretical 'structure' of states[1] was fundamentally transformed by the dissolution of the Soviet Union, offering no alternative power pole around which opposition might coalesce, and the United States found itself in a position to exercise leadership in a unipolar world. The contribution that the United States might make to global stability during the 'unipolar moment' was seen as a 'public good' that the United States should provide in its own geopolitical interest.[2]

States understood that behind any US contribution lay the threat or use of military force.

At issue here is how the power of the United States was to be exercised during the unipolar moment. Bush I drew upon a disposition toward international cooperation to exercise United States leadership in the 1991 Gulf War. Clinton professed a desire to conduct United States diplomacy, as a good international citizen, in accordance with international legality.[3] Madeleine Albright, then Clinton's ambassador to the United Nations, described America's perception of its leadership as 'assertive multilateralism'.[4] Bush II also saw the United States contributing to geopolitical stability during the unipolar moment, declaring his intention to 'work with our allies and friends to be a force for good and a champion of freedom'.[5]

Under Clinton's presidency, the United States intended 'to remain engaged and to lead'[6] because it was compelled to do so by its interests and ideals; the United States would seek an enlargement of the community of democratic nations in the world; and while reserving the right to act unilaterally where its vital interests were at stake, the United States would continue to engage cooperatively with the international community. Bush II wished to project a 'distinctly American internationalism' that favours human freedom by promoting global economic progress and democracy, and that makes the globalised world a safer and better place by addressing threats to US and international security.[7] The United States would work in concert with close allies, great powers and international institutions to establish secure and stable conditions under which economic prosperity and democracy could be built.

Conceptually, the ideal of a negotiated and comprehensive settlement of the Arab–Israel dispute concluded with United States leadership, were it to be achieved, would address significant national American interests, would be a powerful demonstration of the ability of United States hegemony to produce a 'public good', and would provide a tremendous boost to the US's image. As Robert Jervis has observed, images are important in foreign policy and success can bring rewards by influencing the psychological environments and policies of other decision makers.[8]

Despite their desire to work toward an enlargement of the community of democratic states, neither Clinton nor Bush II could really have believed that a settlement of the dispute would promote democracy in the Arab Middle East. Clinton had advocated democratisation as an issue during his 1992 electoral campaign, but had no grand design for its advancement.[9] Bush II's effort to import democracy into Iraq and elsewhere has encountered resistance. Like a number of their predecessors, Clinton and Bush II have practised what Tony Smith has called 'selective liberal democratic internationalism': an expansion of democracy abroad was held to be in the US's security interest, but America's power to promote such reforms was too limited to be used imprudently.[10]

While the United States prosecution of a comprehensive settlement of the Arab–Israel dispute would not contribute directly to a realisation of the global visions of the three presidents, the changed inter-state structure from 1991 offered a tempting opportunity for them to display what they believed would be a benign interpretation of United States hegemony.

A BALANCE OF US INTERESTS IN THE MIDDLE EAST

The United States has significant national interests in the Middle East that a settlement of the Arab–Israel dispute could protect. Moreover, its international image would be enhanced if a peaceful resolution of the dispute could be effected through a skilful projection of United States power. This section will identify those national interests and establish why the United States should have believed that a convincing case existed for its promotion of a peaceful settlement of the Arab–Israel dispute. This is a necessary precursor to discussion in the final section about power in international relations and how it might be employed to effect a desired outcome.

American support for Israel

Contemporary United States support for Israel is anchored in America's Jewish and fundamentalist Christian populations, but includes many others for whom recall of the holocaust inspires a need for atonement, Israel's struggle for survival has sparked admiration, and shared democratic values provide a sense of common outlook. Zionism has appeal to American Christian fundamentalists as well as to America's Jewish community. 'Christian Zionists' see the State of Israel as a fulfilment of Biblical prophesies, as conferring upon this largely secular state a divine right to the land called Israel, and as paving the way for the second coming of Jesus the Messiah.[11] They entered into a coalition with Israeli lobbyists in 1978, and the National Unity Coalition for Israel became the lobbying arm of Christian Zionism with contacts in the Congress and neoconservative think-tanks in Washington.[12] The Jewish vote generally favours the Democrats, core support for the Democrats running at about 55 to 60 per cent against about 10 per cent for the Republicans. The more numerous Christian fundamentalists tend to support the Republicans.[13]

The Jewish community constitutes only 2.5 per cent of the American population, but they vote in greater numbers than other Americans: they are nearly twice as likely to vote as non-Jews.[14] They are far more likely to fund their candidates and political causes, and actively to volunteer their time. Demographically, 81 per cent of all American Jews live in the nine states that cast 202 of the 535 votes (37 per cent) in the Electoral College to choose the President of the United States.[15]

Within the Jewish community there is a schematic division of labour, although in practice there may well be some blurring at the edges. The Conference of Presidents of Major American Jewish Organisations seeks to forge a consensus on Israel from among the diverse views of organised American Jewry, which the American Israel Public Affairs Committee (AIPAC) then translates into political clout in Washington. AIPAC has few registered lobbyists among its staff. Its influence lies in an ability to mobilise volunteers at every level of the electoral process. They quiz candidates about their views on Israel and circulate them.[16] A further source of AIPAC's influence lies in its provision of well-presented research material to members of the Congress. The Washington Institute for Near East Policy has sought to bring an intellectual dimension to the debate in America on the Middle East. The United Jewish Appeal, 'the central engine driving all the other parts of the machine called the organised American Jewish community', raises funds for Israel.[17] Its contributions to the Jewish Agency for Israel, the largest social service provider in that country, form the budgetary core of the Agency.[18]

The Arab American community is very small, officially estimated at 3.5 million people of Arab descent, and is dispersed over all 50 states.[19] They claim descent principally from Lebanon (39 per cent). There are smaller contingents from Syria, Egypt and Palestine. Twenty-four per cent identify their religion as Islam, while 63 per cent are members of various Christian denominations.[20]

An Arab American Institute, committed to the civic and political empowerment of Americans of Arab descent, was founded in 1985. It promotes immigrant rights, and lobbies for enhanced American cultural, educational, diplomatic, and economic and security ties with Arab countries. It supports a viable Palestinian state, the integrity of Lebanon, US assistance to advance economic and political development in the Middle East, and a balanced American role in promoting regional peace and prosperity. The Institute circulates scorecards among its membership indicating how members of the Congress have voted on issues of importance to them.[21] A study undertaken by the Institute in relation to the 2000 presidential election[22] shows that about 40 per cent of Arab Americans generally support the Democratic Party and 38 per cent the Republican Party. There exists a high percentage of swinging voters within the community. Clinton was the preferred presidential choice in 1996, attracting 54.5 per cent of Arab American votes, but the majority cast their votes for Bush II in 2000. Almost half of those Democratic Party supporters who abandoned the party's presidential candidate did so because of the inclusion of a Jewish senator, Joseph Lieberman, on the party's ticket as its nominee for the position of Vice President.[23]

The US total official aid package to Israel from 1949 to 2004 amounted to $93.5 billion,[24] some 28 per cent of which was disbursed during the eight years of Clinton's presidency. To this total amount must be added the voluntary contributions and benefactions to Israel from private sources in the United States. The $2.4 billion per annum US appropriation for defence assistance sustains Israel's qualitative edge over the military capabilities of all of its neighbours. Israel is permitted, under an exceptional arrangement, to spend just over 26 per cent of its military grant within Israel whereas the general practice is that all US foreign military financing is spent in the United States.[25] The access that the American defence production industry enjoys under this scheme broadens the compass of the pro-Israel lobby to include the elected representatives of the states and congressional districts in which Israeli defence contracts are awarded.

An American Administration's susceptibility to the pro-Israel lobby is evident. On four occasions Administrations have informed the Congress that Israel 'may have violated' the provisions of the Arms Export Control Act and the Mutual Defense Assistance Agreement. The Congressional Research Service has recorded that the United States was investigating whether Israel misused US military equipment when Apache and Cobra helicopters were employed to kill Palestinians suspected of insurgency and when F-16 aircraft attacked Palestinian facilities.[26] Also, the State Department concluded in 1992 that Israel had transferred United States arms technology to other states or entities without American permission.[27] Such investigations have rarely resulted in United States condemnation of Israel.

Until an evolution in Arab thinking toward acknowledgement of Israel's existence began in 1981–82, the position of the United States was in fundamental opposition to that of the Palestinians and their Arab supporters. Israel's occupation of territory previously settled by, and still claimed by Palestinians, much of it acquired by conquest in the wars of 1948–49, 1967 and 1973, and denial of Palestinian self-determination, form the core of Palestinian grievances. The Arabs maintain that Israel's actions had been made possible because of the US's support – moral, financial and military. In their view it would be unlikely that Israel would move to accommodate the Palestinians unless or until required to do so by the United States; and pan-Arab orthodoxy precluded resolution of their own differences with Israel before then. For an accommodation to be reached there had to be a change in the US's Middle East policy. The Arab states were determined to impress upon the United States the need to pressure Israel. They had tried unsuccessfully to force the United States and other oil importers to urge the return of Israeli occupied territories to the Palestinians through a reduction in Middle East oil supply in the aftermath of the June 1967 and October 1973 wars. The United States was conscious of the possible employment by Iraq of weapons of mass destruction (WMD), especially chemical weaponry, against its forces in the 1991 Gulf War, and United States installations and agents have been the victims of terrorism in the Middle East by actors keen to impress the Palestinians' cause upon Americans. These actual and potential 'levers' – oil, WMD and terrorism – remain in the hands of Arab and Islamic states.

United States oil demand

A national interest of the United States has been to assure the supply of crude oil from the Middle East at 'affordable' prices. Because of the US's global economic connections, that interest has both domestic and international ramifications. Clinton intervened in 2000 to urge an increase in supply from the Organization of the Petroleum Exporting Countries (OPEC) when prices rose above the $20 to $25 per barrel band that he believed reasonable, but oil prices have exceeded three times that bracket during Bush II's presidency and may rise further.

The US's dependence on petroleum imports could grow to 62 per cent of its requirement by 2020.[28] Despite a policy of diversification of supply following the Arab producers' employment of the 'oil weapon' in 1973–74, access to Middle Eastern oil will become of increasing importance to the United States in the longer term. This is because the countries of the Middle East possess 65.3 per cent of the world's proven oil reserves[29] and an average reserve-to-production ratio that is twice that of the world average. Middle Eastern oil also enjoys a comparative advantage with the lowest production costs in the world.

Unless the world is able to hasten the development of other sources of relatively cheap energy, including petroleum, the United States will not be able in the longer term to insulate itself from the effects of the growing dependence of world consumers on Middle East oil. That oil will come from a diminishing number of Gulf suppliers. Dependence on Middle East oil supply inevitably links the United States to countries that champion the cause of the Palestinians. They have declared their preparedness to accept Israel as a legitimate regional neighbour provided Israel accommodates Palestinian demands for a viable sovereign state. They will continue to importune the United States if it does not press Israel for movement on the Palestinian issue.

Non-proliferation of WMD and delivery systems

The United States has been disturbed about the potential for proliferation of WMD, including within the Middle East, and the possibility that terrorists might acquire such weaponry to target American interests. Chemical agents were used by Iraq against Iran, and SCUD missiles were launched by Iraq against Israel. There was a fear that Iraq might use chemical weapons against

American troops in the 1991 Gulf War, and that Iraq might develop a missile system capable of delivering a chemical warhead. After the war, Clinton worked within the UN Security Council to restrain Iraq's development and use of WMD and associated delivery systems. In 1994 Clinton found that the proliferation of nuclear, biological and chemical weapons, and of the means of delivering them, constituted an unusual and extraordinary threat to the national security, foreign policy and economy of the United States. He ordered that the United States lead and seek multilaterally coordinated efforts with other countries to control the proliferation of WMD and the means of delivering them. He ordered also that national export controls be applied to items likely to contribute to the manufacture of such weaponry and delivery systems.[30]

Predating the Clinton presidency, but continued under his Administration, has been the promotion of normative regimes through the adoption of international instruments embracing nuclear, chemical and biological weaponry and associated missile delivery systems. The United States has also sought to bring associated missile development under a Missile Technology Control Regime (MTCR).[31] The regime has some 30 members, including most states that possess the necessary technological base for missile production.

Despite its pursuit of global non-proliferation regimes, the United States was either unsuccessful in persuading or unwilling to persuade Israel to become a party to the Nuclear Non-proliferation Treaty (NPT). Israel has never acknowledged that it is a nuclear-weapon state. The United States protested Israeli nuclear activity in 1963, but was unable to secure more than a promise that it would not be the first state in the Middle East to test a nuclear device. Israel signed the Comprehensive Test Ban Treaty (CTBT) in 1996.

UN Security Council sanctions adopted after the 1991 Gulf War assisted materially in hobbling Iraqi ambitions for some years, but by 1998 Saddam Hussain's regime was no longer cooperating with the Special Commission (UNSCOM) set up by the UN Security Council to disarm his country, and differences had emerged among the Council's permanent members about its *modus operandi* and a continuing need for UNSCOM. The Commission was replaced in 1999 by another that the Security Council hoped would be more acceptable to the Iraqis.[32] That agency, too, would be unable to complete its work before the United States, at the instigation of Bush II, led a 'coalition of the willing' into Iraq in 2003, ostensibly to destroy Iraq's WMD capability. Bush II's primary objective, however, was to effect a change of regime in Iraq.

Clinton was also concerned about Iran's ability to secure nuclear and missile development material and/or assistance and tried to restrain suppliers. The changes that were secured did not halt Iranian activity. Since Bush II's election to the presidency, Iran has declared its determination to proceed with the enrichment of uranium, ostensibly for electricity generation. Recognising the possibility that enriched uranium could be used for military purposes, the UN Security Council has called for a halt to the process.[33] In the missile field, and despite the MTCR and United States intervention, Iran has been able to develop a capability, testing a missile that brings Israel within range, and an underwater one that could jeopardise oil cargoes transiting the Strait of Hormuz. These developments are worrying to Bush II because of their potential for employment against the national and international interests of the United States.

Terrorism and insurgency

A distinction may be drawn between an insurgent's active rebellion against state authority and a terrorist's attempt to challenge state authority by provoking terror among its citizenry. The form and severity of a state's response to insurgency may, however, inspire rebels to undertake terrorist acts, blurring the line between these two forms of violent political expression and, if the state's response is deemed excessive, lead to allegations of 'state terrorism'.

Terrorist activity has frequently been employed in relation to the Arab–Israel dispute. Palestinian extremists, Lebanese Hezbollah and other groups have been engaged in attacks on Israelis and Americans. Terrorists have been able to demonstrate that, for all its power and resources, the United States has been unable effectively to protect its properties at home and abroad and the lives of its citizens, including those of its official agents. Both Lebanese and Palestinian extremists have received support from Iran since the Islamic revolution of 1979,[34] and Syria is an important point on the supply route to Lebanon. The umbrella Palestine Liberation Organization (PLO) was founded by Arab states in 1964 to represent the Palestinians. Yasser Arafat's Fatah movement embarked on armed struggle in 1965, and took over the PLO in 1969. Both the United States and Israel proscribed official dealings with the PLO until 1993.

In the period from the beginning of the so-called *al-Aqsa intifada* in late September 2000 to May 2006 some 3500 Palestinians were killed by Israelis and 1000 Israelis by Palestinians.[35] These figures contrast markedly with that of the 282 Israelis killed by the PLO in the 13 years from 1968 to 1981.[36] Disturbing though these data are, they do not rate as highly in terms of either the number of attacks or the number of casualties as those recorded in Asia,[37] with the leading instigators being the Tamil Tigers in Sri Lanka.

There is a discernible trend: contemporary terrorism is carried out primarily by loosely-organised, self- or mutually-financed networks with cross-national links. Religion is rarely the root cause of suicide attacks, although it assists in broadening the appeal of the organising agency and in recruitment.[38] Debate is entertained about the efficacy of terrorism in achieving political ends. On the eve of the convening of the Madrid conference in 1991, a view was expressed in relation to the Arab–Israel dispute that as a bargaining weapon terrorism was simply not up to the job.[39] The negotiation process that began at that conference was to prove the author wrong. At its outset both Israel and the United States held that there should be no Palestinian state. By late 2000, Clinton was talking of Palestinian sovereignty, and within a couple of years both the United States and Israel were committed to the realisation of an independent Palestine. This can be attributed principally to the greater understanding of the Palestinian cause gained during the course of the negotiation. Insurgency, which persisted throughout the negotiation process, served to reinforce to Clinton and Bush II the depth of the Palestinians' sense of humiliation and grievance, and to bring them to acknowledge that Israel could never hope to live in an environment free from violence while the Palestinians were a subjugated people.

Palestinian independence could not guarantee Israel's immunity from attack, but for so long as the Palestinians remained subject to Israel, they would command the support of others: Iran rejected the Oslo peace process and has provided material assistance to activist Palestinian elements; Syria provides a sanctuary; and Al-Qaeda lists the Palestinian cause among its anti-Western grievances. The conquest of terrorism became a major foreign policy objective of Bush II following the attacks by Middle Eastern terrorists on buildings in New York and Washington DC in 2001.

Weighing the balance

Linkages exist among the three issues. Iran's oil revenues enable it to undertake nuclear development, to develop missile technology, and to provide support in differing measure to Lebanese and Palestinian insurgents. Oil wealth enabled Iraq to mount military campaigns against Iran and Kuwait, to target Iran with WMD, and to attack Israel by missile. The Gulf oil producers have been able to restrict production for political purposes, causing panic within industrialised countries and distress to Third World importers. Uncertainty about supply, especially in relation to the Iran–Iraq War, the 1991 Gulf War and disturbances within Iraq post-2003, have been reflected in volatile oil prices. American Administrations have had to address these issues. Different, even apparently contradictory policies have been applied. The United States provided intelligence assistance and materiel supplies to Iraq during the Iran–Iraq War, but under changed circumstances led campaigns against Iraq in 1991 and 2003. It has encouraged Saudi Arabia to exercise its considerable influence among oil producers to assure supply and to keep prices at an 'affordable' level despite Saudis forming the largest contingent in the band of terrorists that attacked the US in 2001.

A capability by foreign actors to deploy these instruments in ways detrimental to America's perceived national interests, including in some cases an ability to jeopardise Israel's security, does not translate into a continuing commitment to do so. The ability of Arab oil producers to direct their 'weapon' specifically against the United States is tempered by the nature of the international oil market and their own developmental requirement to accommodate their burgeoning populations. Although Iraq had demonstrated an ability to deploy chemical weapons and to strike into Israel, it is no longer in a position to do so. Iran is clearly aware of United States resolve in relation to non-proliferation, but is resisting international pressure to conform to normative expectations. Hitherto, the three 'levers' have rested in differing hands and have not been used in concert. While collusion has not been achieved in the past among those capable of exercising the instruments, the situation is now different. Iran seems capable of manipulating all three independently of other actors, and has shown a determination to resist United States hegemonic intentions.

The United States had, over many years, tried to encourage regional states to reconcile themselves to Israel's existence. It was clear to Bush I that if Israel's security were to be assured, its place within a Middle Eastern community would need to be legitimised and that this could only be achieved through a process of negotiation with its neighbours. If Arab and Islamic states were to be enticed into negotiation, they would need to be confident that the negotiation sought to resolve the conflicting claims of Israelis and Palestinians to territory under terms satisfactory to both parties. Because of its concern for Israel's security, the United States had a particular interest in encouraging a negotiation that addressed this matter. Resolution of that issue would not resolve all the tensions among regional states, or between them and the United States, but it would defuse the most probable incendiary issue at the heart of the Arab–Israel dispute and could lead to Israel's acceptance as a regional player.

The alliances forged by the United States within the compass of the United Nations to condemn Iraq's invasion of Kuwait in 1990 gave expression to American leadership in a unipolar world. It was not achieved without mutual obligation: the president implicitly acknowledged the relevance of the Arab–Israel dispute when he told Syria's President Hafez al-Assad in November 1990 that he would address the wider issues of the Middle East after the Iraq–Kuwait crisis had been resolved.[40] Bush I's decision to launch a United States-led initiative in search of a comprehensive settlement of the Arab–Israel dispute, and Clinton's persistence in sustaining it, go deeper than being seen to honour a commitment. They suggest a genuine interest in advancing the United States claim to global leadership. By taking advantage of the prevailing generally positive international attitude toward the United States, Bush I hoped the United States could demonstrate that its power could be employed in the production of a 'public good'. A resolution of the Arab–Israel dispute – if it could be achieved – could be expected to bring a greater measure of stability to the region than had existed for half a century. The circumstances for achieving this result seemed propitious in 1991, and the argument for United States intervention compelling.

POWER

Having established why the United States sought a resolution of the Arab–Israel dispute, consideration is now given to how that goal might be achieved. Power is the means by which a state influences 'others' in order to secure its objectives. It may be projected – short of force – through political, economic or cultural means, and through ideas. The identification of United States foreign policy objectives and the conduct of its international relations is a constitutional responsibility of the president. There is a range of instruments that the president may employ to secure United States goals. The choice of instrument and the method in which it is used in relation to the Arab–Israel dispute, and other issues, is a function of statecraft. How a state manages its interaction with other states is the matter of diplomacy. The following passages discuss first the concept of power, then the means of its application in the context of a state's diplomatic relations.

Power is the capacity for producing an event.[41] It is neither the event itself, nor a resource,[42] because it consists of psychological factors as well as situational ones.[43] It is, as Hans Morgenthau put it, about 'man's control over the minds and actions of other men'.[44] Power and influence are frequently conflated. While the capacity to produce an event may inhere in both, the two concepts are distinct. 'Influence' is defined by Peter Morriss 'as *affecting* (in a certain way), whilst "power" is usually defined as the ability to *effect*'.[45] But his interpretation of influence dismisses the pervasive effect of widely held attitudes generated by normative expectations, or the demonstration effect of the achievements of others. Either of these forces could be current and direct contemporary behaviour in certain directions. The line between influencing an 'other' in a way conducive to achieving a desired outcome, and effecting that outcome may be a fine one in some circumstances. The latter suggests both determination and currency, whereas the former is insidious and less insistent.

Joseph Nye's concept of 'soft power' is essentially influential. It involves 'getting others to want what you want ... It co-opts people rather than coerces them.'[46] The reason America's 'soft power' may be attractive to others is that it is underpinned by the US's material, intellectual or cultural attributes: a trenchant critic of United States policies may nevertheless wish to live or study there.[47]

Whether expressed directly to secure an objective, inferentially through its 'soft' form, or through some regime in which 'others' subscribe to the agenda of the dominant actor, power can only be manifest in relation to an 'other'. As such, it is often viewed as a means of attaining a goal, and therefore essentially instrumental. The common conception of power treats it as a causal element in which the power wielder affects the behaviour, attitudes, beliefs or propensity to act of another actor.[48] Such a simple cause/effect dichotomy suggests that the target state acts in accordance with the wishes of the wielder of power because it bears the burden of 'cost'. Kenneth Waltz has rejected so bald an assumption in favour of one implying some measure of 'cost sharing': 'an agent is powerful to the extent that he affects others more than they affect him'.[49] He has also warned that the outcome of the use of power is necessarily uncertain and that powerful agents fail to impress their wills on others in just the way they intend to.[50]

Whichever means a state employs in pursuit of its objective, the objective may be expressed either as the desired ultimate outcome, or an intermediate one. Sometimes a state may find it useful to identify its goal with precision; at other times to express it more broadly. A state may need to co-opt the assistance of other states in pursuit of its objective, in which case it may judge that prospective partners would be more amenable to supporting a broadly-framed objective than to pursuing a narrowly-defined goal patently designed to serve the interest of the power-wielding state.

DIPLOMACY

Diplomacy is the process of dialogue between states. It is the process of dialogue and negotiation by which states conduct their relations and pursue their purposes by means short of war, while foreign policy is the substance of a state's relations with 'others' and the purposes it hopes to achieve by those relations.[51] Put succinctly, foreign policy embraces the identification of objectives, while diplomacy addresses the strategies pursued for their attainment. The means by which a state employs the instruments at its disposal is the matter of statecraft. Craig and George have pointed out that statecraft incorporates force and threat of force as a necessary instrument of diplomacy.[52] While force was never threatened in the search for a settlement of the Arab–Israel dispute, Arab states were aware of America's ability to project military power into the Middle East and it remained a background condition of the negotiation. United States intervention in Iraq in 2003 provided confirmation, if any were needed.

The instruments of diplomacy that may be employed by a state in the exercise of its power are persuasion, financial inducements, sanctions and coercion. It might be expected that in employing any of these instruments, a state would conform to general expectations of normative behaviour. Positive sanctions offer actual or promised rewards, while negative sanctions employ actual or threatened punishments and are usually applied with coercive intent. Each of these measures may be employed discretely or in concert. Whichever instrument or combination is used, the aim is to achieve acceptance of, or support for, a particular objective of the wielding state.

Persuasion

The purpose of persuasion is to appeal to the target state's understanding of its national interest, if necessary by encouraging it to change its perception of its own national interest. The state seeking to engineer a decision in its own interest will suggest that the target state shares with it a common or mutual national interest; there could be advantage to both in concurring in a certain matter. Persuasion may be distinguished from bargaining. The former involves efforts to get the target state to understand why the power wielder's demands are so important to it. Bargaining is characterised by concessions, conditional offers, threats and inducements.

Formal communication between states may be supplemented through public information programmes and public diplomacy. The purpose of public information is to inform others in the expectation that a well-informed public in a target state will understand the goals of the projecting state and seek some accommodation with them. It is an appeal to logic. Public diplomacy introduces a more evident intent to influence others.[53] It deals primarily with non-governmental individuals and organisations, but does not exclude dealings with governments. The differing views of individuals, organisations and governments may be projected by these means. It is an avenue for the projection of so-called 'soft power' in that it seeks 'to entice and attract. And attraction often leads to acquiescence or imitation.'[54]

Positive sanctions

Positive sanctions may be offered either as an inducement to secure an objective or as a reward for a service rendered. They may be made either on a state-to-state basis, or by international organisations drawing upon resources allocated for such purposes principally from the contributions of member states. Both bilateral and multilateral aid may take the form of finance or credits, or technical assistance, or be in kind. How financial inducements may be broken down into grants or loans or assistance for various purposes offers scope for the application of power over the target state. Constitutionally, legislators in democracies need to be satisfied that allocations of taxpayers' funds are for justifiable purposes, and a state hoping to attract aid must demonstrate that it is prepared to meet their expectations. In practice few such analyses are attempted, but the threat of exposure remains.

A financial inducement to a recalcitrant or wavering state to accord with a power wielder's objectives may need to be matched by a reward to a well-disposed one for its continuing friendship or support. The converse is also true. The United States decided that it could not afford to continue to sustain Israel's qualitative military edge in 1990 without also providing some military assistance to Saudi Arabia.[55] Failure to do so in either case could impair what was regarded as a beneficial relationship.

Disbursements to member states from the pooled contributions of members are made by some international organisations. The United States is the major state contributor to the International Monetary Fund (IMF) and the World Bank. Its holding of 25 per cent of the votes on their governing bodies outweighs the voting power of other individual state contributors and places the United States in an exceptional position to guide the governors' decisions in favour of its preferred outcomes, but its dominance is not absolute.

Negative sanctions

Negative sanctions are designed to increase the 'costs' to a target state of continuation of certain policies and, in so doing, to effect a change in its policies.[56] They have the effect of increasing tension between the two parties and may increase the risk of war, which is itself a form of 'cost'. Like other costs, they may be used to add credibility to a signal.[57]

Economic sanctions are the most common form of negative sanctions. They include a denial, or reduction, in bilateral aid; denial of access to capital markets; a freezing of the bank accounts of institutions and citizens of the target country; trade boycotts, including denial of or tariffs on the entry of goods from the target country, restrictions on exports and technology (usually of sophisticated items), and a refusal to supply military materiel to the target country; a proscription on investment in the target country; and a refusal to entertain the conclusion of a free trade agreement with the target country. Production or export subsidies to producers of goods in competition with producers in the target state are other forms of economic sanctions. Many of these tools may involve 'costs' to the state wielding power and will involve implicit, if not explicit, cost–benefit judgements by it before their application.

Negative sanctions may address symbols important to the target state, their impact being dependent upon the significance attached to its image by the target state. Examples could be the denial of a vote for election to the governing body of an international institution, the recall of an ambassador for 'consultations', or the boycott of a national sporting team. Options that would cut to the quick of the relationship between the two parties would be a decision to downgrade or sever diplomatic relations, or to suspend a state's participation in some international body, or to extend material support to citizens of the target state who are known to be antipathetic to their government.

It is often claimed that sanctions do not work. One of the most prescriptive sets of sanctions ever to have been applied to a country was that imposed upon Iraq in 1991 at the conclusion of the Gulf War under UN Security Council Resolution 687. The resolution called for the dismantling of Iraq's WMD and long-range missiles and the means to produce them, and it established machinery to effect and verify this; it also restricted the volume of oil permitted to be exported to that necessary to cover the cost of Iraq's food import needs. The outcome was mixed, not least because the United States kept moving the goal posts in pursuit of securing a change of regime in Iraq. Iraq responded to the UN prescriptions, waging what Anthony Cordesman has called a 'war of sanctions', through which it frustrated the efforts of UN inspection bodies to carry out their mandate; provoked a division among the five permanent members of the Security Council; exploited the sympathy of the Arab world; and used its oil wealth (some of which was generated through sanctions busting means such as smuggling) to win foreign support.[58] The food-for-oil arrangement could not guarantee that food reached Iraq's most needy because its distribution remained largely in the hands of the Iraqi regime. An extensive survey of Iraq after the United States-led intervention of 2003 suggested that, while UN inspections had inhibited the development of WMD, Iraq retained a capability to develop missiles with a range of up to 1000 km, was attempting to obtain ballistic missile technology from North Korea,[59] and retained a capacity to make the liquid fuel to power the SCUD missiles banned under the Security Council resolution.[60]

Coercion

Where force is threatened it must be credible, foreshadowing greater diversion of resources from, and destruction of, the target state than of the threatening state. Coercion may be applied multilaterally under UN collective security provisions, or unilaterally. The United States has used both of these channels. Since the attacks on the United States in 2001, the US has led an attack on Iraq under a proclaimed policy of pre-emptive self-defence. Its preparedness to exercise its military superiority under such terms has sent a warning of United States disposition to act unilaterally in accordance with its own perception of its national interests.

International norms

There is a general expectation that in exercising the instruments described above a state will conform to normative behaviour. The place of international norms[61] in influencing state behaviour is a complex one. The strength of a norm, and thus the strength of its influence in international relations, depends on two properties: on its commonality (how many actors of a social system share a value-based expectation of behaviour), and on its specificity (how precisely a norm distinguishes appropriate from inappropriate behaviour).[62] The situation is complicated by the fact that not all international norms are codified in international law,[63] or where codified, upheld.

Normative expectations do not operate mechanically in regulating conduct in international relations: 'they are always subject to contestation, interpretation, and reinterpretation. But the norms and rules themselves set the terms of the interpretive discourse.'[64] Monitoring compliance is frequently entrusted to international organisations within the area of their jurisdiction. Egregious behaviour may also be brought to the attention of the world community by other actors, including non-state ones.

The United States has played a formative role in the creation of many global institutions, including the United Nations and its Specialised Agencies. The weight of its commitment, even during the decades of bipolarity, was such that it is difficult to envisage the inauguration of the world's most significant international organisations in the absence of its support.[65] The importance of the institutions to the global community ensured their survival when United States financial contributions came later to be withheld or tardily delivered. Among the organs conceived with United States participation is the UN Security Council. Its responsibility for peace and security, and endowment with distinctive power, accords it a singular place among international institutions. It has been used by the United States both to prescribe acceptable international behaviour and to frustrate the adoption of measures where they depart from United States interests.

In short, while states that wish to receive the benefits of some normative regimes must accept restraint on their domestic or international behaviour, this is not invariably realised, and states – especially great powers – may choose to ignore peer pressure where they believe that an overriding interest would be compromised by observance of some normative requirement.

LEGITIMACY OF US INTERVENTION

In the light of this discussion of power and the means of its application by a state, this section will address briefly the extent to which the actions of

United States presidents and their advisers in seeking to effect a settlement of the Middle East dispute may be said to have exercised the power of the United States.

Bush I, Clinton and Bush II acted in their search for a settlement of the Arab–Israel dispute in accordance with the constitutional responsibility of the President of the United States for the conduct of America's foreign policy. In a pluralist democratic society there will be citizens who do not share the president's view. Within the Congress, contrary views may find expression in the passage of prescriptive legislation, the adoption of resolutions, or in criticism expressed in congressional committees and debate. Within the government some agencies may acquire and seek to advance agendas of their own, vying for influence within the Administration. 'Turf warfare' within bureaucracies, particularly competition among agencies to gain an ascendant position of influence, is an established phenomenon. Non-governmental organisations also struggle to gain influence among the Administration's decision makers. The support of legislators may be enlisted by agencies and non-governmental organisations for their cause. These less-than-tidy manoeuvrings are inherent in America's democratic processes and challenge the president when engaged in the development of a policy capable of commanding broad public support. He may adjust his policy to accommodate divergent opinion where he deems it in the interest of his government to do so. But even where domestic dissent is evident, only the president has the constitutional authority to direct the course of the country's foreign policy. He may entrust the day-to-day conduct of affairs to officials, notably the secretary for state. When a choice is made among the instruments to be applied to effect a possible settlement of the Middle East dispute, it is by the president – or made in his name with his approval by his designated agents – acting for the state. Many of the contributions of American Administrations that are considered in this study are attributed to the president rather than to his agents because of his overall responsibility for them.

EFFICACY OF POWER

The relational nature of power has been discussed, as have the instruments of diplomacy that may be employed at the command of a state to secure a goal. The response, or responses, of the targeted state(s) go to the nub of the definition of power, namely the capacity of the wielding state to effect a desired outcome.[66]

A predisposition to exercise power involves choosing among alternative courses of action, and an examination of their probable costs and benefits. The comparison is between the costs and benefits of the power wielder's different policy options, not between costs to the wielder and to the target state. Although the ultimate aim of the power-wielding state is to increase the cost to the target state, an increase may not be achievable without also some increase in cost to the wielder. It is impossible, however, for decision makers to make precise comparisons. At best, their choice involves the making of intelligent guesses. At the heart of decisions about the projection of power are questions about the usual effects of various techniques, and counterfactual ones about likely outcomes were power not to be projected. The latter may not amount to much more than an educated guess, but such factors have to be taken into account by decision makers.

The objective of a comprehensive and peaceful settlement of the Arab–Israel dispute encompasses many subsidiary issues. The attainment of the overall objective must address, and resolve in some form acceptable to the parties principal, fundamental questions relating to territory, security and sovereignty. A resolution of these issues is dependent upon solutions being found to many other critical ones: the future of Israeli settlements in occupied territory; the status of Jerusalem; the return of Palestinian refugees to some place of permanent resettlement and possible compensatory payments to them; the access of Palestinian labour to employment in Israel; and access to water by the riparian states of the Jordan valley and inhabitants of the West Bank. Effecting satisfactory outcomes for each requires the employment in varying degrees of different instruments or mix of instruments and challenges American statecraft. This study will analyse how effectively the diplomatic instruments and resources at the disposal of the United States were used to produce an outcome of all these issues satisfactory to Israel and its neighbours.

An assessment of the efficacy of state power must ask whether modified behaviour by the target state can be ascribed to the wielder's power. Rosenau believes that it can,[67] although the task is not likely to be easy. Some commentators argue that attainment of objectives is always a matter of degree.[68] The outcome may not be precisely that sought by decision makers, and an overall assessment may need to conclude that near enough may be good enough. Modification of behaviour due to the application of positive or negative sanctions may be relatively easy to assess. Less readily identified are the target state's responses to intellectual or psychological influences. Depending upon the circumstances, it may be possible to determine with reasonable precision that the target has been persuaded to modify its behaviour in response to the wielder's intellectual argument, but the extent to which a state or actor may be influenced by the wielder's 'soft power' would be virtually indistinguishable. Nor need it necessarily be immediately apparent that modified behaviour by the target, however encouraged, represents a permanent change of direction, for the target could be seeking some tactical advantage through what it intended to be a temporary accommodation. Some subjectivity cannot be avoided in assessing the target's response, but the objectives of the target may become more apparent with the passage of time. So too, may the strength of the wielder's commitment to the objective, for the more protracted the process, the more likely it is that other issues will arise to compete for the attention of the power wielder's decision makers.

An imprecise result does not mean that the task of analysing the efficacy of United States power should be set aside. The methodology of *post hoc* evaluation is widely practised with the particular intent of identifying inefficiencies. It involves recognition of imperfect choices among available options, and limitations on the part of the instruments used. The diplomatic instruments discussed in this chapter offer a basis for critical analysis that should facilitate identification, with some certitude, of areas of strength and weakness in American diplomacy in relation to the Arab–Israel dispute. While some assumptions may need to be declared where facts have not been stated, employment of these analytical tools offers scope for a disciplined assessment. The *post hoc* evaluative technique to be followed in this study also offers a prospect of remediation for the United States in other diplomatic applications.

CONCLUSION

The President of the United States has constitutional responsibility for the conduct of his country's foreign relations. The domain and scope of any projection of American power is at the disposition of the president, who may apply various instruments in pursuit or defence of his country's interests. The legitimacy of his action in accordance with normative behaviour is evaluated domestically and internationally, and there may be divergence of opinion about the policies chosen or the means by which they were prosecuted.

The advent of the unipolar moment in 1991 provided the United States with space in which to exert its dominance substantially free from contestation by another great power. The broader interest of the US in engaging with and leading the international community toward a realisation of its global vision required that it address contentious inter-state issues. One of those was the Arab–Israel dispute, at whose heart lay United States concern for the security of Israel. Israel, the United States and other states supportive of Israel were vulnerable to actions by Arab and Islamic state and non-state actors who were opposed to Israel's existence and who were prepared to bring pressure to bear in the Palestinians' cause. United States national interests were at stake. The United States had sought over many years to resolve the dispute, and was challenged to try again after the 1991 Gulf War. Success would demonstrate that United States hegemony could be employed to produce a significant 'public good' concurrently with the defence of its national interests. If the United States were to effect a resolution of the Arab–Israel dispute, it would have to persuade the parties principal that it was in their interest to reach accommodations with one another. Its ability to do so would depend upon the efficacy with which the instruments available to it were employed.

Although a convincing argument could be made in favour of the United States demonstrating leadership during the unipolar moment, there could be no guarantee that it could deliver a resolution of the Arab–Israel dispute. Much would depend upon the dynamics of the diplomatic process. The preliminary objective of the US was to get the parties principal into negotiation with one another. The next chapter will address this. Were the negotiation to fail and the United States to be unsuccessful in attaining its overall objective, the Middle East would remain unsettled and United States interests vulnerable. The United States would have to continue living with the attendant uncertainties. Its authority would be questioned for its inability to attain one of its hegemonic ambitions, the more so for its goal having been launched in a generally benign international environment. Convinced of the need for a settlement and that the conjunction of forces and timing was right, Bush I decided to give the search for a comprehensive settlement his best shot.

As this study is about the application of power by a state in order to achieve an objective, the outcome of its projection is properly a matter for evaluation. The point of departure for any *post hoc* evaluation of the efficacy of a state's projection of its power must be a clear statement of the objective. Negotiation is, however, a dynamic process and objectives may be modified in response to changing circumstances. In the case of a comprehensive settlement of the Arab–Israel dispute, attainment of the overall objective must resolve fundamental questions within which many critical matters may be subsumed. Prior identification of all contentious issues would be complex and confusing. Bush I and Clinton preferred to express their objective in broader, more general terms. By the time Bush II took office, the objective had contracted. A comprehensive settlement was no longer on the agenda. Bush II was to focus only on the question of a possible settlement between Israel and the Palestinians, and then only to the extent that he was moved to do so.

An analysis of the efficacy of the instruments employed for the projection of American power will provide the basis for an assessment of the limits of American power in relation to this case study. It should be possible to observe modification of the target states' and Palestinians' behaviour in response to positive or negative American sanctions. Their responses to American intellectual or psychological influences may prove harder to assess. Some subjectivity cannot be avoided in evaluating the effectiveness of the employment of American instruments. Despite these qualifications, shortcomings might be identified that could be remedied in other American diplomatic applications.

NOTES

1 Waltz (1979) p.79.
2 Rodman (2000) p.53.
3 Krauthammer (2002) p.11.
4 Ibid.
5 Bush, G.W., *Public Papers of the Presidents of the United States* (hereinafter *Public Papers*) – *President Bush, 2001*, p.145.
6 Clinton, W.J. *Public Papers, 1993*, p.1614.
7 US Department of State (2002).
8 Jervis (1970) p.8.
9 Smith (1994) p.325.
10 Ibid. p.322.
11 Wagner (2001) p.18.
12 Fisk (2002).
13 Buruma (2003).
14 Goldberg (1996) p.30.
15 Ibid. pp.30–1.
16 Ibid. Ch.8; Melman and Raviv (1994) Ch.16.
17 Goldberg (1996) pp.352–3.
18 Ibid. p.353.
19 Arab American Institute (2006).
20 Ibid.
21 Arab American Institute (2004).
22 Zogby (2004).
23 Ibid.
24 Mark (2006) p.12.
25 Ibid. p.3.
26 Ibid. p.7.
27 Ibid. p.7.
28 Abraham (2002).
29 British Petroleum (2002) p.5. If the reserves remaining at the end of any year are divided by the production in that year, the reserve-to-production ratio is the length of time that those remaining reserves would last if production were to continue at that level.
30 Clinton (1994).
31 Ozga (1994) pp.66–93. US sanction laws are triggered when non-MTCR participants transfer controlled goods to other non-participants.
32 The United Nations Monitoring, Verification and Inspection Commission (UNMOVIC) was created by UN Security Council Resolution 1284 of 17 December 1999. UNMOVIC was to replace UNSCOM and continue with the latter's mandate to disarm Iraq of its weapons of mass destruction (chemical and biological weapons and missiles with a range of more than 150 km), and to operate a system of ongoing monitoring and verification to check Iraq's compliance with its obligation not to acquire weapons prohibited to it by the Security Council.
33 United Nations (2006).
34 US Department of State (2003) p.77; Perl (2003) p.3; Christopher (1995a) p.2.
35 B'Tselem (2006).
36 Herman and O'Sullivan (1989) p.30. The data are drawn from official Israeli police statistics.
37 Perl (2004) p.1. Most of the attacks in Iraq do not meet the US definition of international terrorism because they were directed at American and coalition forces on duty.
38 Pape (2003).
39 Schelling (1991) p.29.
40 Baker III (1995) p.414.
41 Morriss (1987) p.22.
42 Ibid. p.19.

43 Dougherty and Pfaltzgraff (1990) p.126.
44 Morgenthau (1978) p.30.
45 Morriss (1987) p.30. Morriss instances the fact that the work of an artist or philosopher can influence or affect the attitudes of others long after the creator's death, to demonstrate that influence is not an exercise of power.
46 Nye (2002) p.9.
47 Friedman (2003).
48 Baldwin (1993) p.192.
49 Waltz (1979) p.16.
50 Ibid. p.192; Rosenau (1968) p.315.
51 Watson (1982) p.11.
52 Craig and George (1995) p.258.
53 US Information Agency (2002); Djerejian (2003) p.13.
54 Nye (2002) p.9.
55 Bartholomew (1990) p.169.
56 'Cost' is used in the sense of value foregone as a result of a decision.
57 Baldwin (1985) p.112.
58 Cordesman (1999) p.1.
59 Kay (2003).
60 Knowlton (2003).
61 Chayes and Chayes (1995) p.306 (25n). The authors define 'norm' in a generic sense as including the concepts of principles, precepts, standards, rules, and the like.
62 Boekle et al. (1999) p.5.
63 International Court of Justice (1945). International law is stated to derive from international treaties, customary international law, 'the general principles of law recognised by civilised nations' and (as 'subsidiary means') judicial decisions and 'teachings of the most highly qualified publicists of the various nations'.
64 Keohane (2002) pp.120–1.
65 Keohane and Nye Jr (1989) p.271. The authors note that international regimes can be 'valuable to great powers, such as the United States, that want to create, but are unable to dictate, the terms of a stable world environment'.
66 Morriss (1987) p.38.
67 Rosenau (1968) p.321.
68 Simon (1957) p.177; Waltz (1979) p.192; Baldwin (1985) p.131.

2. Failures and success: the road to Madrid

President Bush I found the argument for United States engagement in a search for a comprehensive settlement of the Arab–Israel dispute compelling. The United States having tried in 1989, and again two years later, to pursue a peaceful resolution of the dispute, Bush's Administration employed various instruments of statecraft to persuade the parties principal to participate in an international conference at Madrid in October 1991. The Arabs' agreement to negotiate with Israel marked a significant reversal of a long-held position.

FAILURES – THE BACKGROUND

Bush I decided in early 1989 to explore a common basis on which Israel and the Palestinians could engage because geopolitical circumstances in the Middle East were changing markedly.[1] By the end of 1988 superpower competition was in decline; the PLO had met the United States on matters of principle, having accepted the land-for-peace proposition implicit in UN Security Council Resolutions 242 and 338, and Israel's right to exist, and had condemned terrorism;[2] and Israel was under pressure from primarily domestic, not external forces. The moment seemed opportune.

A rehearsal of the history of the various American attempts to broker a settlement of the Arab–Israel dispute is unnecessary. It is sufficient to record some of the perceptions held by prospective participants in any negotiation, including those of Bush's Administration. The policy to which Israel's Prime Minister Yitzhak Shamir was committed derived from the position taken by a predecessor from his own Likud Party when negotiating the Camp David accords in 1978. Menachem Begin had insisted that in return for relinquishing the Sinai Peninsula to Egypt he had secured Israel's right to retain the West Bank. From the United States perspective, important determinants were carried forward from the presidency of R.W. Reagan. In 1982 Reagan advanced the proposition of self-government for the Palestinians of the West Bank and Gaza in association with Jordan.[3] Drawing upon the Camp David accords, he advocated a transitional period 'to prove to the Palestinians that they can run their own affairs and that such Palestinian autonomy poses no threat to Israel's security'. His proposal contained three important qualifications: the United States would not support the use of any additional land for the purpose of settlements during the transitional period; peace could not be achieved by the formation of an independent Palestinian state; and Jerusalem would remain undivided, but its final status should be decided through negotiation. Fundamental to the United States position was UN Security Council Resolution 242, adopted after the war of June 1967 and setting the parameters for 'a just and lasting peace in the Middle East'. The key principles of such a peace included the withdrawal of Israeli forces 'from territories occupied in the recent conflict' and the right of every state in the area 'to live within secure and recognised boundaries free from threats of force'. The Americans held that the resolution's terms applied to the West Bank and Gaza, a view clearly at odds with the policy of the Likud Party.

The first Palestinian uprising, or *intifada*, broke out in December 1987. By the following month Israelis were acknowledging that they had an unprecedented situation on their hands. Their heavy-handed response, seen by American viewers on television, contributed to a decline in public support for Israel,[4] and gave impetus to the suggestion of a peace conference under the auspices of the United Nations. The United States was loath to see an intrusion by the United Nations where its ability to influence outcomes would be constrained, and responded in 1988 with another initiative that was less overtly prescriptive about the possible final outcome than Reagan's. It sought to imbue negotiations with a sense of commitment and urgency by introducing timeframes within which various stages of the process were to be completed, telescoping those set out in the Camp David accords.[5] Palestinian representation would be within a Jordanian–Palestinian delegation, confirming the United States predilection for some form of Palestinian association with Jordan. An international conference would be held before the commencement of the bilateral negotiations, at which all parties would be required to accept UN Security Council Resolutions 242 and 338, and to renounce violence and terrorism.[6] That plan, too, ran aground. Shamir did not support an international conference, and he rejected the foreshortening of the Camp David process. The Palestinians, though happy that the *intifada* should have sparked an initiative by the United States, were unhappy with their proposed 'associate' status within the Jordanian delegation. The whole proposition foundered on 31 July 1988 when King Hussein formally relinquished all Jordanian legal and administrative ties to the West Bank, stating that henceforth the PLO would be responsible for the Palestinians living there. In handing over the Palestine question to the PLO, the king shattered the Israeli Labor Party's long-held belief that the West Bank's future lay with Hashemite rather than PLO rule, thus avoiding the creation of an unstable third state between Israel and Jordan.

These developments had proceeded concurrently with an evolution in Palestinian thinking and influenced the PLO's attitude toward a negotiated settlement with Israel. UN Security Council Resolution 242 characterised the Palestinians as refugees, a description that the Palestine National Council had been determined to broaden in a revision of the Palestine National Charter adopted in July 1968. It emphasised the right of the Palestinian people to self-determination and sovereignty over their homeland. In November 1981 an Arab Summit in effect endorsed a proposition for an Arab state alongside a Jewish one in the former territory of Palestine.[7] The Arab states had rejected a two-state solution when the UN partition plan was adopted under General Assembly Resolution 181 in 1947,[8] but the idea had been implicitly resurrected at a meeting of the Palestine National Council in 1974.[9] The question of which Arab state or body should become heir to any occupied territory to be vacated by Israel was addressed in a declaration by the heads of Arab states in 1984. Their conference formally acknowledged the right of the Palestinian people to a separate homeland, but without specifying that its territory was restricted to the West Bank, and it recognised the Palestine Liberation Organization as the sole legitimate representative of the Palestinian people. Henry Kissinger informed Israel that the United States would not recognise or negotiate with the PLO unless and until the PLO recognised Israel and accepted UN Security Council Resolutions 242 and 338. The US Congress codified the pledge into law, and added that the PLO must also renounce terrorism.[10]

A confluence of events in 1988 saw a further transformation of the PLO's position. The *intifada* had brought the Palestinian cause to a wider audience and the Palestinian leadership was anxious to capitalise on the sympathy generated. It was concerned, however, that the uprising was indigenous to the West Bank and Gaza and that it threatened a divergence between the Tunis-based leadership and the Palestinians living in the territories, exacerbated by the impact that radical Islam was beginning to have on Palestinian nationalism under the *intifada*. Within Israel, opinion was divided on whether to pursue repressive measures or a political solution. There was a growing realisation among Israelis that the *intifada* demonstrated the high price to be paid for retention of the West Bank and Gaza, not only in terms of hostility from the Arab world but also in the form of a threat to Israel's Jewish and democratic character, and possibly to its military security as well.[11] The Labor Party, which demanded compromise, threatened to quit the coalition government in the light of the conservative component's support for the status quo. Elections were held in both Israel and the United States that year, and informal explorations were in train between the outgoing Reagan Administration and the PLO over the terms under which the United States could commence negotiation with that organisation. Particular sticking points for the Americans were that the PLO renounce terrorism, and that while the Palestinians had the right to pursue an independent state through negotiation this did not amount to acceptance of a Palestinian right of self-determination.[12] Under US urging and after some prevarication, Arafat stated publicly in December 1988 'the right of all parties concerned in the Middle East conflict to exist in peace and security ... including the state of Palestine, Israel, and other neighbours according to the resolution 242 and 338 [*sic*] ... [and] ... that we totally and absolutely renounce all forms of terrorism, including individual, group, and state terrorism'.[13] The United States effected the desired outcome because the PLO recognised that progress toward attainment of the Palestinian objective could not occur without United States intervention.

It was against this background and an appreciation of the key players' perceptions that Bush I decided to explore the prospect of negotiation between Israelis and Palestinians. His secretary of state, James Baker, chose to start by inviting the Likud-led coalition government of Yitzhak Shamir to offer a plan, influenced by a desire to establish a good rapport with the notoriously truculent prime minister at their first meeting. Shamir submitted four points: the need for negotiations with Arab states to conclude peace treaties; the importance of settling the refugee problem; the necessity for the Camp David partners to renew their commitment to the agreements and to peace; and a requirement that elections be held in the West Bank and Gaza to select non-PLO Palestinians with whom Israel would then negotiate an interim agreement on self-government, according to the Camp David formula.[14] Baker then elicited a proposal from the Egyptians, which he understood to have benefited from considerable private input from Israelis and members of the PLO.[15] He boiled down the two sets to five points that he claimed met Shamir's concerns and protected Israel,[16] including: that a meeting would be convened in Cairo only after Israel had approved a list of non-PLO Palestinians with whom they could treat; that all sides would agree to accept Shamir's plan as the basis for negotiations; and that the Palestinians would be free to raise their own ideas about elections and the negotiation process. As Shamir stalled, Bush I reminded him that he was equivocating on his own suggestions, notwithstanding that they had been modified by Baker. During the down time the situation became clouded by the building of Israeli settlements in the West Bank.

Many states contend that Israeli settlement in the occupied territories and deportation of Palestinians from occupied territories are illegal under international law, specifically the sixth paragraph of Article 49 of the Fourth Geneva Convention on the Protection of Civilian Persons in Time of War, which states: 'The occupying power shall not deport or transfer parts of its own civilian population into territories it occupies'. Israel became a party to the treaty in 1949. The illegality of Israeli settlements has been affirmed in resolutions of the UN Security Council and General Assembly, according the proposition substantive status in international law. Some American spokesmen have stated formally a United States view that the settlements are illegal.[17] The State Department's legal adviser provided an opinion to the Congress in 1978 which concluded that Israel's establishment of 'civilian settlements in those [occupied] territories is inconsistent with international law'.[18] American Administrations held to this view until the early 1980s when Reagan declared that such settlements were not 'illegal'. All subsequent Administrations have opposed settlements as an obstacle to peace. The Israelis deny the central proposition that the territories are occupied. They maintain that Jordan's annexation of the West Bank in 1950 was not recognised by the international community and was therefore illegal, and that Egypt never claimed the Gaza Strip. Moreover, Jordan had relinquished its claim to the West Bank in 1988. Israel argues that the two territories thereby rightfully belong to it: they cannot, therefore, be 'occupied territories' and the provisions of the Geneva Convention do not apply to them.[19]

Bush I adopted a firm position on the matter, consistent with that which he had expressed in 1971 when he was Permanent Representative of the United States to the United Nations. Baker had told the American Israel Public Affairs Committee in May 1989 that Israel should lay aside its unrealistic vision of a Greater Israel, forswear annexation and stop settlement activity.[20] Then on 1 March 1990 he told a congressional committee that the United States would support a request for $400 million in loan guarantees to build housing for Soviet Jewish immigrants provided that Israel agree to halt the construction of new settlements in the territories. Two days later the president confirmed that there should be no new settlements in the West Bank or East Jerusalem, the specific mention of Jerusalem provoking an outcry from Israel's American supporters.[21]

Detail relating to Palestinian representation under Baker's five-point plan was introduced into the Israeli cabinet in this context. Determined not to concede any possible basis for a Palestinian claim to any part of Jerusalem, Shamir objected to a proposition that it might be possible for a Palestinian who had residential addresses in both the West Bank and East Jerusalem to be a representative at the proposed conference. The proposition was submitted to the cabinet of Israel's coalition government, where it was endorsed with Labor support. The prime minister and conservative members of the cabinet opposed it. Labor then left the coalition and secured a vote of no confidence against the government on 15 March. It took Shamir until June to reconstitute a government, this time with hard-line right-wing support. These developments, and an attack on Israel by the Palestine Liberation Front on 30 May contrary to Arafat's assurances, ensured that by mid-1990 another United States initiative to promote a peace settlement was dead.

Iraq's invasion of Kuwait and America's forging of an international alliance to counter Iraqi aggression saw a revival of the question of a peaceful and comprehensive settlement of the Arab–Israel dispute. Prior to Iraq's invasion of Kuwait, President Saddam Hussain had sought to promote his pan-Arab credentials by disparaging the United States record in relation to the Palestinians. Later, he tried to create a linkage between the questions of Palestine and Kuwait. In the context of the imposition of UN sanctions against Iraq, Baghdad criticised America's passivity in the face of Israel's refusal to withdraw from occupied territories in accordance with UN Security Council Resolutions 242 and 338, and demanded that the United States show the same attention to all Security Council resolutions.[22] Bush I was determined to maintain a clear distinction between events in the Gulf region and those in the Mediterranean littoral,[23] and to ensure that Saddam's attempt to forge a linkage between the two issues did not gain currency beyond the Palestinians and, to a lesser extent, Jordan.[24]

While the United States was successful in preventing a direct linkage, there was a growing climate in favour of a Middle East peace settlement, including among America's Western allies. The Administration recognised that Arab countries' deployment of military forces under US leadership required some reciprocal gesture. The United States had promised that it would address the larger issues of the Middle East after the Iraq–Kuwait crisis had been resolved.[25] The matter was discussed at Bush's meeting with President Hafez al-Assad in Geneva in November 1990. Prime Minister Shamir visited Washington and met with Bush in December 1990. The US and Israeli leaders agreed on the need to try to reinvigorate the peace process after the Gulf crisis had been solved.[26] A month later, the US and Soviet foreign ministers agreed that mutual efforts be made by them to promote Arab–Israel peace and regional stability[27] in the aftermath of the crisis in the Gulf. The Israeli prime minister immediately criticised the statement, which dealt with his country's affairs, for having been issued without either consultation with, or prior notice to, his government.

The complaint was insufficient, however, to deter the two superpowers from continuing to work together toward a peace settlement. It was in the interests of the United States to engage the Soviet Union in cooperative endeavour in the Middle East, demonstrating the advantages of its proclaimed 'new world order'. Their cooperation in relation to the Arab–Israel dispute fostered an illusion of continuity with US and Soviet co-sponsorship of the Geneva Conference of December 1973. In reality the power lay with the United States, particularly as the Soviet Union became increasingly preoccupied with its domestic affairs. As early as March 1991, Baker had made it clear to the Soviet leadership that the price of co-sponsorship would be the Soviet Union's establishment of full diplomatic relations with Israel.[28] In July, Presidents Bush and Gorbachev announced that the United States and the Soviet Union, acting as co-sponsors, would work to convene a peace conference in October. In preparation for a conference – and in accord with the new era of cooperation – the foreign ministers of the two countries met in Jerusalem on 18 October. The Soviet Union's restoration of full diplomatic relations with Israel, after a break of 24 years, was pre-emptively announced by the United States that day, coinciding with the formal issuance of invitations by their heads of state to a conference in Madrid on 30 October 1991.

SUCCESS

How the United States succeeded in bringing all the major actors in the Arab–Israel dispute into negotiation is an outstanding example of the efficacy of the projection of American power. Ideas were explored, inducements offered, coercion exerted and leverage maximised through the co-optation of third parties in order to persuade the parties principal to participate in the negotiation.

Bush I's analysis of the geopolitical situation in late 1990 and early 1991 suggested that the broad coalition of states forged to contest Iraq's occupation of Kuwait, the newly emergent pattern of cooperation among the permanent members of the Security Council, and the United States demonstration of leadership in prosecuting the Gulf War, offered the prospect that the outcome of the war might create conditions conducive to productive negotiations between Arabs and Israelis. A resolution of the Arab–Israel dispute became a formal objective of the United States when the president addressed a joint session of the Congress on 6 March 1991, saying that it was time to end the Arab–Israel conflict. The principle of an exchange of territory for peace should be realised, Israel's security assured and legitimate Palestinian rights recognised.[29] While his statement focussed on Israel and the Palestinians, he was concerned to express the Palestinian question in the context of closing 'the gap between Israel and the Arab states'. The plural is instructive, even though the states were not specified. It would be necessary to convince all disputants to come together in order that they might proceed to negotiate a resolution of their differences.

The intermediate objective of convoking an international peace conference was not without attendant difficulty because Israel's Arab neighbours had never to that point agreed to negotiate with Israel. It was not until agreement had been reached on the convoking of a conference to address a resolution of the Arab–Israel dispute that greater precision was given to defining the scope and objectives of the process. Bush I's contribution during his first presidential term was to bring the parties principal together: he would have hoped that a second term would have provided the space in which to pursue a comprehensive settlement of the dispute.

The centrepiece of what was to become a new US initiative was based on a proposal in September 1990 by a senior aide to the Israeli foreign minister.[30] There should be two tracks, the first leading to an Israel–Palestinian dialogue; and the second engaging Israel and the Arab states in a regional conference, co-sponsored by the United States and the Soviet Union, where all the parties directly concerned would be represented.[31] This would be in lieu of a conference under the aegis of the United Nations, sought by a number of Arab and other states but anathema to Israel and the United States because so many resolutions adopted by UN agencies went against what they believed to be Israel's interests. The hope was that, once the parties had been brought to the negotiating table, the dynamic would produce a comprehensive and peaceful settlement of the Arab–Israel dispute. Three things are apparent from even this minimalist description: the Bush Administration's proposed structure would draw upon an Israeli concept; the focus would be on the negotiating process rather than upon negotiating an outcome related to some expressed objective; and the negotiating process would accord *de facto* recognition by Arab states to Israel as a Middle Eastern state, thus conferring upon Israel a measure of legitimacy denied by Arab states since 1948. Further, the principle of self-determination for the Palestinian people would be qualified: it would not extend to a separate independent state, but application of the principle would not be excluded in the context of a confederation with Jordan.[32]

Baker knew that in order to convoke a conference it would be essential to demonstrate to the Arabs and to the Israelis that both sides were prepared to be flexible. As neither side would be prepared to move first, parallel reciprocal steps would need to be taken.[33] A tentative move by one Arab state might be sufficient to encourage movement by another, until gradually an Arab consensus could be framed around participation in an international conference. Baker's tactic was to acquire and apply accumulative authority through persuasion and leverage. He began by seeking support in Saudi Arabia and Egypt before engaging with Shamir and Assad. Egypt, which had been cold-shouldered by the Arab world after signing a peace treaty with Israel in 1979, enthusiastically supported the American initiative. The Saudis traditionally felt more secure when occupying the middle ground, but Baker was able to gain their commitment to attend the conference under the cloak of representing the six states of the Gulf Cooperation Council.[34] King Fahd and President Mubarak were asked to help bring Syria on board, and in the meantime to keep the PLO at bay because of Arafat's pro-Iraq stance during the Gulf War.

Syria's primary interest in any eventual settlement of the Arab–Israel dispute related to recovery of territory in the Golan Heights occupied by Israel under the terms of the 1974 Disengagement Agreement. Baker decided to focus on that issue. Shamir had shown him a letter from President G.R. Ford to the Prime Minister of Israel dated September 1975 pledging that in formulating future policy with respect to the terms of a peace settlement, the United States would give 'great weight to Israel's position that any peace agreement with Syria must be predicated on Israel remaining on the Golan Heights'.[35] Baker asked Shamir what the position would be if there were American troops stationed there, and was told that the situation would then be different.[36] Armed with this hint of flexibility, Baker told Assad that he was prepared to explore the concept of a formal United States pledge guaranteeing the security of the Israeli–Syrian border along the Golan Heights, comparable with the Multinational Force and Observers (MFO) on the Israel–Egypt border, but that such a commitment could be offered only after Israel and Syria had negotiated a full and complete peace. Baker said also that he would not explore the question of security guarantees with his president unless Assad were willing to drop his insistence that an international conference convened as part of the proposed peace process be in continuous session with all members of the UN Security Council present.[37] Later Assad was to claim that Baker had promised the return of the Golan to Syria and that America was backing away from its offer of guarantees, a charge that Baker flatly denied. He reminded Assad that an American security guarantee offered the best prospect for gaining Israeli withdrawal from the Golan Heights and Syria should not underestimate its importance.[38] Baker co-opted others, this time Egypt and the Soviet Union, in persuading Syria to agree.

The United States had always anticipated that Israel would have difficulty with the form and composition of Palestinian representation, especially after Arafat had applauded the Iraqi cause in the 1991 Gulf War and Palestinians had cheered Iraqi SCUD missile attacks on Israel. The notion of a joint Jordanian–Palestinian delegation would require some fence mending. Jordan's king would have to assure the United States of his support for its initiative, and Bush I would have to reclaim him as an ally after Jordan's opposition to America's position in the Gulf War. Both parties were quick to recognise the value in terms of their own interests in a resumption of cooperation. King Hussein appreciated the importance of Jordan's participation in a regional conference, and agreed to exercise his influence to secure the nomination of individuals likely to prove acceptable to Israel in their guise as Palestinian representatives. That would mean inclusion in the Jordanian delegation of Palestinians from the West Bank with no institutional links to the Tunis-based PLO leadership and with only nominal association with East Jerusalem. To that end, the king pledged to tell the PLO to keep a low profile,[39] and Bush signalled his appreciation by rewarding Jordan with $27 million in food aid, despite congressional objections.[40]

Arafat was not easily mollified and tried to get someone from East Jerusalem on to the delegation. For their part, the 'West Bankers' insisted that if they participated in any joint delegation, they had to be able to raise issues of concern to them at the conference, including their objective of an independent Palestinian state.[41]

Israel also had a fundamental problem with the basis for the conference. The notion of exchanging territory for peace in accordance with UN Security Council resolutions was contrary to Likud's objective of the realisation of *Eretz Yisrael*. Begin had succeeded at Camp David in 1978 in reaching agreement with Sadat on UN Security Council Resolution 242 as the basis for a peace settlement while avoiding explicit reference to the question of territorial exchange. Shamir wished to carry the same approach into any new negotiation. Baker responded that while the parties could interpret the formula however they wished, the Arabs would never agree to language modifying Resolution 242 as the basis for a meeting.[42] Further, Shamir had difficulty with the notion of inviting a representative of the European Community and an observer from the United Nations to the conference, given the expressions of sympathy for the positions of the Arabs that had emanated from these two institutions over a number of years. A personal letter to Shamir from Bush on 31 May failed to persuade him to compromise, confirming Baker's suspicion that Shamir simply was not interested in peace.[43] For Baker, the hope of convening a peace conference now lay with Assad. If he could be persuaded to compromise, Shamir would be thrust on to the defensive.

Concurrently with his letter to Shamir, Bush had written to the other prospective participants. Assad was warned that the peace process would proceed with or without him and that the bilateral relationship would suffer if Syria was not on board. Assad agreed to Syrian participation. Having now mustered Arab states' agreement to engaging in direct negotiations with Israel, something Israel had sought for 40 years, Baker calculated that 'neither Shamir nor the Palestinians could possibly remain intransigent in these circumstances'.[44] Shamir's suspicions were not easily allayed, however, and he remained concerned that the Arab states would find a way to bring the United Nations more intimately into the negotiating process. In order to gain Shamir's acquiescence, Bush offered an inducement, committing the United States to a serious effort to secure the repeal of UN General Assembly Resolution 3379 equating Zionism with racism, which had been adopted in 1975. He was not prepared, however, to acquiesce in Shamir's claim for two years of automatic vetoes in the UN Security Council on any measure Israel opposed.[45]

As the process of negotiating with the principal parties had proceeded, Baker had given certain assurances to each. Assad and Shamir used the opportunity presented by discussion on draft letters incorporating their assurances to secure marginal gains in terms of their respective interests. A public announcement of the invitation to a peace conference was designed to halt such erosion. The Palestinians were the last party to announce that the terms of the conference were acceptable. In the face of death threats and the opprobrium of PLO headquarters, Palestinians living in the West Bank produced the names of 14 persons who could be accommodated within a joint Jordanian delegation. All of them were acceptable to Israel.

Throughout this exercise of American diplomacy, the Israelis had persisted with the building of settlements in the occupied territories, ostensibly to accommodate some Jewish immigrants from the Soviet Union. This could only raise doubt about Israel's preparedness to display flexibility at any peace conference. In the view of one historian: 'Settlement activity was not just incompatible with the peace process; it was intended to wreck it'.[46] The United States had obtained public assurances from several Arab states that they would suspend the Arab League's economic boycott of Israel if settlement activity in the occupied territories were halted.[47] Through carefully balanced policies the Administration sought to deny assistance to Israel for its settlements, while continuing to extend support in other areas such as the repeal of the 'Zionism/racism' resolution.[48]

Six days after the US-led coalition launched its air attack against Iraqi forces in Kuwait in January 1991, Israel's finance minister announced that his government would ask for $13 billion in additional aid from the United States – '$10 billion in loan guarantees for settling Soviet Jews, and $3 billion in compensation for the damage inflicted on Israeli cities by SCUD attacks'.[49] Bush I seized the opportunity presented by this request to coerce Israel into attending a peace conference. Baker suggested that Israel curtail the expansion of settlements in the West Bank as a gesture for peace, but this was turned down by Ariel Sharon, Israel's housing minister. Then, against the wishes of a powerful domestic lobby group, Bush gained the Senate's agreement in September 1991 to defer the loan guarantees for 120 days, although it transpired that deferral was to continue after the expiry of the designated period. Shamir retorted that the expansion of the settlements would continue, and no power in the world could prevent this construction.[50] For its part, the United States rejected any idea of a compromise short of a settlement freeze.[51] For many years American Administrations had held that no United States assistance to Israel could be used in the occupied territories, because they wished to avoid the appearance of endorsing Israel's annexation of the territories without negotiation. The Congress incorporated this position into law in 1992.[52]

Israel eventually caved in to United States pressure and voted to attend the peace conference. It is possible that the government thought that it had little to lose in acquiescing: it could always impede developments that threatened its national interest during the conference. Inadvertently, the Israeli loan guarantee request and the prime minister's obduracy had played into the hands of the Bush Administration, whose response was not wholly motivated by concern over Israel's settlement policy. Shamir had been difficult to deal with and, by playing the loan guarantee question as it did, it contributed in some measure to his electoral defeat in June 1992.[53]

Although Bush's Administration was successful in bringing all relevant Arab parties into face-to-face negotiation with Israel at an international conference, the prospect of its producing a negotiated settlement of the Arab–Israel dispute was at best tenuous. Baker's diplomacy had suggested a possible means of resolving the Golan Heights issue, but profound uncertainty had to be entertained about any accommodation between Israelis and Palestinians.

The Madrid conference was ambitiously conceived and was to be comprehensive in scope, addressing the vexed questions of Israel's bilateral relationships with the Palestinians, Jordan, Lebanon and Syria, and multilateral issues such as arms control and regional security, water, refugee issues, the environment, economic development and other subjects of mutual interest. Although linkage among the elements was explicitly denied, the United States expressed a hope that agreement in all negotiations would serve the interests of a comprehensive settlement.[54] The withdrawals of Israeli and Syrian forces from Lebanon, under the terms of UN Security Council Resolution 425 and the Taif Agreement of 1989 respectively, were viewed by the United States as separate issues to be treated independently of any Israeli withdrawal from occupied territory in accordance with UN Security Council Resolutions 242 and 338.[55] Bush's Administration made explicit its continued opposition to Israeli settlement activity in Syrian and other territories occupied in 1967 as an obstacle to peace; its refusal to recognise or accept the extension of Israeli sovereignty to the Golan Heights; and its opposition to the Israeli annexation of East Jerusalem and the extension of Jerusalem's municipal boundaries.[56] These, and other undertakings were incorporated in the letters of assurances to the parties in lieu of the more binding memoranda of understanding that had originally been planned.

While a principal element of the conference would be the question of Palestine, a significant omission from the agreed arrangements was any vision of the probable outcome of negotiations between Israel and the Palestinians. All that Israel was prepared to concede was that the Palestinian question would be tackled according to an agreed phased framework comparable to that in the Camp David accords. The United States was not prepared to go beyond a restricted interpretation of the principle of self-determination as it related to Palestinian aspirations. Although the principle is expressed in the first Articles of the UN Charter, and the International Covenant on Civil and Political Rights and the International Covenant on Economic, Social and Cultural Rights adopted by the UN General Assembly in 1966, there is no absolute right to national self-determination.[57] A theoretical right to national self-determination is recognised in some circumstances, but there is no disposition among nation-states to countenance a wholesale devolution of sovereignty to minority groups within, or across, existing borders,[58] which could pose significant challenges to the sovereignty of many nation-states.[59] The principal manifestation of the right has been the transformation of colonial dependencies into nation-states, commonly within borders established by the metropolitan powers and generally recognised internationally. The post-colonial model does not apply to the Palestinian case, a UN plan for the partition of the British mandated territory of Palestine into Arab and Jewish states having been rejected by Arab and Islamic nations in 1947.

The Palestinians were seeking separation from a regime whose imposition, substantially by military conquest, does not enjoy international recognition and whose withdrawal from occupied territory has been demanded through UN Security Council resolutions. The Palestinians seek the recovery of a 'national sovereignty' that had not previously been recognised. Palestinian sovereignty, in these terms, would be accomplished to the satisfaction of some Palestinians by Israel's progressive withdrawal from occupied territory in accordance with the two UN Security Council resolutions.[60] But even this would not satisfy those Palestinians who contest Israel's right to a state on any part of the former Ottoman administrative district known as 'Palestine'.

When Mahmoud Abbas, the chief PLO architect of the Oslo accord, published that concept in 1995, Palestinian thinking was to express such 'complete national sovereignty' in confederal form: confederation being, as he saw it, a contractual agreement between two or more independent entities. The goal of independent statehood was therefore a necessary precursor to confederation. Later, the Palestinians were to amend their position and to seek a sovereign Palestinian state alongside Israel. In constructing the framework of the Madrid conference the Bush Administration held to an objective that they shared with Israelis for some available solution to the question of Palestine other than self-determination, denying the possibility of a 'two-state solution'. A decade later both countries were to profess support in principle for an independent Palestinian state.

CONCLUSION

If a settlement of the Arab–Israel dispute were ever to be achieved, it would be necessary for the parties principal to negotiate with one another. An essential intermediate objective attained by the United States was the parties' agreement to enter into negotiations. The Madrid conference was 'designed to launch a process, not conclude it'.[61] The Bush Administration fondly hoped that by 'breaking the symbolism of denial – a taboo on direct talks between Arabs and Israelis'[62] – the participants might declare their determination to make peace and avoid attacking their negotiating partner, Israel. The conference succeeded in getting negotiation under way.

The United States had employed the instruments at its disposition to get Israel and its four Arab neighbours to the negotiating table. That had required its unwavering commitment to its interim objective, a flexible approach, and the expenditure of considerable energy.[63] International legitimacy would be accorded to the negotiations through participation, in some measure, of the United Nations, the European Community and the Gulf Cooperation Council,[64] and a formula had been devised that allowed for what one observer questionably termed 'authentic but non-PLO Palestinian'[65] representation. In the event, Israeli acceptance proved to be the hardest to extract, requiring both inducements and the application of leverage. Inducements were also broached with other states. In essence, the conference had been secured through an intelligent analysis of the parties' interests, clever tactics and persuasion, backed by selective offers of rewards.

The outcome was, however, an unbalanced one. In adapting an Israeli structure and ensuring that negotiations did not transgress upon Israel's bottom line, the United States created a framework that formalised the disparity between Israel and the Palestinians. On the core issue before the conference, the future relationship between Israel and the Palestinians, one party to the negotiations was formally separated from its political leadership and denied identity as a separate people. The Palestinians, especially the 'West Bankers' from among whom many representatives were chosen, could not afford to let the opportunity to address the Palestinian cause pass. Circumstances that were to restructure the negotiation process fundamentally will be addressed in the next chapter.

For decades Palestinians had hoped that United States liberalism and power could be engaged to their advantage. It is probable that a memorandum addressed to the United States in April 1949 was the first appeal by Palestinians to a foreign government for help after having been driven from their homeland.[66] Forty years on, a 'national' Palestinian delegation had been deliberately excluded from a peace conference, one of whose principal issues was the future of the Palestinian people. While the United States had declared that it would support any outcome achieved through negotiation with Israel, the Palestinians knew even before the negotiation began that a right of national self-determination had been denied. Given Israel's comparative strength, this would mean recognition of any outcome based on what Israel was prepared to concede to the Palestinians. In his opening address at the Madrid conference, Bush I spoke about the need for peace to be based on fairness, 'above all to the Palestinian people';[67] and Baker claimed that the United States 'is and will be an honest broker'.[68] The Palestinian representatives may well have been somewhat sceptical about such assurances in view of the record of the United States to that point.

The Palestinians were not the only Middle Eastern party to the conference to harbour reservations about the conference. Assad had never been enthusiastic, and the right-wing government of Shamir accepted it only grudgingly and under American pressure. Assad was known, however, to keep his word.[69] While Assad might prove to be a tough negotiator, Syria would presumably stick to any agreement reached. Doubts were entertained in Washington, however, about the strength of the commitment of the Shamir government. The most robust support for the launching of the peace process had come from Egypt and Jordan, both of which stood to gain from a successful outcome, and Saudi Arabia. For Egypt a comprehensive peace settlement would prove the value of its risky undertaking in concluding a peace treaty with Israel. Jordan would hope to see a pacification of a troublesome issue on the River Jordan's western bank that had spilled over into the demographics and politics of the Hashemite Kingdom. The Saudi royal family would be able to demonstrate to the Islamic world and to its own people that it was genuinely concerned about the fate of the Palestinians.

These inauspicious beginnings were to influence events during 1992, but they were not the only factors to inhibit the negotiation of a comprehensive settlement during that year. The Israeli and American electoral cycles intervened, and Bush was to recall Baker from his diplomatic duties to act as his campaign manager. Without Baker's commitment to the attainment of an outcome from the process launched with fanfare at Madrid's Royal Palace, it stalled.

NOTES

1 Baker (1995) p.118.
2 Tessler (1994) pp.717–22.
3 Reagan (1982/1998) p.124.
4 D'Amato (1991) p.356.
5 Europa Publications (1998) pp.119–20.
6 Shultz (1988/1998) p.125.
7 Al-Saud (1981/1998) p.124.
8 UN General Assembly Resolution 181 (II) was adopted on 29 November by 33 (for) – 13 (against, including all states with significant Muslim populations) – 10 (abstentions).
9 Muslih (1990) pp.3–29.
10 Mark (2003) p.2.
11 Tessler (1994) pp.726–7.
12 Quandt (2001) pp.277–85.
13 Ibid. pp.284–5; Abbas (1995) pp.27–35.
14 Quandt (2001) pp.296, 453 (12n). There must be some doubt whether Shamir's plan was a genuine contribution toward peace. He let slip at the time that it was merely 'an idle fancy'; Morris (2001) p.609.
15 Baker (1995) p.124.
16 Ibid. p.125.

17 Mark (2003) p.9. Statements to that effect were made by US Permanent Representatives to the United Nations in 1971 and 1976 and by Secretary of State Cyrus Vance in 1980.
18 US Department of State (1978) p.1578.
19 Mark (2003) p.9.
20 Baker (1995) pp.121, 127.
21 Ibid. p.128.
22 Aronson (1991a). Statement by Iraqi Foreign Minister Tariq Aziz at a press conference after his meeting with Secretary of State Baker, in Geneva, 9 January. p.142; Baker also held a press conference after the meeting at which he referred to his personal efforts over 14 months to bring about a dialogue between Palestinians and Israelis, and said that he had made it very clear to the Iraqi Foreign Minister that 'there would be no linkage ... of that issue to Iraq's withdrawal from Kuwait.' p.163.
23 Bush, G.H.W. *Public Papers, 1990*, p.1679.
24 Aronson (1991a). In his last interview on 13 January 1991, the prominent Palestinian figure, Abu Iyad, said that 'it is important to work for two declarations of principle: an Iraqi declaration concerning the withdrawal of Iraqi troops from Kuwait, and a UN declaration establishing a link between the problems of the Middle East and of the Gulf.' p.146; Jordan's King Hussein juxtaposed the two issues without making the linkage between them explicit. pp.148–9.
25 Baker (1995) p.414.
26 Aronson (1991a). Briefing on Bush–Shamir Talks, 11 December 1990 by US Under Secretary of State John Kelly. p.157.
27 Ibid. Joint U.S.–Soviet Statement on the Gulf, 29 January 1991. p.137.
28 Baker (1995) p.428.
29 Bush, G.H.W. *Public Papers, 1991*, p.220.
30 Baker (1995) p.513.
31 Ibid. p.416.
32 Ibid. p.496.
33 Ibid. p.416.
34 Ibid. p.459; Ross (2004) p.75.
35 Ford (1975).
36 Baker (1995) p.424.
37 Ibid. pp.455–6.
38 Ibid. p.461.
39 Ibid. p.451.
40 Ibid. p.465.
41 Ross (2004) pp.77–8.
42 Baker (1995) p.445.
43 Ibid. p.469.
44 Ibid. p.488.
45 Ibid. pp.494–5.
46 Shlaim (2000) p.486.
47 Bush, G.H.W. *Public Papers, 1991*, p.959.
48 Rabil (2001) pp.423–4. The resolution was revoked by the UN General Assembly on 16 December 1991.
49 Baker (1995) p.544.
50 Rabil (2001) p.422.
51 Rabil (2001) p.422, citing testimony by Secretary of State Baker to the Senate Operations Committee in February 1992.
52 Mark (2006) p.5.
53 Quandt (2001) p.314. The incoming Prime Minister, Yitzhak Rabin, announced that more than 6000 housing units planned for the West Bank would be cancelled, although some 10000 units under construction would be finished. The Congress voted for the $10 billion in loan guarantees in October 1992, with the president retaining the authority to make deductions from the appropriation of amounts that Israel might spend on settlements beyond the completion of the 10000 units already under way.
54 Baker (1992d) pp.119–20.

55 Baker (1992b) p.120.
56 Baker (1992c) pp.118–9 and Baker (1992d) pp.119–20.
57 Freeman (1999) p.368.
58 Ibid. p.367; Keal (2003) p.136.
59 UN General Assembly Resolution 1514 (XV). Operative para. 6 states: 'Any attempt aimed at partial or total disruption of the national unity and the territorial integrity of a country is incompatible with the purposes and principles of the Charter of the United Nations'.
60 Abbas (1995) pp.219–20.
61 Ross (2004) p.81.
62 Ibid. p.80.
63 Baker (1995) p.488. Baker has described the process as 'a rich tale of determination, false starts, personal and political courage, blind alleys, perseverance, misjudgments, lost tempers, endless negotiations, scores of creative compromises, and both good faith and bad. In the end, the courage and determination of the parties themselves to give peace a chance – bolstered by the psychological sustenance, credibility, and catalytic creativity of the last superpower – somehow prevailed over years of enmity and chaos'.
64 Aronson (1991b) p.121. The United States had been able to secure the agreement of the parties principal to the involvement of the President of the European Community as representative of that body. The Secretary-General of the Gulf Cooperation Council would have a role in relation to multilateral issues, thus formally associating oil and gas producing states of the Gulf with the peace process. The United Nations would have a token presence through the attendance of an observer representing the Secretary General.
65 Hudson (1998) p.121.
66 Sharabi (1998) p.2; Gendzier (1989) pp.108–9. The Memorandum concludes: 'If the United Nations Organization has proved so far so weak as to be unable to force the Jews into behaving in accordance with international law, it is enough reason for people like us to come to you, the Government of the United States for help … [M]ost of the small countries of the world look to the United States as the all-powerful generous nation, which has been and still is prepared to defend the rights of man and the freedom of peoples.'
67 Bush, G.H.W. *Public Papers, 1991*, p.1363.
68 Baker (1991b) p.808.
69 Baker (1995) p.425.

3. Expectation and disappointment: the United States, Israel and the Palestinians, 1991–96

Marked progress was achieved in the negotiation between Israelis and Palestinians from 1991 to the election of Netanyahu as Israel's prime minister in 1996. President Clinton, who was in office for most of that period, committed himself to the peace process and mustered international support for it. Early progress toward an accommodation between Israelis and Palestinians was, however, to be set back by extremists on both sides opposed to the probable outcome of the negotiation, and by Israel's continuing construction of settlements on occupied territory. Clinton moved to protect the process, which had produced the only substantive agreements between the two contestants.

THE MADRID PROCESS

Bush I had devised a two-track structure under which the negotiation would be pursued, with bilateral negotiations commencing in Madrid in November 1991, and multilateral negotiations being launched in Moscow in January 1992. The intent was that the former would resolve the core bilateral issues at the heart of the Arab–Israel dispute: namely, land, peace and security. It would be broken down into separate negotiations between Israel and the Palestinians, Jordan, Syria and Lebanon. There would be no binding link among the different fronts, which implied that Israel would be free to play one off against another if it were so inclined.[1] The multilateral track would address functional issues on a region-wide basis. It was designed to foster broader human contact between Israelis and Arabs, tackling those regional problems that were themselves a source of tension and instability.[2] The multilateral negotiation will be discussed in Chapter 4.

The Madrid conference did not make much progress; nor did subsequent bilateral meetings in Washington in December 1991 and during 1992.[3] Also, Israeli and American elections in 1992, which produced changes of government in both countries, interrupted the process. For the remainder of his term Prime Minister Shamir remained uncommitted to the peace process, letting slip that he intended to drag out the negotiations without result for at least ten years, but he claimed later to have been misquoted.[4] The Israeli delegation persisted through the early part of 1992 with procedural objections to direct negotiation with the Palestinian representatives. They restricted negotiation to modalities for handing over to the Palestinians certain matters concerning their daily life, while declining to address the principles underpinning the Palestinian cause.[5] To break this deadlock, the United States persuaded the Palestinians to engage with the Israelis by stating in detail their points of agreement and disagreement to every proposition.[6] But the Palestinian delegates were kept on a tight rein by Arafat and lacked authority. The whole procedure was characterised by a Palestinian delegate as one of 'paralysis and inertia'.[7] At one stage the United States organised weekly meetings of all delegations in order to keep them at the table, but the effort proved futile. It had been within the power of the United States to facilitate the process and to bring the parties to the negotiating table: how it exercised its power to effect its desired outcome is the subject of this study.

Bush I had outlined the proposed framework for the core Israeli–Palestinian question at the Madrid opening ceremony:

> Negotiations will be conducted in phases, beginning with talks on interim self-government arrangements. We aim to reach agreement within one year. And once agreed, interim self-government arrangements will last for five years. Beginning the third year, negotiations will commence on permanent status ... Nothing agreed to now will prejudice permanent status negotiations. To the contrary, these subsequent negotiations will be determined on their own merits.[8]

The proposition that the Israeli–Palestinian negotiation should proceed by confidence-building stages towards some 'final status' derived from the Camp David accords of 1978. The devil was in the principles: Israel wanted to focus solely on interim arrangements, while the Palestinians' focus was on eventual self-government. Bush I found the Israeli concept of 'interim self-government' fundamentally flawed as Israel seemed reluctant to accept that, by definition, interim self-government was a stage leading to full self-government. But, having lost the presidential election in November 1992, he was not in a strong position during the transitional period to influence the Israelis.[9] As negotiations progressed it became clear that for the newly-elected Israeli Labor government, as for the defeated Likud government, 'interim' was code for 'limited'.[10]

As the Madrid process had produced little beyond getting the principal actors on to the same stage during the presidency of Bush I, Clinton decided upon taking office in January 1993 that an early assessment needed to be made of the prospect of success. At that stage, neither he nor his principal advisers were attracted to becoming engaged in a resolution of the Arab–Israel dispute.[11] The need for an assessment gained urgency from Israel's deportation in December 1992 of 400 Palestinians for allegedly being supporters of the Islamist group, Hamas. Clinton worked closely with the Israelis to develop a solution that involved the return of 100 of the deportees in 'a timely fashion', with half of the rest to return in September 1993 and the remainder in 1994.[12] In order to prepare the assessment, the president sent Secretary of State Warren Christopher to the Middle East. On his return Christopher reported: 'Nearly everyone I spoke to ... agreed that there may be now a one-time opportunity to promote peace. History tells us that such opportunities may be fleeting, especially in the Middle East, and we believe it is now time to re-launch the negotiations'.[13] A factor in Christopher's assessment was that Rabin had shown some flexibility, reversing Shamir's policy that UN Security Council Resolution 242 did not apply to the Golan Heights. The negotiations resumed in April 1993.

An American initiative to stimulate the Israel–Palestinian negotiations was made in May and June. The Administration submitted a paper purporting to be a synthesis of ideas raised by Israeli and Palestinian delegates and by American coordinators.[14] The document retraced some old ground in proposing that the two parties should agree on a declaration of principles to guide the negotiations. Arafat's analysis of the American synthesis identified some 65 per cent as having been taken from an Israeli paper and only 7 per cent from Palestinian sources and fumed over the United States lack of even-handedness.[15] Christopher's first essay at peace making, like those of so many of his predecessors, was unsuccessful. Indeed, the Administration's good offices were probably unnecessary at the time, for by then a back-channel had been established at Oslo. The Administration was aware of this, but seems not to have enquired about the credence then being given by both parties to it, including Israel's official participation in it from 21 May.

Israel decided to participate in the Oslo negotiations because the Labor government, elected in June 1992, had become disenchanted with the Washington talks. Arafat required that everything be referred back to the PLO leadership. In May 1993, the foreign minister, Shimon Peres, with the somewhat sceptical backing of Prime Minister Rabin, decided that the time had come to test the PLO's true intentions. He did so as a member of the first Israeli government to have accepted UN Security Council Resolutions 242 and 338 as applicable to the achievement of peace.[16] A secret dialogue between the Israelis and Palestinians had begun in December 1992 under Norwegian auspices. The Palestinians were to demand that Israel match the 'ministerial' rank of their delegate,[17] and Uri Savir, Director-General of the Israeli Foreign Ministry, attended the May round of negotiation in his official capacity.

DIRECT ISRAEL–PALESTINIAN NEGOTIATIONS

It was not intended that the backchannel replace the Washington process, but that it help to get it on track.[18] The unofficial exchange of views transmuted into official negotiations[19] and resulted in the initialling of a Declaration of Principles on Interim Self-Government Arrangements by Israeli and Palestinian officials on 20 August 1993.

The terms of the Declaration were concluded without US input. During a visit to the Middle East, Christopher asked Rabin how the talks with the Palestinians in Oslo were progressing. Rabin fobbed him off with a hand gesture, suggesting 'It's not worth talking about'.[20] Mahmoud Abbas, who coordinated the Palestinian position from PLO headquarters, records that there was agreement between the Israelis and Palestinians that the American Administration and the Egyptian Government should be kept informed, with Israel assuming responsibility for informing the United States and the Palestinians for informing Egypt.[21] Rabin's apparent dissimulation may well have been due to a number of factors: a desire to keep details of progress at Oslo secret; the convenience of the Washington track as a cover for the discussions in Norway; a disinclination to jeopardise the Washington talks because they offered a fall-back position should the Oslo negotiations fail; and a prospect that Israel could threaten the Palestinians with a return to Washington if the Oslo rounds got stuck.

The Palestinians confided in the Egyptians, and the Egyptian foreign minister informed the US ambassador in Cairo.[22] Washington's reaction was such as to discourage any further attempt to pass on information received from Egyptian sources. The Norwegians also tried to apprise the American Administration of developments. Yossi Beilin states that, when Norway's deputy foreign minister, Jan Egland, applied to travel to America to brief the State Department on progress, he was asked not to go and contented himself with regular conversations with an official in Washington over the American Embassy's secure telephone lines.[23] The question remains why a country which had learned of the backchannel from diverse and friendly sources, and which possesses a sophisticated intelligence capability, should have been so ill-prepared for the Oslo outcome. It is possible that Rabin had put Christopher off the scent, and that Washington was inclined to view Norwegian advice as somewhat self-serving. More weight might be given to the proprietary view which the United States had of the Madrid process, its attachment to Washington as the locus of negotiations, and to the newly-installed Clinton Administration's preoccupation with an attempt to reinvigorate the process.

Although the United States had been excluded from the Oslo talks, the imprimatur of the world's superpower was highly valued by both parties. During the negotiation, the Israelis and Palestinians had discussed the possibility of providing the Americans with the text of their Declaration, which the United States would, in turn, present as a final 'American' proposal to both parties at Washington, but the content of the document was published on the same day that Christopher was apprised of the Oslo breakthrough. The two parties had hoped that such a ploy would ameliorate criticism from within their own constituencies. So remote was the United States from the detail of the Oslo negotiations that Peres was fearful of an adverse reaction when on 29 August 1993 he presented Christopher not only with an initialled document but also a proposal for mutual recognition between Israel and the PLO.[24] The United States acknowledged the historic significance of the two propositions, and Clinton agreed to host a signing ceremony at the White House.

The president responded promptly to these changed circumstances, which required amendment to United States diplomatic practice in exchange for certain guarantees from the PLO. Reception of the PLO and its chairman, Yasser Arafat, at the White House would convey a more formal level of recognition than had been conferred by ambassadorial contact in Tunis in 1988–89. Israel had acted in early 1993 to end legal sanctions against Israelis who might talk to PLO officials; comparable action would be required from the United States. An imperative precondition imposed by the United States was that Arafat dissociate his movement from terrorist groups outside the PLO.[25] That was achieved on 7 September when the PLO Executive Committee in effect voided the provision within the Palestinian National Covenant that had called for Israel's extinction; and it opened the way for an exchange of letters between the Israeli prime minister and Arafat establishing formal mutual recognition. On 13 September 1993, the Declaration of Principles was executed at the White House.

Clinton was quick to reposition the United States at the centre of what seemed like a winning proposal. He threw the weight of his Administration behind the accord, and mobilised international assistance for the Palestinians, but not before extracting further assurances from Arafat. Speaking at the signing ceremony, Clinton pledged United States support 'to implement the difficult details that will make real the principles'[26] contained in the Declaration, endorsing in principle the creation of a Palestinian Interim Self-Government Authority and an elected Council for the Palestinian people, but his commitment was heavily qualified. He made it clear to Arafat that he was prepared to take a lead in trying to organise the finances necessary to carry this through and to try to build the political support for it but that it was imperative that Arafat honour the commitments made to Israel's security, to denouncing terrorism and to assuming responsibility within the areas of self-government for maintaining law and order.[27]

The president had more in mind than reminding Arafat that financial assistance would be dependent upon observance of such factors. He used the occasion to convey an important message to the Arab and Islamic world 'that the United States and all of the nations which help us … are prepared to work with and support Islamic nations as long as they are willing to adhere to the international rules governing human rights and peace and democracy'.[28] He believed that, in offering the Palestinian people the chance of a normal life, the peace process would contribute to the removal of 'one of the great causes of fundamentalism and political extremism'.

One week after the signing of the Declaration, Christopher announced that the United States and Russia would convene a Conference to Support Middle East Peace. On 1 October, representatives from some 43 foreign governments, the World Bank and other international organisations pledged more than $600 million to meet the immediate needs of the Palestinians and over $2 billion over the following five years to help establish Palestinian self-government.[29] The need for international assistance had been anticipated, and the World Bank had been commissioned by the European Community to estimate the resources that would be required to start the building of an economic base in Gaza and the West Bank. The Bank's initial estimate was that $3 billion would be needed over ten years; Arafat's advisers had estimated that $11 billion would be needed in the first three years. The participants also agreed to encourage trade and private investment through export financing programmes and investment incentives. While the United States had initially found it difficult to get the Israelis to treat with the Palestinians, it was able quickly to mobilise rewards. In the space of 33 days since the secretary of state had been informed of the Oslo accord, the former outcast, Yasser Arafat, had been received by the President of the United States at the White House, the PLO had been accorded recognition by the United States, and much-needed international assistance had been pledged for the benefit of the Palestinian people.

If Clinton envisaged the employment of United States power to help realise the Declaration, what would this mean in practice?[30] The Declaration was opaque on a number of significant matters, including two elements that related to the area of occupied territory to be transferred to the Palestinians, and the responsibility of the Palestinian police force. The former is stated to 'cover West Bank and Gaza territory, except for issues that will be negotiated in the permanent status negotiations', like Jerusalem, settlements and borders.[31] Nowhere does the Declaration state the total amount of territory to be transferred to the Palestinians or the timetable for further transfers of territory beyond an initial disposition of Gaza and Jericho. The provision relating to the Palestinian police places upon them the obligation to 'guarantee public order and internal security for … the West Bank and the Gaza Strip'. The Palestinian police were, in effect, to be co-opted as an agency of Israel's security apparatus, obliged to act as guarantor of Israel's internal security from its most vulnerable quarter.[32] There was much else that would be left to negotiation under an Interim Agreement. The emotional question of the right of return of Palestinian refugees would be deferred to the permanent status negotiations, along with that of the future status of Jerusalem. It was envisaged that the Palestinian Authority's writ would be limited initially to 'education and culture, health, social welfare, direct taxation, and tourism'.

The allocation of responsibility for Palestinian health, education and welfare to a Palestinian Authority presented little problem for the United States. The Administration also seems not to have been particularly concerned about the lack of specificity in the Declaration about the more contentious issues,[33] apparently content to rest on the Declaration's provision that the two parties would address these matters in the permanent status negotiation. Such was the general euphoria surrounding the conclusion of the first agreement between Israel and the Palestinians, that there was an expectation that the parties would have little difficulty in moving to the next stage by 13 December. The step-by-step process that underpinned the negotiation was designed to foster a sufficient measure of trust and cooperation between the parties that a resolution of the more intractable issues could be tacked in a more benign atmosphere at the end of the process. Despite Israel's settlements policy, the Administration did not act to forestall developments that could adversely affect the process in the interim. Further settlement construction would change the situation on the ground and complicate a resolution of the question of territory. It would have been possible for the president to have expressed a hope that nothing would be done by either party that would make more difficult a resolution of the permanent status issues, but he did not do so.

A crisis in Palestinian fortunes, including the PLO's deteriorating financial situation, had brought it to the negotiating table; and the imbalance of power between Israel and the Palestinians had determined the nature of their agreement.[34] Arafat had taken a close interest in the drafting of the Declaration,[35] but seems never really to have understood the implications of the Oslo process or the detail. He placed his faith in its leading toward recognition of the PLO, which it did, and subsequently toward realisation of a vision of Palestinian statehood. As Article VIII on the Palestinian police shows, his understanding of the obligations of statehood was fuzzy.[36]

POST-OSLO NEGOTIATIONS

The environment during the last quarter of 1993 seemed to the Americans, as facilitator, to augur well for success. The United States was encouraged that both the Israeli and Palestinian leaderships had received convincing, though not overwhelming, endorsement of the Declaration from their respective legislatures. Both sides contained a minority that strongly rejected its central proposition that an independent Palestinian entity of some kind should be created alongside Israel. The leaderships' first task was to give effect to the Israeli withdrawal from Gaza and Jericho. When Arafat and Rabin met to discuss the matter it became clear that the Declaration's imprecision provided ground for divergent interpretations. Arafat asked the United States and Russian governments to intercede with Rabin, but neither was prepared to intervene unless requested to do so by both parties. They argued that it was natural that disagreements should arise during the process of turning a vague agreement into something workable. As the Israelis and Palestinians sorted out their differences, support for the Oslo accord in the occupied territories fell from 68 per cent in September 1993 to 44 per cent in January 1994.[37] An agreement on the 'redeployment' of Israeli troops from Gaza and Jericho was initialled at Cairo on 9 February, and signed after further elaboration, on 4 May 1994. The Cairo Agreement started the clock on the five-year transitional period envisaged in the Oslo accord and provided for final status talks to begin no later than May 1996, with 4 May 1999 as the envisaged end of the transitional period. It also paved the way for Arafat's residence on Palestinian soil and the creation of a Palestinian Authority.

The United States had to intercede to keep implementation of the process moving after an Israeli settler, Baruch Goldstein, tried to derail it by massacring Muslim worshippers at Hebron on 25 February 1994. The attempt was timed to block the withdrawal from Gaza and Jericho, which was planned to begin on 17 March, and to inflame religious feeling.[38] An immediate attempt to have the UN Security Council condemn the settler's murderous rampage was delayed by Washington and not adopted until 18 March. Clinton and Christopher telephoned Arafat urging that the assassin not be allowed to stop the peace process, Christopher telling Arafat that a Security Council resolution would complicate matters. The direct call from the President of the United States impressed Arafat and Clinton's influence was evident in a statement issued by Arafat's Fatah faction a few hours after the attack: 'The negotiations with the Israelis are not suspended: on the contrary these acts demonstrate the urgency of peace'.[39] It was immediately obvious that Fatah was out of step with Arab capitals, and the PLO Executive Committee reversed Arafat's decision. By the time the Security Council acted, nearly three weeks after the massacre, all the Arab parties principals had suspended their participation in the Washington talks. Agreement was eventually reached on the resumption of negotiations and the temporary deployment to Hebron of an observer force from Norway, Denmark and Italy.

From the United States perspective it was paramount that the Oslo process, which offered the only prospect of a peaceful settlement, be preserved and that negotiations be resumed within its framework. There were three options available to the Administration if the UN Security Council were to be prevented from adopting a resolution inimical to the peace process. It could persuade other members to address the matter in terms acceptable to it, if necessary by threatening use of the US veto to effect changes to any draft resolution to ensure that the final document accommodated American interests; or persuade members of the Council to adopt a non-binding presidential statement in lieu of a resolution, again possibly by threatening to use its veto; or, as a last resort, prevent the adoption of a resolution by the exercise of its veto. On this occasion, the United States was able to persuade the Security Council, in adopting Resolution 904, to condemn the massacre without holding the Israeli government accountable. Chastisement of Israel was confined to the less-weighty preambular portion, while the operative paragraphs focussed on a resumption of bilateral negotiations.

On 6 April, hours after the completion of the Muslim 40-day period of mourning, a Hamas activist from Gaza detonated a suicide bomb in Israel, killing eight and injuring 42 people. The United States demanded that Arafat condemn the incident. He agreed to comply on condition that the Israeli government condemn any future killings of Palestinians by Israeli settlers. The US demand put Arafat in an awkward position, and he hesitated. He knew that the bombing would be regarded by Palestinians as justified retribution for the massacre at Hebron. The Israeli government responded to his hesitation by sealing the routes that Palestinian commuters normally used to travel to their regular jobs in Israel. The blockade was to become 'an economic fact of life in the West Bank and Gaza, a permanent system that … introduced a host of new and intractable problems into an already weakened and structurally distorted economy'.[40]

Terrorism and insurgency was one of the major United States interests discussed in Chapter 1. It was a phenomenon that was to bedevil the peace process, affecting relations between Israel and both the Palestinians and Syria. For the Palestinians, a culture of terror and violence, developed over the preceding decades, was seen as a legitimate tool to force the world to pay attention to them and to address their grievances. In Dennis Ross's appreciation, the Palestinians saw themselves as victims because Israel 'had taken by force what had been theirs, and … kept them under occupation'. Such was their self-view that they admired those who stood up to and threatened Israel or its benefactor. The 1987 *intifada* was 'an expression of Palestinian frustration and anger … [T]he Palestinians felt degraded and humiliated under occupation. Israeli actions to try to prevent Palestinian acts of terror … deepened Palestinian resentment, and fostered their sense of victimisation.'[41] For Clinton, terrorism was a global scourge that had impacted upon American interests at home and abroad. In his concluding days in office the president identified possible collusion among terrorists, narco-traffickers and organised criminals 'with smaller and more difficult to detect weapons of mass destruction and powerful traditional weapons' as the main security threat to the United States in the twenty-first century.[42] Throughout his engagement in the search for a resolution of the Arab–Israel dispute Clinton recognised the capacity of terrorists to frustrate and inhibit progress and urged Arafat and Assad to clamp down on terrorist activity undertaken or sponsored by actors within their spheres of responsibility.

The Hebron 'exchange' was significant for its violence, and illustrative also of the havoc retributive closures were to wreak on the Palestinian economy. It was only one of many acts initiated by Arab and Jewish opponents of the peace process directed at both the other party and the leaderships of their own communities.[43] Rabin was to be assassinated by an Israeli in November 1995 for his peace policies. Arafat, too, faced a crisis of public confidence.[44] A significant challenge for Clinton became that of encouraging movement toward the objective of an Israel–Palestinian settlement in the context of growing public dismay, disillusion and distrust occasioned by terrorist activity and retributive action. Israelis and Palestinians were both at fault. Islamist Palestinians played a major part in organising and perpetrating Palestinian violence. Israeli retribution caused economic and social hardship and discontent in the occupied territories, which aided the recruitment of activists and insurgent 'martyrs'. The United States urged Israel to honour its commitment to an initial transfer of territory to the Palestinians and both sides to press ahead with negotiations on the application of the principles of the Declaration to other parts of the West Bank. The Palestinian leadership welcomed the US's interest in seeing the Declaration implemented: it was important that the Oslo formula of 'Gaza first' should not be allowed to turn into 'Gaza last'.

THE PALESTINIAN AUTHORITY

Congressional authority to participate in Palestinian institution building was conferred by a presidential waiver to the Middle East Peace Facilitation Act (MEPFA) of 1993, but was dependent upon the Palestinians honouring specified commitments, and the State Department was required to report on Palestinian compliance. The Administration used this provision to pressure Arafat to abide by his commitments to Israel.

The Administration's concern about Palestinian terrorism necessarily transferred to an interest in the development of Palestinian security forces. The establishment of 'a strong police force' is one of the provisions of the Declaration. Although the size of the force is established by various agreements between Israel and the Palestinians, its limits have not been observed by the Palestinian Authority, Israel or the Palestinian Authority's various international sponsors.[45] If the United States hoped that international sponsorship would help create a conventional police force, this hope was misplaced. The Palestinian Authority spawned a complex network of anywhere from four to nine PA intelligence forces, depending on how they are classified.[46] The array gave Arafat enormous scope for political patronage. The absence of a clear chain of command entrenched power in his hands, and the proliferation of forces enabled him to exert authority through any one agency while portraying a softer approach through another.

In order to help constrain the violence, Clinton issued Executive Order 12947 of 23 January 1995 Prohibiting Transactions with Terrorists who Threaten to Disrupt the Middle East Peace Process, which lists the Islamist group Hamas that rejected the Oslo accord. By January 1995 some 95 Israelis had been killed since the Gaza–Jericho withdrawals and the Israeli Government was under considerable domestic pressure to demonstrate the value of the Oslo process. The majority of Israelis now thought that Israel should reinforce its military capabilities rather than pursue peace. Over the preceding months Rabin had applied punitive measures to impress upon the Palestinian leadership the need to restrain the Hamas and Islamic Jihad militants operating from the Gaza Strip. The newly installed Palestinian police did make arrests and on one occasion used live ammunition to control rioting, which led to their being compared unfavourably with Israeli forces by their own community.

Unable to prise enough money out of the World Bank trust fund to meet the salaries of the nascent Palestinian civil service, and hurt by defections from the PLO executive committee,[47] Arafat faced an increasingly uncomfortable situation in 1995. Between the end of 1992 and the end of 1996, real GNP in the Gaza Strip and West Bank fell 18.4 per cent, primarily due to the loss of employment in Israel and reduced trade flows that resulted from the closure of the border. Talk of civil war was no longer fanciful, and Peres had to intercede with Rabin to make some conciliatory gestures. Clinton summed-up the situation as the toughest issue he faced between the Israelis and the Palestinians.

> When the borders were open, it made Israel more vulnerable to terrorism. When innocent people are killed, it undermines support in Israel for the peace process and weakens the government's ability to go forward. When the borders are closed, the incomes of the Palestinian people drop dramatically, and it makes young people more vulnerable to the appeals of the terrorists.[48]

Convinced of the ameliorative effect of economic development in the Palestinian territories, and of the role of free enterprise as the engine of long-term economic development, the United States made arrangements for another international conference to commit additional economic assistance to the Palestinians. It also initiated discussion with Israeli and Palestinian officials about the granting of reciprocal duty-free status for products manufactured in the West Bank and Gaza. Its ability to buttress the peace negotiations with economic and technical assistance to the Palestinians was hampered, however, by congressional attitudes and differences between governmental officials. The State Department, looking for early results, often complained about the slowness of USAID programmes in the territories, while USAID complained that the programme was being diverted from meaningful development objectives. USAID was constrained by a prohibition on direct US assistance to the Palestinian Authority; its projects in the West Bank and Gaza had to be contracted out to non-governmental agencies. The subcontractors often initially underestimated the political and economic difficulties that lay ahead. Congressional suspicion of the Palestinians meant periodic congressional review of the assistance programme, making the USAID budget a battle-ground for those critical of foreign aid and the peace process.[49]

TOWARD AN INTERIM AGREEMENT

It had become evident to the United States by 1995 that popular support for the Oslo peace process was declining and the spirit of the Declaration was dissipating. Israel continued to expand its settlements in the occupied territories and increased construction in and around East Jerusalem, and it repeatedly halted, in response to Palestinian terrorist attacks, the talks on further withdrawals from the West Bank towns to which it was committed. An Arab summit in Alexandria in December 1994 registered regional concern, expressing a fear that Israel, which had by then concluded a peace treaty with Jordan, was trying to split the Arab world. In order to re-energise the process, Christopher invited his Egyptian, Israeli and Jordanian counterparts and the PLO negotiator to Washington in March 1995. They reached agreement there on a new target date of 1 July for concluding negotiations on implementation of the stalled parts of the Oslo agreement, but that timetable was also to slip.

When the Israelis and Palestinians were eventually persuaded to embark on negotiation of the Interim Agreement, and consistent with the approach of the United States that the terms of any agreements were for the parties to decide, the Administration stood aside. A 'hands off' approach would help to disabuse any Arab expectation that the United States could deliver Israel. The United States was to intercede, however, when the parties needed its help. The Israelis refused to declare their final position on the amount of territory that they would transfer to the Palestinians. The Palestinians expostulated that they were being asked to enter into an agreement without knowing what the outcome would be.[50] The United States urged Peres to ring Arafat to express impatience with the lack of progress – the 1 July target date having passed – and to engage with him personally. It was successful: Arafat and Peres issued a joint statement on 11 August 1995, and agreement was reached on an Israeli proposal for the transfer of further security powers to the Palestinians every six months over an 18 month period, without defining the amount of territory involved in each of the three phases. At Arafat's insistence, this would be subject to the opening of a Palestinian police station in Hebron. His qualification defused the issue by diverting the discussion from the strategically important question of territory to an issue of immediate importance to Palestinian opinion. Tension in Hebron was real and the predominant Arab community there was insisting that the Israeli Defence Force (IDF) be redeployed from Hebron as was happening in other towns to be transferred to the Palestinians. Peres secured his government's approval to the proposal.

Not only did Ross, as Clinton's envoy, maintain close contact with the negotiating teams, but he also encouraged his American compatriots to lobby Rabin and Peres. At that time, Israel's Likud opposition was encouraging its own friends within the US Congress and the American Jewish community to oppose further aid to the Palestinian Authority.[51] To counter that, Rabin and Peres instructed the Embassy of Israel in Washington to step up a campaign in the Congress in favour of aid to the Palestinians, explaining that aid for the purpose of raising the standard of living in Gaza was part of the fight against terrorism.[52] Ross also told Arafat that if agreement were not attained before 1 October 1995, the Congress would not extend the waiver that permitted the PLO to maintain its quasi-embassy in Washington.[53] Savir suggested to his Palestinian counterpart that Ross be approached about a signing of an Interim Agreement in Washington on 22 September. That artificial deadline also imposed its own constraints, including a requirement that Peres and Arafat resolve some 25 difficult issues that had eluded officials.

The principal issue in contention was the allocation of territory to the Palestinians. Savir has recalled that a senior Palestinian negotiator had spoken of the need to benefit from the experience at Gaza and to fight terrorism in the Palestinian interest, not as something done for Israel's sake. It was in the context of mutual security that Savir attributed to him a new concept for crafting the Interim Agreement. 'He spoke of establishing three security areas in the West Bank: one under Palestinian control, one under Israeli control, and the third to be patrolled by a joint force'[54] as part of the transitional process. The delegate claimed that the concept had been discussed with Arafat. The Israelis only revealed the map showing their proposed allocations to the Palestinians 24 hours before the planned conclusion of the talks. Ross, who had been in telephone contact with the Israeli delegation every few hours during the final stages of the negotiations, must have been aware of its intention to produce the map toward the end of the negotiating process. When Arafat saw the proposed division, which allocated the Palestinians about 22 per cent of the West Bank, he stormed out of a meeting complaining that the Israelis wanted to destroy him by making him accept cantons.[55] In fact, the area under discussion was home to 98 per cent of the Palestinian population.[56] Arafat and Peres both indulged in brinkmanship as they fought for their respective interests. They were able eventually to ring Christopher and Ross to inform them that the Interim Agreement had been concluded.

THE INTERIM AGREEMENT

The Israeli–Palestinian Interim Agreement ('Oslo II')[57] was signed in Washington by Rabin and Arafat in the presence of Clinton, Egypt's President Hosni Mubarak and King Hussein of Jordan on 28 September 1995. Among its principal provisions are:

- direct election of a Palestinian Legislative Council of 82 members and a *ra'is* (or head) of the Executive Authority by the Palestinian people of the West Bank, Jerusalem and the Gaza Strip. The Council and the *ra'is* together will constitute the Palestinian Interim Self-Government Authority;
- the Israeli civil administration in the West Bank will be dissolved, and the Israeli military government withdrawn, after the inauguration of the Council. Special arrangements are made for Hebron where IDF withdrawal will take place by 28 March 1996;
- the West Bank shall be divided into three types of areas: area A consists of Palestinian towns and urban areas; area B consists of Palestinian villages and less densely populated parts; and area C consists of the lands confiscated by Israel for settlements and roads. Area A will be placed under exclusive Palestinian control and area C under exclusive Israeli control, and in area B the Palestinians will exercise civilian authority while Israel continues to be in charge of security;
- the role of the Palestinian police in support of security is reaffirmed, with its location, size, weaponry and responsibilities spelled out in some detail; and
- within two months of the inauguration of the Council the Palestine National Council will formally approve changes to those provisions of the Palestinian Covenant which deny Israel's right to exist.

The Interim Agreement disappointed many Israelis and Palestinians. The Israeli right could see in it the evaporation of their dream of an *Eretz Yisrael*.

The Knesset ratified the agreement by the tight vote of 61 in favour and 59 against. The Palestinians acted in accordance with the agreement, electing the Palestinian Authority's executive and legislature in January 1996, and convening a meeting of the PLO's National Council in April to remove articles from the Palestine National Covenant calling for the elimination of Israel. The Council voted 504 to 54 (with 214 abstentions) to amend the Covenant, revealing considerable scepticism about the direction of Palestinian policy.

Five weeks after the signing of the agreement, Yitzhak Rabin was murdered by a Jewish zealot who confessed that his aim was to derail the peace process. Disaffected Palestinians also took direct action. Palestinian expectations of a freer and better way of life independent of Israeli authority had not been realised. Between 1992 and 1996 real per capita GNP declined by 37 per cent in the West Bank and Gaza, and the situation was to worsen, with 19.1 per cent of the population of the two areas living under the poverty line of $650 per person per annum by early 1997.[58] Palestinian terrorists undertook suicide bombings in Ashkelon, Jerusalem and Tel Aviv in February and March 1996, causing 58 deaths, mostly of civilians. The incidents prompted the Israeli government to postpone the March redeployment from Hebron, which was to be deferred again until after the Israeli general election scheduled for 29 May 1996.

Rabin was succeeded as prime minister by Peres, but Peres was never able to exert the same authority over the peace process as Rabin. Albright felt that he lacked Rabin's military credentials and charismatic bluntness.[59] Peres was admired for his faith in human nature, and had been at his most successful in exploring options under the authority and resolve of Rabin. Clinton backed him, but lacking Rabin's strength of purpose, the somewhat visionary Peres was vulnerable.

PROTECTING THE PEACE PROCESS

Clinton's pledge in September 1993 to build political support for the Olso process took him to the United Nations, where he was able initially to turn matters to the US's advantage. Its concern to control the process launched at Madrid contradicted a UN General Assembly (UNGA) decision to convene an international conference on Palestine under UN auspices. His Administration saw an opportunity to muster the weight of international opinion behind the Madrid conference and to isolate irredentist states opposed to dealing with Israel. It used the United Nations to garner international support for the Madrid process, turning to its advantage the votes of an overwhelming majority of the members of the United Nations, including especially those of formerly trenchant critics of Israel within the Non-Aligned Movement and the

Organisation of the Islamic Conference. After the signing of the Declaration of Principles in 1993, the US and Russian co-sponsors of the Madrid process combined with 108 other states in co-sponsoring UNGA Resolution 48/58, which expressed full support for the Declaration. The United States elicited comparable support in the General Assembly and the Economic and Social Council (ECOSOC) in ensuing years.[60]

Clinton's Administration also tried to capitalise on the moment to create a clean slate for the negotiating parties, removing from consideration prescriptive formulations adopted by the United Nations, many of which favoured the Palestinian cause. Madeleine Albright, then Permanent Representative of the United States to the United Nations, wrote to the President of the General Assembly on 8 August 1994 suggesting that 'contentious resolutions that accentuated political differences without prompting solutions should be consolidated, improved, or eliminated … [and that] … resolution language referring to "final status" issues should be dropped, since these issues are now under negotiation by the parties themselves … These include refugees, settlements, territorial sovereignty and the status of Jerusalem.'[61] Albright sought to avoid the constraint of established UN formulations, but hardly dared expect that this could be achieved through a letter to the presiding officer. Had the General Assembly supported Albright's claim, it would have diminished, if not destroyed, the bases on which key Palestinian claims rested.

It is curious that Palestinian negotiators had not insisted on the precepts of significant instruments such as the Fourth Geneva Convention being incorporated into the Declaration of Principles in 1993. Israel was a signatory to the Convention, and the PLO had committed itself to it. Earlier, at the third round of the Washington talks in January 1992, the Palestinians had presented a document to the Israelis demanding an immediate halt to settlement activity and the application of the Convention to the occupied territories.[62] During the Oslo negotiations the Palestinians had secured Israeli recognition of the West Bank and the Gaza Strip as forming 'a single territorial unit, whose integrity will be preserved'[63] and may have judged this sufficient guarantee that the Arab character of the territory would be maintained. Whatever the reason for the absence of any specific reference to the Convention, the fact that its principles were not mirrored in the Declaration enabled the United States to shelter behind the formula that such matters had been reserved for the final status negotiations.

The US use of the United Nations to bolster the peace process was set back as Israel continued building settlements. Opinion within the world body became increasingly critical of Israeli action. The Israeli government declared that it would not negotiate on settlements during the interim period. The question was brought before the UN Security Council in February and May 1995 where the US was obliged to address it. In February France, Italy and the United Kingdom declared the Israeli activity illegal, essentially in terms of the Fourth Geneva Convention, while Russia called for restraint from acts that would prejudice an Israel–Palestinian peace settlement. The United States representative, too, sought to preserve the integrity of the Oslo process, and the February session adjourned without the Council taking any action. The Security Council's consideration of May 1995 focussed on Israel's planned land expropriations in East Jerusalem. Again the Western allies of the United States, including Canada, spoke against the decision of the Israeli government. All other members of the Security Council voted in favour of the draft, but the United States vetoed it. The Administration had protected Israel on a matter of fundamental significance to the shape of any final outcome.

LEGITIMACY OF THE PALESTINIAN AUTHORITY

Clinton's pledge to assist the formation of a Palestinian Authority was conditional on adherence 'to the international rules governing human rights and peace and democracy'. In the same speech he had seen the peace process as contributing to the removal of 'fundamentalism and political extremism'.[64] The legitimacy of the Authority would be critical to the peace process, imputing responsibility and accountability to Palestinian institutions. The European Community assumed the role of the Authority's principal sponsor. When the first elections were held for the *ra'is* and legislature, the Europeans took the lead in organising international election monitors. Former President Carter was the principal American observer. Although the monitors reported that the conduct of the elections was fair, the scope of their observation was confined to the possibility of coercion and ballot rigging. The United States would have known of pre-election irregularities; that the Europeans had expressed reservations about the electoral process; and that local observers had called on 25 January for a re-vote throughout the West Bank and Gaza.[65] The success of Arafat's Fatah organisation also cast suspicion upon the conduct of the elections. All members of the leadership who had returned from Tunis won. The Palestinian opposition largely boycotted the elections.

The contest for the Palestinian presidency also deserves qualification. The exit poll conducted by the eminent Palestinian political scientist, Khalil Shikaki, showed that the electorate was evenly divided over whether Arafat should have comparable or lesser power than the legislature. Only 20 per cent thought that he should have more power than the council.[66]

Notwithstanding these reservations, Shikaki concluded from his detailed analysis of the elections that they passed four critical tests of political legitimacy.[67] The President of the UN Security Council issued a statement on behalf of the members of the Council on 22 January noting that the elections were an accurate reflection of the wishes of the Palestinian electorate. Over the ensuing years, grave doubts have come to be entertained about the Authority's system of governance: from the very beginning power gravitated toward Arafat's executive authority; no senior official had ever been held accountable for any violation of the law;[68] and human rights abuses had been perpetrated by the Palestinian Authority on its own people. Arafat has often been unreceptive to the legislators' democratically formulated proposals. To what extent could the United States rely upon the Palestinian Authority to deliver upon its commitments? Ross has recorded that Washington tended to side with Israeli leaders who preferred an authoritarian Palestinian regime that could fulfil its security obligations. Israel's concern was that the Palestinian Authority fight Islamic militancy and terrorism, regardless of its stance on human rights and due process.[69] For his part, Arafat preferred that Palestinian extremists focus on Israel, not on him. It was not until after President Bush II took office that the United States began in earnest to pressure Arafat to reform his administration.

As this digression into the creation of the Palestinian Authority shows, the United States was confused about the means of prosecuting its objectives with the Authority; was treating with an imperfect instrument; was more concerned with law and order than the realisation of principles of liberal and accountable governance; and was reliant upon an unformed and nascent 'state' to deliver on internationally brokered agreements. That was to remain the case for the remainder of Clinton's term of office and beyond, complicating the realisation of a peace agreement.

Persuasion and pressure remained the Administration's principal means of influencing the Palestinian leadership. Arafat was well aware of the US's expectation of him in terms of the Middle East Peace Facilitation Act. He showed that he was able to crack down on terrorism, on which Israeli and Palestinian security forces cooperated; and he responded to bomb explosions in Jerusalem and Tel Aviv in March with imprisonments, outlawing several Islamic groups and closing some of their schools, orphanages and charitable organisations. He also concurred in Peres's decision to defer withdrawal of the IDF from Hebron until after the Israeli election in 1996, hoping that cooperation would facilitate Peres's return to office.

The efforts of Palestinian insurgents to set back the peace process, and of Hezbollah in Israel's self-declared southern Lebanon security zone, presented particular difficulties to the United States. In order to bring international pressure to bear to restrain, if not halt, the violence, Clinton persuaded the Egyptian president to host a meeting at Sharm el-Sheikh in March 1996. Clinton secured international condemnation of terrorism, and was able to demonstrate to terrorist groups that they were running against the tide of regional opinion. He also praised Israel's efforts to date, promising support in its campaign to thwart Islamic violence.[70] While Clinton achieved his political objective, it was obtained in the absence of the two states that abetted terrorist groups, Iran and Syria, and also of Lebanon, from which some terrorist activity was launched. Moreover, the summit's conclusions lacked material substance, and international condemnation did nothing to persuade terrorist groups or their state supporters to halt terrorist activity in the region.

Although the ostensible focus of the conference was terrorism, Clinton had an additional objective. He sought regional support for the peace process. The best prospect for its continuance lay in the return of an Israeli government led by Peres. Peres's principal challenger for the premiership, Binyamin Netanyahu, had already signalled his disagreement with the process. During the two months remaining before that regional support could be reflected in an electoral victory, Lebanon's Hezbollah responded vigorously to Israeli shelling into southern Lebanon. Israel launched Operation Grapes of Wrath against Lebanese sites on 11 April. Peres hoped that the assault would show the Israeli public that while he was deeply committed to the peace process, he could be firm where questions of security were involved. Public opinion surveys were showing increased support for the Arab–Israel peace process, but most supporters of the religious and right-wing parties remained opposed to, or sceptical about it. The military adventure played indirectly into the hands of the Israeli political right. On election day many Arab Israelis abstained from voting because IDF action had caused casualties among Lebanese civilians.

Netanyahu had promised that if he attained office on 29 May, he would not renege on any of the country's international commitments. He implied, however, that he would freeze the Oslo process. He won Israel's first direct election for prime minister under new procedures by less than one-half of one per cent of the vote. His party actually won fewer Knesset seats than Peres's Labor party, but was able to form a governing coalition with minor parties of the right. It was hardly a convincing mandate to frustrate the Oslo peace process. The United States now had to deal with the third Israeli government, and the fourth prime minister, since the negotiation had been launched in 1991. How it sought to persuade the new government to effect a peaceful settlement with the Palestinians will be discussed in Chapter 6.

CONCLUSION

The contrast between Bush I's robust application of power to bring Israel and the Arab parties into face-to-face negotiation and Clinton's restrained use of American power during his early period in office is patent. Under Clinton, the ideational power of the United States was, in general, relegated to the realm of the possible in the light of agendas set by others rather than an instrument to be used for the advancement of discrete objectives. There were significant exceptions. The United States effectively marshalled international assistance for the Palestinian Authority after the signing of the Declaration of Principles, and secured almost universal approbation of the peace process within the United Nations. Later, when the United Nations became seized of Palestinian concerns about an expansion of Israeli settlements in the occupied territories, United States diplomacy was employed to protect the process.

Clinton's Administration was constrained in its dealings with Israel and the Palestinians by congressional attitudes, but was able to turn some congressional requirements to its advantage, especially in respect of the Palestinians, for whom the threat of negative United States sanctions outweighed the positive sanctions that were extended. The United States used this to effect the removal from the Palestinian National Covenant of clauses that called for Israel's extinction. But with an annual pledge to the Palestinians amounting to just 3.3 per cent of the $3 billion allocated to Israel each year, any authority the United States might hope to exercise through the aid element of positive sanctions was limited.

For Clinton, keeping the peace process afloat became an imperative if the overall strategic objective were ever to be realised. He believed that its progress could easily be disrupted and that it needed to be preserved at almost any cost. Such was the importance given to protection that the United States came to view the process as an end in itself, rather than the means toward an end. With the benefit of hindsight, Ross has concluded:

> By never holding either side accountable, by never being prepared to disrupt the process and put it on hold, we contributed to an environment in which commitments were rarely taken seriously by either side, knowing there would never be any real consequence. In the future, there must be a consequence for nonperformance – and to have real meaning, it must be publicly seen. When all sides have to explain publicly why a particular step has been taken, why they are being blamed, why they have not acted in accordance with an obligation, they will feel the consequence.[71]

That argument does not satisfactorily address the need to prevent, or minimise, disruption to the peace process. A public charge by the United States of non-performance by one party would almost inevitably have produced assertions that the fault lay in the other's provocation. Once the airwaves had become saturated with accusations and counter-accusations, negotiation would have become more difficult.

The unbalanced nature of the structure launched at Madrid was presented in the previous chapter. Why did Arafat initially agree to negotiate within a structure that formalised Israel's supremacy over Palestinians, and then later place his trust for remediation in the hands of Israel's most fervent supporter? Therein lies the paradox that Israel's receptiveness to an exchange of land for peace depends upon the unwavering commitment of the US to its security.

The United States is the only external power possessing the necessary authority to effect some change in Israeli perceptions. Although not an ideal situation, Palestinian reliance upon the United States was not without some countervailing advantages. Personal contact with the president flattered Arafat's vanity, a toehold had been created through the Declaration of Principles that offered the prospect of a Palestinian state, and the United States had encouraged foreign assistance for his people.

The United States concentration on protection and preservation of the process meant that it failed to answer fundamental questions about the nature of any future Palestinian entity dotted with Israeli settlements; how the continuing construction of settlements might complicate the controversial issue of Palestinian statehood; how an undivided Jerusalem could satisfy the contradictory aspirations of Israelis and Palestinians to locate their capitals there; and, above all, how to handle such matters as they arose during the transition to final status negotiations. Its apparent disinclination to address and resolve the last of these questions led to a gradual erosion of confidence in a United States-designed process whose tactical objective was to proceed to a negotiated settlement through confidence-building stages.

An option available to the United States, consistent with that objective, would have been to insist that settlement activity be halted pending the outcome of the final status negotiations. The 1993 Declaration does not prescribe a halt to settlement-building, but there are many precedents in international relations for freezing contentious issues pending their resolution. If Clinton had determined the relevance of these precedents to the settlements question, the United States could have exerted pressure on Israel to conform. He chose the softer option of leaving the matter to the two parties to resolve, notwithstanding that by the time they addressed the matter the situation on the ground would have been irrevocably altered.

A further shortcoming on a matter of principle was revealed in 1994 when Albright tested the receptivity of the UN General Assembly to the creation of a clean slate for Israeli and Palestinian negotiators. Jerusalem, refugees, and again, settlements, were among the matters whose UN prescriptions the Clinton Administration sought to excise.

The United States could reasonably expect that there would be some opposition to the Oslo accords among Israelis and Palestinians. It could not have anticipated the cycle of violence and retributive action that eventuated, or the murder of an Israeli premier. It responded to these unintended consequences. The United States secured significant regional condemnation of terrorism, although some key states that facilitated, if not actually supported terrorism, were not party to the condemnation. Clinton also proscribed assistance to Hamas through an Executive Order.

The United States had explicitly conditioned support for a Palestinian self-governing agency on its ability to maintain law and order within its jurisdiction. Arafat showed that he was able to restrain his opponents when it suited him, as he did in helping to create a climate conducive to Peres's election to the premiership. When Arafat did so, it was in ways that were often contrary to international human rights norms. The Palestinian Authority was not alone in this: breaches of customary international law affecting human rights were committed by both Israelis and Palestinians.[72] These might be presumed to have troubled a president who was championing global observance of human rights and democratisation and who had explicitly denied particularism in human rights.[73] But priority was accorded to security, without which the peace process was stymied.

Progress had been made in the Israeli–Palestinian negotiation during the tenure of Israel's Labor government, but it was tentative. Much of the address of Clinton's Administration had perforce been the protection of a process whose vulnerability had been exposed by extremists opposed to the accommodations that were being concluded.

NOTES

1 Mansour (1993) p.6.
2 Djerejian (1993b) p.696.
3 Heikal (1996) pp.412–25; Mansour (1993) pp.10–28.
4 Morris (2001) p.615.
5 Mansour (1993) p.16; Parsons (1996) p.16.
6 Mansour (1993) p.15; Bush, G.H.W. *Public Papers, 1992*, p.1506.
7 Morris (2001) p.614.
8 Bush, G.H.W. *Public Papers, 1991*, p.1363.
9 Shlaim (2000) p.509.
10 Reich (2002) p.92. Reich cites Rabin informing the Knesset during ratification of the Israel–Palestinian Interim Agreement of 1995 that: 'The borders of the State of Israel, during the permanent solution, will be beyond the lines which existed before the Six Day War. We will not return to the 4 June 1967 lines.'
11 Ross (2004) pp.98–9.
12 Rubenberg (2001) p.1.
13 Christopher (1993) p.141.
14 Djerejian (1993a) p.569.
15 Heikal (1996) p.449.
16 Clinton, W.J. *Public Papers, 1993*, p.307. Stated by Prime Minister Yitzhak Rabin in answer to a question at a press conference.
17 Morris (2001) p.619.
18 Waage (2002) p.608.
19 Abbas (1995) pp.51–2; Beilin (1999) p.62.
20 Beilin (1999) pp.114–5.
21 Abbas (1995) p.194.
22 Interview with former US ambassador Robert Pelletrau Jr in Washington DC on 26 March 2001.
23 Beilin (1999) pp.79, 120.
24 Savir (1998) pp.66–7.
25 Clinton, W.J. *Public Papers, 1993*, p.1457.
26 Ibid. p.1476.

27 Ibid. p.1480.

28 Ibid. p.1479.

29 Ibid. p.1643; Djerejian (1993c) p.876; Savir (1998) p.82. Savir records the amount pledged as over $3 billion in grants and loans, primarily from the United States, the European Union and Japan.

30 In broad terms it would mean pursuit of a peace settlement according to the timetable set out in the Declaration of Principles. By 13 December 1993 an agreement was to be concluded on Israel's withdrawal from Gaza and Jericho and the withdrawal begun; the withdrawal should be completed by 13 April 1994 when a five-year transitional period should begin. The transitional period would comprise an interim period, and permanent status negotiations must commence not later than the beginning of the third year of the interim period (that is, by 13 April 1996). By 13 July 1994 a Palestinian police force should have been established, the Israel Defence Force redeployed in the West Bank and Gaza outside of populated areas, and elections held for a Palestinian legislative council. Clinton's commitment would also mean support for the creation of a Palestinian Authority, which would become a principal actor in the peace process.

31 Declaration of Principles on Interim Self-Government Arrangements, 13 September 1993.

32 Khalidi (1996) p.9.

33 Neither Clinton's autobiography nor Ross's memoir mentions this matter. Ross worked on the Arab–Israel peace process within the Bush and Clinton Administrations from 1988 to 2000. He has described himself as 'the architect of our policy toward the Arab–Israeli conflict in the first Bush administration and the lead negotiator in the Arab–Israeli peace process throughout the Clinton presidency.' Ross (2004) p.7.

34 Heikal (1996) pp.463, 469. After listening devices were discovered in the residence and office of the PLO's ambassador to Tunisia, it was clear to the PLO that the Israelis must have known everything about the organization's internal splits and the gravity of its financial situation.

35 Beilin (1999) p.102. The Israelis had seen Arafat's minutes in the margins of the draft Declaration.

36 Interview with Dennis B. Ross in Washington DC on 20 April 2001, in whose view Arafat had never shown that he understood what was meant by a two-state solution.

37 Heikal (1996) p.484.

38 Ibid. pp.492–507. Baruch Goldstein chose the Mosque of Ibrahim, built over the burial place of the religious messenger of monotheism. The site is celebrated in Judaism as the Tomb of the Patriarchs. UN Security Council Resolution 904 states that 'the massacre in Hebron and its aftermath ... took the lives of more than fifty Palestinian civilians and injured several hundred others'.

39 Ibid. p.495.

40 Roy (1998) p.2.

41 Ross (2004) pp.38–43.

42 Clinton (2004) p.890.

43 Shlaim (2000) pp.551, 521. Rabin was accused by some Israelis of grovelling before foreign statesmen, of having no mandate for his policies because his majority in the parliament depended on non-Jewish Knesset members, and Binyamin Netanyahu compared his actions with those of Neville Chamberlain in appeasing Hitler.

44 Heikal (1996) p.511. Arafat was charged with having over estimated the authority of the United States in the post-Soviet Union world order, leading to unnecessary retreats; Ma'oz (1996) p.14.

45 Usher (1996) p.22; Christopher (1995b) p.725.

46 Usher (1996) p.23–4; Abu Amr (2002) p.17. Abu Amr has said that it was the Palestinian Legislative Council, not the United States or Israel, that first called for a reduction in the number of security services.

47 Heikal (1996) p.537. Four members had resigned in protest against the signing of the Declaration of Principles in September 1993, only six members agreed to go to Gaza, and the majority stayed out.

48 Clinton, W.J. *Public Papers, 1995*, p.468.

49 Brynen (1996) p.80.
50 Savir (1998) p.200.
51 Noyes (1997) p.146. Noyes records that several Likud-supporting groups vigorously questioned US policy on providing aid to the Palestine Liberation Organization (PLO) and other measures that Rabin and Peres considered vital to the peace process.
52 Savir (1998) pp.205–6.
53 Ross (2004) p.204.
54 Savir (1998) pp.158–9.
55 Ibid. p.234.
56 Cordesman (2005) p.4.
57 Israeli–Palestinian Interim Agreement on the West Bank and the Gaza Strip, 28 September 1995.
58 Roy (1998) pp.30–1.
59 Albright (2003) p.291.
60 UN General Assembly Resolutions 48/58 and 50/21 and ECOSOC Resolution 1994/44.
61 Goodman (1994); Bennis (1995).
62 Mansour (1993) p.12.
63 Declaration of Principles.
64 Clinton, W.J. *Public Papers, 1993*, p.1479.
65 Andoni (1996) pp.6, 14.
66 Shikaki (1996) p.21.
67 Ibid. p.22. Shikaki assessed the electoral results, largely on the basis of exit polls, against voter participation, voter perception of the fairness of the electoral processes, voter perception of the role of the council, and whether clan or family loyalties took precedence in the voting over political affiliation.
68 Abu Amr (2002) p.17.
69 Schenker (2000) p.xiv.
70 Clinton, W.J. *Public Papers, 1996*, p.445. Clinton promised $100 million toward combating terrorism. The United States would provide Israel with additional equipment and training; would work together to develop new anti-terror methods and technologies; would enhance communication and coordination; and would increase intelligence sharing and coordination with the assistance of the U.S. Central Intelligence Agency.
71 Ross (2004) p.771.
72 Ibid. p.193. When Arafat arrested a number of operatives from the Hamas military wing in 1995 and created 'security courts' to try them, Rabin urged the US not to pressure Arafat on the human rights questions raised by these courts.
73 Clinton, W.J. *Public Papers, 1993*, p.1056. Clinton said that 'democracy and human rights are not Western imports. They flow from the internal spirit of human beings because they reflect universal aspirations.'

4. Progress and regional cooperation: the United States, Israel and Jordan, and the multilateral negotiations, 1992–97

President Clinton's peace objective in the Middle East included a requirement that 'peace must be comprehensive … [with the expectation that] … the wider Arab and Muslim worlds … [would] … normalise their relations with Israel'.[1] The United States wished to engage Israel's Arab neighbours in a constructive partnership with Israel that would assure Israel's legitimacy as a Middle Eastern state. Significant steps along that route had been taken by Egypt (1979) and the Palestinians (1993). A peace treaty was to be concluded between Israel and Jordan in 1994. Clinton's Administration used the multilateral channel established under the Madrid conference, and regional economic conferences, to help secure Israel's peaceful integration into the region.

THE UNITED STATES, ISRAEL AND JORDAN

Clinton received King Hussein in June 1993 and obtained a firm undertaking of his intent to pursue peace with Israel. A week later the king wrote to the president describing his vision of peace, and Clinton passed a copy of the letter to Israel. Soon afterwards, and in recognition of Jordan's rehabilitation as a helpful associate in the search for a comprehensive peace settlement, Clinton asked the Congress to resume military and economic assistance to Jordan.[2] Jordan's agenda for peace had been ready since October 1992, but King Hussein had preferred to wait until some progress had been made between the Israelis and Palestinians. He had also overseen the composition of a Jordanian Parliament likely to be receptive to a peace treaty with Israel. The path had thereby been cleared for Jordan to move quickly once there were clear indications of movement on the Palestinian side.

The Israel–Palestinian breakthrough in 1993 opened the way. While in Washington for the signing of the Declaration of Principles, the Israelis and Jordanians initialled a substantive agenda for their own negotiation. Then, during a further visit for the pledging conference on 1 October, Crown Prince

Hassan and Shimon Peres announced the creation of a joint economic committee. The United States linked this to the changed Israel–Palestinian circumstances, creating a trilateral US–Israeli–Jordanian working group to look at the next steps for economic development in the two Middle Eastern countries and how they would work with the Palestinians in Gaza and Jericho.

The antecedence of the Israel–Jordan agenda of September 1993 lay in many years of discreet, informal contact between the two parties. Despite the hostile character, at times, of the Israeli–Jordanian relationship, King Hussein and Prime Minister Rabin revealed to Clinton that they had known each other for some 20 years. The king's contact with other Israeli leaders dated from the late 1960s. The king and Peres, also then Israel's foreign minister, had drafted an agreement in London in 1987 on a framework for formal negotiation between their states, but it was to founder on suspicion and tension between Peres and his then prime minister, Yitzhak Shamir. Anticipating a deceptive ploy that was considered again in relation to the Oslo Declaration, the two parties had hoped that their draft could be presented as an 'American' addendum to the Reagan plan of 1982.[3] Secretary of State Shultz was initially well-disposed toward it, and was prepared to visit the Middle East to see how the matter could be taken forward, but was discouraged from doing so by Shamir. The king was to remain somewhat distrustful of Peres's ability to 'deliver' in view of his experience in 1987, and had greater confidence in Rabin, with whom he chose to work on the political negotiations, leaving the economic dimension largely in the hands of Peres and the Crown Prince.

Consistent with his commitment to Clinton, the king proceeded with negotiations with Rabin. Less than a week after the October pledging conference, King Hussein and Rabin met secretly to discuss a peace agreement between their two countries. The king was conscious of the inconclusive nature of the Palestinian Declaration, and insisted that every issue between Israel and Jordan be resolved before he would agree to sign a peace treaty. In a critical reference to the Palestinian Declaration, King Hussein characterised to the US Senate Foreign Relations Committee as 'an unstable surrender treaty' any declaration that left major issues for resolution at a later date.[4] He sought the Israeli prime minister's endorsement of several principles: Israel's guarantee of his 'preferred status' in the Muslim shrines in East Jerusalem deriving from his direct descent from the Prophet Mohammad; Israel's withdrawal from a stretch of land that the Israeli army had captured during the 1948 and 1967 wars; and a more generous division of the water of the Yarmuk River between Israel and Jordan. He achieved all of these objectives, although the area of land returned to Jordan was slightly less than that claimed.

When the king met again with Clinton on 22 June 1994 and briefed him on progress, the president suggested that he make public his secret meetings with Rabin, adding that the Congress would be more receptive to the idea of granting Jordan the economic assistance that it needed were that to occur. The king responded positively, suggesting a public meeting with Rabin in October, but later advanced the date to 25 July 1994. A sense of urgency had been imparted by the conclusion of the Palestinians' Cairo Agreement on 4 May. The Palestinians had set the pace, but the Jordanians were concerned not to lose touch with the front runners. They were also apprehensive that Israel would conclude a separate agreement with Syria, and that there would be very little left for Jordan.[5] Accordingly, Jordan and Israel raced against the clock to complete their Declaration of Principles (known as the Washington Declaration, distinguishing it from the Palestinians') in time for a signing ceremony at the White House. Although the American Administration had been apprised of developments from time to time, a copy of the final draft was only made available to it on the day before its execution. And, indicative of an uneasy truce between Rabin and Peres, Rabin told the press that Peres had been totally excluded from the secret initiative with Jordan.[6]

Clinton, who had already had to address Assad's concerns about Israel's negotiating priorities, did not want the Israel–Jordan agreement to complicate the tentative negotiation under way between Israel and Syria. King Hussein was also concerned about Syria's possible reaction to the Washington Declaration. Its signature represented a breach of Jordan's commitment to keep its formal relations with Israel within an Arab consensus. Clinton telephoned Assad on the eve of its signature to assure him that the United States would continue to mediate a peace agreement between Israel and Syria and that he would accordingly be sending Christopher back to the Middle East.[7] Later, after the signing of the Israel–Jordan peace treaty on 26 October 1994, the Syrians were to complain that relations between the two countries were too warm. The king was determined, however, that Jordan's peace with Israel would not be like the 'cold peace' between Egypt and Israel.[8]

The US contribution to the conclusion of the peace treaty was an indirect one. It was not a participant in the negotiations, but it had established the framework within which they were able to take place. That involved a reassessment of United States interests in Jordan, and the re-establishment of friendly relations with it. Bush I had presided over the change in United States policy, and Clinton built upon it, urging the parties to continue their negotiations, and encouraging King Hussein to believe that US aid would be forthcoming.

The Clinton Administration used Jordan's economic difficulties to its advantage. The suspension of aid to Jordan by Congress in 1991 had contributed to Jordan's problems, but the kingdom's economic woes were longer standing. By 1990, because of unmet financial pledges from the Gulf states, Jordan had been forced to reschedule its external debt and resort to revenue extraction from domestic sources in its quest to balance the budget.[9] The United States wanted the Jordanian government to be able to demonstrate that the peace treaty was of benefit to the people of that country. Jordan has a population with significant links to the Palestinians, which is sympathetic to their condition. American economic assistance might not be sufficient to ensure their support for the peace process, but tangible benefits might moderate opposition to it.

From their first official meeting in June 1993, Clinton was to find King Hussein a committed partner of the United States in the search for an Arab–Israel peace settlement. The president was to call upon the king's assistance a number of times in his dealings with the Palestinians, and in his attempts to build a regional consensus against terrorism. The king proved to be an active and helpful ally. Clinton's gratitude was evident in his promise to King Hussein in mid-1994 to seek forgiveness of Jordan's debt to the United States, which at that time amounted to $702.3 million (including $309.9 million in military loans). The Administration also urged Jordan's other creditors to forgive Jordan's debt, but they were largely unwilling to do so and at the turn of the twenty-first century Jordan's indebtedness remained at over $7 billion. After the signing of the Israel–Jordan peace treaty, the Administration reinstated economic and military assistance to Jordan at about $220 million a year and, as a special dispensation in recognition of King Hussein's contribution to the Wye River negotiations of October 1998 (see Chapter 6), Clinton sought an additional $300 million appropriation to be spread over three years.[10] Jordan also earned America's favour for hosting one of the four economic summits, complementary to the peace process.

The level of American aid to Jordan has not been large, especially when compared to the volume of US assistance to Israel and Egypt. The Administration offered Jordan an economic benefit in another form. In October 2000 Clinton and the new monarch of Jordan, King Abdullah II, witnessed the signing of a US–Jordan Free Trade Agreement. Clinton explicitly linked the conclusion of this treaty to the peace process.[11] The treaty's relatively early conclusion was a signal development: it was only the fourth to be implemented by the United States. The agreement with Jordan had its provenance in the 1985 agreement with Israel. In 1996, in recognition of developments in the Middle East, the agreement with Israel was extended to cover goods produced or manufactured in the West Bank and Gaza Strip, thus providing Palestinian exporters with duty-free access to the United States market; it was also to cover products from qualifying industrial zones between Israel and Jordan, and Israel and Egypt. Ten Jordanian industrial zones qualified under this provision by 2001. Originally Egypt did not register its industrial zones under the provision, preferring to await the conclusion of a comprehensive regional peace. It was to list three zones during the tenure of Bush II. The possibility of a bilateral American free trade agreement with Egypt was also considered by Clinton, who received representations from 26 senators in August 2000 urging him to negotiate a free trade agreement with Egypt that would form the basis for a

Middle East free trade region embracing all of the places mentioned above. The United States felt that Egypt was not in a position economically to satisfy the requirement for an agreement.[12] The more ambitious regional free trade zone proposal is unlikely to prove politically feasible before a settlement of the Arab–Israel dispute.

MULTILATERAL NEGOTIATIONS

The United States objective of expanding the number of Arab and Muslim countries to engage with Israel was pursued through Madrid's multilateral channel. By encouraging closer functional links among all regional states, the United States sought to foster broader social and political understandings and to encourage adaptation to a new perception of shared concerns.[13] Further, the Administrations of both Bush and Clinton saw the well-being of their country linked to an expansion of the world's free market. Baker, the architect of the Madrid framework, said in another context: 'the free markets … will support global – and American – prosperity'.[14] Clinton had advanced a global vision of democracy underpinned by free market forces. An easing of political tension in the Middle East could facilitate the opening of markets, thus encouraging the movement of foreign capital and enterprise, and promote nationally-sponsored or internationally-assisted economic development, which in turn could lead to a normalisation of relations among regional countries.[15] Israel's involvement in this circular process would assure its legitimacy as a regional partner. A Middle East regional development bank was postulated, which could provide technical expertise and finance. And American business would be a direct beneficiary.

The United States had other reasons for instituting the multilateral channel. It was designed to draw in the international community, which had been largely excluded from the Madrid conference, and to send a powerful signal that all the participants, regional and non-regional, were fully committed to the ending of the Arab–Israel dispute. Also, the Administration had concluded that the United States could not afford to shoulder the entire promise and obligation of peace as it had done at Camp David.[16] Some sharing of the financial burden would be necessary, and the chairmanships of the working groups established under the rubric of the multilateral channel would be distributed essentially among the Organisation for Economic Co-operation and Development (OECD) states committed to the peace process and deemed likely to contribute financially toward its realisation.

Madrid's multilateral working groups

Bush I had been content that the multilateral channel be launched in Moscow, given that the critical bilateral negotiations were being conducted in

Washington. This occurred in January 1992. Most of the 36 participants initially took part in order to go along with the United States. The 11 Middle Eastern and North African states widened by seven the number of Arab states prepared to work alongside Israel within the Madrid framework, but key Arab states were not as enthusiastic about the multilateral track as they were about bilateral negotiations. Lebanon and Syria refused to participate in the working groups, without giving reasons, and tried to enlist Arab support for their position. Later, they said that they would not participate until there was more progress in the bilateral negotiations.

The framework devised by Bush I's Administration had been so constructed that the working groups would remain a bit behind the pace of the bilateral negotiations where real progress had to be achieved. This perception was shared, to some extent, by regional participants who were wary of letting Israel gain too much in terms of improved regional relations before it had made substantive progress in negotiations with the Palestinians and Syria in particular.[17] The US architects hoped that developments within the groups would have a positive effect on the bilateral negotiations through a 'pre-negotiation process' of defining and redefining their conflictual relationship, moving from problem recognition to problem solving,[18] and reaching agreement on confidence-building measures.

The working groups covered water, economic development, refugees, the environment, and regional security and arms control[19] and were linked through a Steering Group under US and Russian joint chairmanship. The contributions of the various working groups differed, as did the import of the matters under discussion. During Clinton's presidency contentious matters were raised in the groups on arms control and regional security, and on refugees, and in connection with the group on regional economic development. The non-participation of Lebanon and Syria precluded discussion of the Jordan River basin in the working group on water.

The United States co-chaired the arms control and regional security (ARCS) working group. All issues related to the arms control debate were on its agenda. In a region in which the asymmetrical power balance lay in Israel's favour, it was inevitable that the United States and Israel would have to find some way to deal with the questioning of Israel's assumed nuclear capability when confronted with the argument that it was no longer acceptable for one Middle Eastern country to remain exempt from the international arms control regime that applied to all other regional states. The United States deflected discussion for some time from the nuclear question by encouraging the group's focus on matters in an 'operational basket', where significant progress was achieved. Egypt was concerned, however, that a comprehensive peace settlement would result in a challenge by Israel for regional hegemony in view of its technological and nuclear supremacy. In

Egypt's self-view, its identity as the leader of the Arab world was at stake. In the first half of 1995, and as the Nuclear Non-Proliferation Treaty (NPT) Review and Extension Conference approached, Egypt used the ACRS forum to demand that Israel sign the NPT as the price of Egypt's support for an indefinite extension of the treaty. The United States was investing heavily in an extension of the treaty and the United States asked Israel to find some means of addressing Egypt's concerns. Israel suggested embarking on discussion of a nuclear weapon free zone (NWFZ) in the Middle East two years after having signed peace agreements with all regional states, including Iran and Iraq. It would then consider joining the NPT. Egypt countered with demands for the opening of discussion of an NWFZ in the Middle East before the NPT conference, and Israel's commitment to sign the NPT within two years of signing peace agreements with Lebanon and Syria. Signature of the NPT would, of course, require Israel to open its nuclear facilities to IAEA inspection, which it was loath to do.

Egypt tactically targeted the United States on the question of Israel's assumed nuclear capability. By 1995, European organisations had advanced their own set of initiatives to establish regional security partnerships between countries in Europe and the Mediterranean. This involved some Middle Eastern and North African countries.[20] They adopted the Barcelona Declaration in November of that year, acknowledging the complementarities of the Madrid and Barcelona processes. But Egypt did not insist on a specific clause in the Barcelona Declaration requiring all parties to adhere to the NPT in the near future.

Israel's assumed nuclear capability presented a particular difficulty for the United States. Clinton was challenged about preparedness to pressure India to conform with non-proliferation norms while not doing so to Israel. He responded that 'the fewer countries who become nuclear powers, the better off we're all going to be'. The president's objective was 'to keep the number of people in the nuclear club as small as possible and then reduce the nuclear arsenals that they have, including our own'.[21] In his view, it ought to be possible for nations to guarantee their security in other ways and it was up to the United States to assist in that process. This longer-term vision has attraction, but it did not address immediate questions relating to constraining states outside the regime that possess a nuclear capability, or the value of norms that are not uniformly applied or upheld by one of their principal proponents.

The United States had to weigh which would better serve its interests – the peace process, or Israel's subscription to the NPT. It rated preservation of the peace process as important and the more likely of the alternatives to be achieved. Clinton was later to put in writing: 'From the beginning of my administration, one factor has guided me: to take no action that I judged would harm the peace process'.[22] A number of reasons may be adduced for the prioritisation. First, President Kennedy's Administration had failed to uncover evidence of Israel's development of nuclear weaponry, and America would not wish to place itself in a similar position again. Second, Israel had honoured its commitment to Kennedy that it would not be the first state in the Middle East to test a nuclear weapon, and Israel signed the Comprehensive Test Ban Treaty in 1996. Third, accordingly there is no publicly available evidence that Israel possesses a nuclear capacity. Fourth, the NPT and the non-proliferation regime had shown a robust ability to survive without Israel's signature. Fifth, Clinton would not have wished to press a matter that could alienate his Jewish supporters a year out from his re-election for a second term. And finally, the ambiguity that surrounded the question of whether Israel possessed nuclear weaponry suited the broader purposes of both Israel and the United States in the Middle East. They found it convenient that other states believed that Israel had such a capability and that they factor this into their own foreign policy equations without the necessity of Israel declaring it. Convinced that no accommodation was possible between Israel and Egypt on this issue, the United States suspended the ACRS talks indefinitely in order that they not adversely affect the peace process or Israel–Egypt relations in general.

The working group on refugees became a forum for the discussion of matters germane to any bilateral settlement between Israel and the Palestinians. No other community of refugees was discussed. 'Refugees' having been reserved under the 1993 Declaration for consideration in relation to final status negotiations, doubt could be entertained about progress being achieved within this working group. Such progress as was achieved tended to be 'technical'. The group decided to seek reliable data on the Palestinian population, especially in Jordan, Syria and Lebanon, and Israel agreed to increase four-fold to 2000 the number of family reunion applications it would process annually.

United States hegemony over the Madrid process was challenged within the regional economic development working group (REDWG). This group, more than any other, was predicated on the functionalist thesis that the 'adaptive' role performed by the economy would drive and strengthen the foundations for political agreement. It was convened by the European Union, whose predecessor institution had tasked the World Bank to produce a report on the economy of the occupied Palestinian territories and to draw up a list of priority projects to overcome the infrastructural constraints on economic cooperation in the region. The Bank's report provided the basis for directing the aid pledged in Washington in October 1993. The pre-emptive calling of that donors' conference by the United States, and the US's subsequent desire to remove economic development of the occupied territories from the remit of REDWG, was seen by the Europeans as diminishing their role in the peace process. They suspected Washington of seeking to marginalise them as 'payers, not players'. A compromise was devised, after what has been described as 'intense discussions',[23] whereby the World Bank's Paris office would provide the operational headquarters for aid to the Palestinians, monitored by an *ad hoc* liaison committee that would report to both REDWG and the Steering Committee, on which the United States was joint chairman.

During the course of their brief life span, the working groups were successful in realising one of the United States objectives. They initiated acceptance of Israel as a partner in regional affairs. Official Israeli delegations were received at meetings with delegations from Arab and Muslim states, including in Egypt, Morocco, Oman, Qatar and Tunisia. With the exception of Egypt, none had diplomatic relations with Israel, but several were to open 'liaison' offices in the Jewish state. One of the criticisms levelled at Arafat by the Palestinians was that the Oslo accords had opened the way for the normalisation of relations with Israel by a number of countries normally supportive of their cause, including China. The process of legitimating Israel was set back by Netanyahu's uncompromising attitude toward the Palestinians and abruptly halted after a botched attempt by Israeli agents to assassinate a senior Hamas official in Amman in September 1997. The United States had to pressure Qatar to go ahead with its previous decision to host the fourth Middle East and North Africa Economic Summit in November 1997 with Israeli participation. Most Arab countries boycotted the conference, dramatising the deterioration in the peace process. Such was the dynamic between the bilateral and multilateral negotiations that when implementation of the Oslo process stalled, the working groups ceased to meet.

The Middle East and North Africa economic summits

After the dissolution of the Soviet Union, the United States espoused the view that democratisation, backed by market economics, would contribute to international stability. Clinton's Administration had made its view clear that supporting American business overseas would be at the heart of its foreign policy interests.[24] Secondary and tertiary boycotts had been imposed by the Arab League on American and other foreign-owned companies that traded with Israel. For Clinton, such discriminatory arrangements had to be removed in the context of normalising Israel's relations with Arab states, and the Administration applied itself to securing that objective. Clinton had initially seemed prepared to accept that the peace process may have to be finished first,[25] but his position was to become firm in favour of an early lifting of the boycott.[26] Saudi Arabia was receptive to the argument for the ending of the boycott, and under its leadership the members of the Gulf Cooperation Council (GCC) declared on 30 September 1994 that they would no longer enforce the secondary and tertiary aspects of the economic boycott and that they would support a move in the Arab League to end the primary boycott of Israel. Qatar began supplying natural gas to Israel.

With arrangements in train for the removal of this obstruction, the Administration engaged the attention of the American and international business community in the commercial prospect offered by a Middle East peace. It concurred in a proposal broached by Peres with the World Economic Forum of Davos, Switzerland, that the Forum and the New York-based Council on Foreign Relations sponsor a Middle East and North Africa Economic Conference at Casablanca in 1994.[27] The participants at that conference agreed:

- to establish a Middle East and North Africa Development Bank, and called for a group of experts to examine different options for funding mechanisms;
- to establish a Regional Tourist Board;
- to encourage the private sector to create a Regional Chamber of Commerce and Business Council; and
- to institutionalise the process through a Steering Committee and Executive Secretariat in Rabat, Morocco.

Israel's institutional links to the regional community seemed to have been affirmed and expanded.

After the success of the first conference, the United States decided to incorporate economic summits, now to be managed by the US government, into its overall strategy for the attainment of a comprehensive peace settlement. Subsequent conferences were held in Amman (October 1995), Cairo (November 1996) and Doha (November 1997).[28] Because the Israel–Palestinian negotiations had stalled by late 1997, no progress was made on the implementation of the various proposed instruments of regional economic cooperation, and no decision was taken to hold a fifth conference.

The United States had seen the conferences as offering a substantive inducement to Israel. Normalisation of relations with Israel by regional states would bring a 'peace dividend' to Israel that would compensate it for expected territorial concessions in the bilateral negotiations with the Palestinians and Syria. This precept reflects some of Peres's ideas.[29] For him, security was not just a military phenomenon: it also had political, psychological and economic components. Arab states found Peres's vision disturbing for it seemed to foreshadow Israeli economic hegemony in the region. The fear that Egypt had expressed in the ACRS working group about Israel's emergence as the dominant regional power also had an economic dimension. United States support for a regional development bank located in Cairo was intended to assuage Arab concern that direct foreign investment, encouraged into the region by an improvement in political relations, would be channelled preferentially to Israel, where socio-economic conditions were receptive, enabling it to build upon an already strong economic base. A development bank would channel investment capital into approved projects in Arab developing countries.

Despite American hopes that multilateral diplomacy would result in a broadening of ties among the countries in the region, the record shows that, with few exceptions, the relationship between Israel and its Arab and Muslim neighbours remained conditional and dependent on political factors.[30]

CONCLUSION

Despite the failure of the multilateral negotiations, the Madrid framework that Clinton inherited from his predecessor was not fundamentally flawed. The bilateral channel produced movement between the Israelis and Palestinians and the conclusion of a peace treaty in October 1994 between Israel and Jordan, which showed that it provided an appropriate setting for the attainment of a negotiated settlement of the Arab–Israel dispute.

Although the Israel–Jordan peace treaty was achieved without direct US intervention, it was pursued in the context of the power of the United States to dispense positive sanctions. Clinton was aware that Jordan's economic difficulties had been compounded by the cessation of US aid. He encouraged the king's predisposition to resolve his country's differences with Israel, and held out the prospect of assistance to his country. Jordan's debt to the United States was forgiven. Signature of the peace treaty brought a resumption of American aid to Jordan; a supplementary allocation to Jordan in gratitude for the king's personal contribution toward an agreement at Wye in 1988; and a US–Jordan Free Trade Agreement in 2000. The United States continues to back the Israel–Jordan peace treaty, as it has the peace treaty between Israel and Egypt concluded in 1979, finding assistance to Egypt and Jordan less expensive than the cost of war were hostilities to break out among the parties once again. Both treaties survive, despite the evident tensions between Israelis and Palestinians and elsewhere in the Middle East.

The multilateral channel fostered the development of links among all regional states and supported the bilateral negotiations by clarifying some issues that transcended Israel's borders. By incorporating Israel into the community of states interested in working through such matters, the United States broadened acceptance of Israel as a regional partner and facilitated its attendance at meetings in some Arab and Islamic countries. Concern began to be expressed, however, by some Arab states which felt threatened by a process that seemed to be moving inexorably toward enshrining Israel as the dominant regional nuclear and economic power. The United States was not particularly successful in assuaging these concerns. The working group on arms control was closed down under challenge from Egypt over Israel's refusal to subscribe to the NPT, in order to protect the peace process and the broader Israel–Egypt relationship; and a proposed regional bank to assist the development of Arab countries did not get off the ground.

For a brief period, from 1992 to 1997, the multilateral channel had seemed productive and the engagement of the United States in the overall peace process looked like producing a favourable political and economic outcome. The prospect of a Middle East peace settlement had attracted global attention, and the convening of economic summits complementary to the Madrid process had commanded considerable interest among governments, international organisations and the business community. The United States failed to achieve its objective because the prospective economic outcome was dependent upon the political one. Neither Arab nor Islamic states, nor some other participating states, would commit themselves to an 'adaptive' functionalist role when confronted with evidence of a continuing conflictual relationship between Israel and the Palestinians. Because that core issue was stalemated, the process had become dysfunctional.[31] An attempt by Israel to assassinate a Palestinian leader in the capital of a country with which it had concluded a peace treaty barely two years earlier brought to the surface deep-seated suspicions of Israel among regional states, and the whole multilateral process ground to an abrupt halt. It is unlikely that the United States will feel sufficiently confident to resume the process before a significant accommodation is reached between Israel and the Palestinians.

NOTES

1. Clinton, W.J. *Public Papers, 1994*, p.1497.
2. Segev (1998) p.299; Mr Marwan Kassim, former foreign minister of Jordan, said in an interview in Amman on 8 May 2002, that it was Israel that had first hinted to the Jordanians of American debt forgiveness or military assistance if a peace treaty were to be concluded with Israel.
3. Shlaim (2000) p.448.
4. Segev (1998) p.302.
5. Interviews with Senator Zeid Rifai, former prime minister of Jordan, Amman, 12 May 2002, and Dr Munther J. Haddadin, former minister of water and irrigation, Amman, 9 May 2002.
6. Segev (1998) p.304.
7. Clinton, W.J. *Public Papers, 1994*, p.1311.
8. Segev (1998) pp.310–11.
9. Brand (1994) pp.409–10.
10. Prados (2001) pp.2, 11–12.
11. Clinton, W.J. *Public Papers, 2000*, p.2609.
12. Interview with Mr Gene Cretz, US Embassy, Cairo, 5 May 2002.
13. In the functionalist view, a society has an underlying tendency to be in equilibrium. Functionalism tends to emphasise consensus among the members of society on basic values, social order and stability in the social system. The term dysfunction is used to refer to negative

social consequences. On occasion some element may disrupt the social balance, being functional in one respect and dysfunctional in another. Silver, *Functionalist Theory*.

14 Baker (1992e) p.322.
15 Clinton, W.J. *Public Papers, 1993*, p.1644.
16 Djerejian (1993b) p.697.
17 Landau (2001) pp.7, 10.
18 Zartman (1989).
19 Djerejian (1992) p.218.
20 Egypt, Israel, Lebanon, Morocco, Syria, Tunisia and the Palestinian Authority are members of the Euro–Mediterranean partnership.
21 Clinton, W.J. *Public Papers, 1994*, pp.955–6.
22 Clinton, W.J. *Public Papers, 2000*, p.1855.
23 Peters (1994) p.28.
24 Pelletreau (1994) p.795.
25 Clinton, W.J. *Public Papers, 1993*, p.1644.
26 Clinton, W.J. *Public Papers, 1994*, p.1498.
27 Savir (1998) pp.84–5. The summits had their genesis in a meeting in Jordan between Peres and King Hussein in November 1993. Representatives from 61 countries attended the Casablanca conference, together with more than 1100 businessmen and the senior executives of various international organisations.
28 All commanded the attendance of large numbers of states and businessmen, as well as officials of relevant international organisations. Even the Doha summit, which was boycotted by Arab states, attracted 2000 people including official delegations from 66 countries.
29 Peres (1993).
30 Brackman (2000) p.1.
31 See 13n.

5. Advance and retreat: the United States, Israel and Syria, and Lebanon

When Presidents Bush I and Assad met in 1990, they discussed the importance of moving ahead toward a peaceful resolution of the Middle East dispute in accordance with UN Security Council Resolutions 242 and 338. For the United States, Arab acceptance of these resolutions as the basis of any negotiation was fundamental because it conveyed acceptance of Israel's existence. In 1991, Bush I's Administration successfully persuaded Syria to attend an international conference, and was able to use Syria's agreement to pressure Israel into doing so too, thus bringing the Madrid conference to fruition.

THE UNITED STATES, ISRAEL AND SYRIA

The United States facilitated negotiation between the Israelis and Syrians in Washington in 1992. It became the go-between in their dialogue because Assad refused to extend the recognition to Israel that would have been implicit in direct negotiation. For Syria, it was one thing to participate in an international conference attended by an Israeli delegation, another to deal with Israel bilaterally on the basis of sovereign equality while Israel remained in occupation on Syrian soil. The United States began the negotiation process as a facilitator, later becoming a mediator and a full participant, realising that in order to pursue its objective of a comprehensive settlement of the Arab–Israel dispute it had to become fully engaged in the Israel–Syria dialogue. This was accepted more readily by Syria than Israel.

The Rabin government's ambassador to the United States and principal Israeli negotiator with the Syrians, Itamar Rabinovich, described the early rounds of bilateral meetings in Washington as defined by reluctance, scepticism and suspicion on both sides. The two countries assumed that the negotiations were likely to fail. As the intermediary, the United States found itself retailing diametrically opposed points of departure. Assad sought Israel's 'full withdrawal' from the Golan Heights, although in the negotiations with Baker leading to the convening of the Madrid conference he had entertained the possibility of some international peace-keeping force being stationed in the

Golan Heights upon the withdrawal of Israeli forces. Assad's objective was irreconcilable with Shamir's view that Israel had met the requirement of UN Security Council Resolution 242 when the Sinai had been returned to Egypt.[1]

Whatever outcome was reached in respect of the Golan would be measured against the return of the Sinai to Egypt. Egypt's recovery of the peninsula was, in part, a function of Anwar Sadat's penchant for the grand gesture, such as his visit to Jerusalem. His public diplomacy had helped to establish his credentials among Israelis. Assad had an entirely different personality; both Baker and Rabinovich attest to his formalistic and legalistic negotiating style. His call for a 'dignified comprehensive peace that will be acceptable to our peoples, that would entail no retraction of any of our national rights and would not hurt in any way the pride and dignity of our nation … [a] peace of the brave',[2] lacked public appeal. The Americans tried to get him to meet personally with the Israeli leadership, as did the Egyptians, French and Israelis, but he declined their overtures. While a summit probably could not have produced a major breakthrough, its convening would have carried an important signal of the earnest of the two parties to negotiate a settlement that must inevitably address the future of the Golan region. Assad held tenaciously to his requirement that an Israeli commitment to withdraw from occupied Syrian territory was a precondition for negotiation, whose purpose would be confined to the modalities of the withdrawal.

Any Syrian expectation that the Golan region could be returned in much the same way as the Sinai had been returned to Egypt was questionable. The Golan area had been annexed to Israel, whereas the Sinai had not; and the act of annexing the Golan in 1981, after the return of the Sinai, was an unambiguous Israeli declaration that no further occupied territory would be ceded. The United States position on Israel's occupation of the Golan Heights had been put in a letter to Rabin by President Ford in 1975. Baker explicitly reconfirmed Ford's view that 'any peace agreement with Syria must be predicated on Israel remaining on the Golan Heights'[3] in his letter of assurances to Israel on the eve of the Madrid conference. He also affirmed the applicability of the 'land for peace' principle to the Golan Heights; asserted that the United States would continue to oppose Israeli settlement activity in the occupied territories; and stated that the United States did not intend to recognise any unilateral extension of Israeli laws, sovereignty or administration to the Golan Heights.[4] The apparent contradiction provided, at the very least, sufficient ambiguity for Clinton to be able to mediate on the Golan question when he took office.

The United States had to address conflicting interpretations of the area of land in question. The territory, like that of the West Bank, was susceptible of differing claims. Israel regards the boundary as the international border

MAP 5.1 GOLAN HEIGHTS, 1923–2000

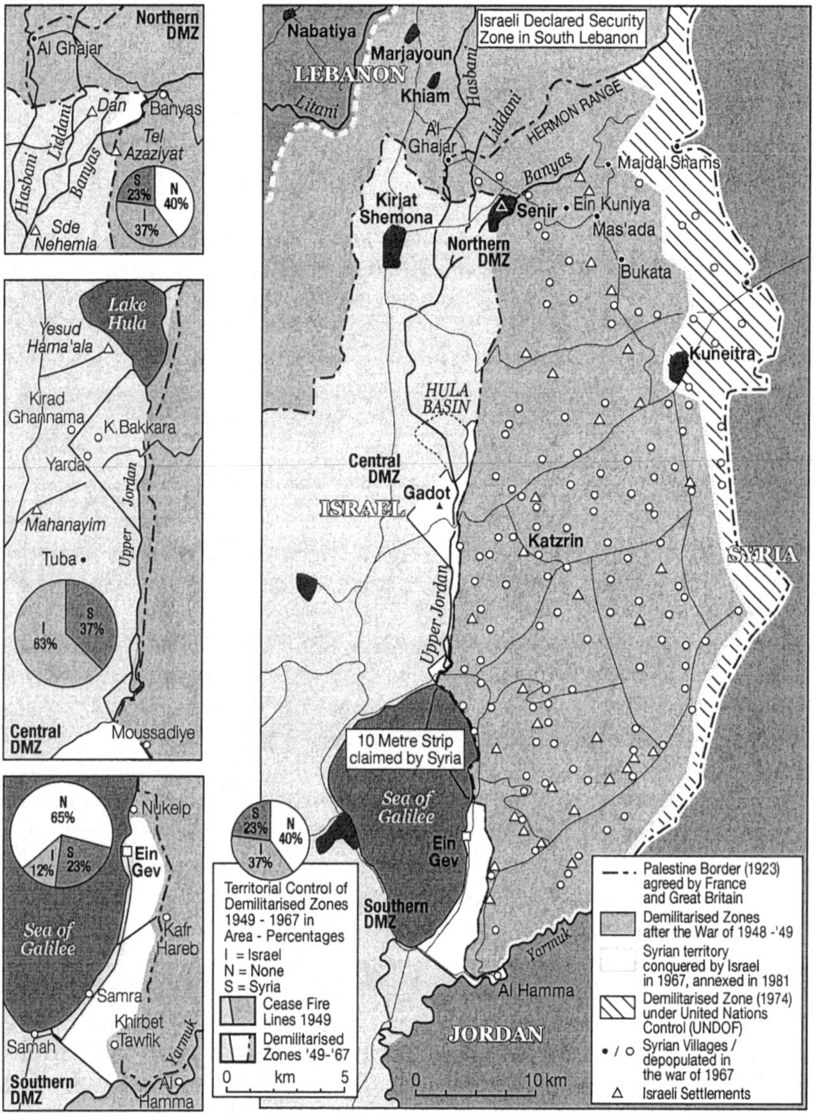

established in 1923 between what was then the British-mandated territory of Palestine and the French-mandated territory of Syria. Syria believes it should be the line where Syrian and Israeli forces were deployed on the eve of the June 1967 war.[5] On this matter of principle, Syria's position was the same as the Palestinians'. The 4 June 1967 line would give Syria access to the north-eastern shore of the Sea of Galilee, Syria having advanced 10 metres to the water's edge from the demarcation line established during the 1948–49 war (Map 5.1).[6]

Members of Clinton's Administration hoped that Syria might find it attractive to establish a relationship of trust with the United States in the light of the dissolution of the Soviet Union, its former supporter; the enhanced role of the United States in the post-Cold War world; and the ability of the United States to constrain Syria's eastern neighbour (Iraq). In seeking to establish a cooperative relationship with Syria, Clinton was at odds with prevailing sentiment in the Congress. Even before either Clinton or his predecessor had assumed office, the International Security Assistance and Arms Export Control Act of 1976, and the Export Administration Act of 1979 required the secretaries of commerce and state to notify the Congress before licensing goods and technologies to countries that support acts of international terrorism. A by-product of the two laws was the so-called 'terrorism list', prepared annually by the State Department. The list identifies those countries that have repeatedly provided support for acts of international terrorism. Syria has appeared on it ever since it was first prepared in 1979, although it has not been implicated in a terrorist incident since 1986. No United States aid had been provided to Syria since 1981.

United States legislation also required that normal relations with Syria be contingent upon improvements in its human rights record; a clear renunciation of terrorism and narcotics trafficking; and a reversal of other policies deemed inimical to United States interests. Syria's alignment with the Gulf War coalition and participation in the Madrid process was viewed by some as tactical moves that offered Syria an end to regional isolation, a free hand in Lebanon, and access to financial support from the Gulf States. They believed that Syria would remain a threat to regional stability. An alternative view, advanced by both the Bush I Administration and some within the Clinton Administration, was that a better relationship with Syria could enhance prospects for achieving United States objectives. The proponents of this view did not advocate the immediate termination of sanctions without further action on Syria's part. Rather, they supported wider contacts between diplomatic and security officials of the two countries and the conclusion of a series of small, reciprocal steps that could lead to a warmer relationship over time.

The 'pre-negotiation process'

Clinton gambled upon an eventual relaxation of congressional attitudes if a peace agreement were to be concluded between Israel and Syria. He told Rabin that 'he saw peace with Syria as the key to an Israeli–Arab settlement and to a new geopolitical order in the region'.[7] The prime minister remained sceptical that Assad would move, and was reserved about Israeli domestic opinion were an agreement to be concluded on the basis of withdrawal from the Golan Heights. The subject had not formed part of his election platform and withdrawal would need to be put to the public at a referendum. So Clinton sought a clarification of Syria's concept of peace; whether Assad was prepared to engage in public diplomacy; and whether Syria was prepared to participate in a back channel, apart from the Washington talks, that could improve communication with Israel. The response to the US overture was negative. In respect of any discrete channel, Assad said that the way to move forward was for the United States to serve as 'a repository' of the two parties' positions.[8]

For his part, Christopher was prepared to act as a special channel between Rabin and Assad. The Israelis were pleased to endorse his role as go-between, particularly in view of his success in working with the Syrians to obtain a ceasefire agreement with Hezbollah in southern Lebanon, effected on 31 July 1993. Rabin posed three questions that he asked Christopher to put to Assad when they met in Damascus on 4 August. Predicated on a hypothetical 'assumption' that Israel would 'withdraw fully' from the Golan in exchange for peace and security, they were: whether Syria would be willing to sign a peace treaty with Israel without linkage to the pace of progress with others; whether Syria was ready for a real peace including normalisation, diplomatic relations and the other paraphernalia of real peace; and whether Syria was ready to offer elements of peace before the completion of withdrawal from the Golan.[9] Christopher returned to Israel on 5 August, briefed Rabin on Assad's response, and then flew back to Damascus to convey Rabin's reaction. The United States was encouraged by the general tenor of the exchange and believed that Assad had accepted the basic equation of peace in return for withdrawal and thought that the Syrian response was worth pursuing further, but Rabin felt that Assad had attached too many conditions to his hypothetical 'offer'. He also had to take into account Israel's concurrent secret negotiation with the Palestinians at Oslo. While Christopher knew that Israel was participating in the Oslo talks, the United States was unaware that a breakthrough on that front was imminent.

Rabin sensed that the Israeli public would have great difficulty in accepting agreements that postulated roughly simultaneous withdrawals from the Gaza Strip, Jericho and the Golan region, should the Palestinian and Syrian tracks be concluded at about the same time. Indeed, Clinton acknowledged that he had urged the prime minister to prepare the Israeli public for the need to make sizeable concessions. Rabin told Christopher that in the event of an agreement with Syria, the agreement with the Palestinians would have to be limited to 'Gaza first', but that if the first agreement were to be made with the Palestinians, both Gaza and Jericho would be included.[10] He seems to have concluded privately in early August that the Palestinian track offered the better immediate prospect. Peres pressed ahead and wrapped it up later that month, thus effectively putting the Syrian track on hold.

On learning of the breakthrough with the Palestinians, Clinton ensured that the tenuous sense of trust thus far established with Assad was not lost. He rang Assad on 9 September to reassure him that the United States remained committed to a Syria–Israel agreement, and to ask him to send a representative to the signing of the Palestinian Declaration of Principles on 13 September 1993. Assad reportedly sought reassurance of Clinton's commitment to continue with the Syrian track, leading Clinton to conclude that Syria did not want to be abandoned. While welcoming this, Rabin told Clinton that he needed time for the Israeli public to digest developments with the Palestinians and asked for the president's help in persuading Assad to wait until the end of the year. Rabin's preferred tactic was to effect a real change on the ground, let the Israeli public digest it and appreciate the accruing benefits, and then move on to the next agreement.[11] So Clinton called Assad again, reassured Assad of his and Rabin's commitment to move forward with Syria in a few months, and asked him specifically to restrain the 'rejectionist' Palestinian leaders residing in Damascus who vilified Arafat for selling out through the Oslo accords.[12] Despite the United States and Israeli commitment, Assad remained aggrieved at Arafat's pre-emption. His concern about being marginalised may have been due to the Administration not having provided sufficiently robust assurances of the importance attached to an Israel–Syria agreement. Rabinovich attributes this diplomatic glitch to the Americans not having wholly accepted Rabin's decision in favour of the Palestinian track.

What the United States did not know at the time was that Rabin was becoming uncomfortable with the intermediary role of the United States. He feared that the United States, which had found Assad's responses in early August encouraging, would pressure him to make concessions in the interest of concluding an agreement with Syria. Ross had visited Rabin in October 1993 conveying Christopher's view that agreement had actually been reached in August, and that Christopher 'preferred to move with Syria for a whole host of reasons, including the fact that his own credibility was at stake'.[13] The reference to 'credibility' seems to refer to Christopher's response to a question from Assad on 4 August. Asked whether he thought Israel had any claim on Golan territory, the secretary replied that Rabin had spoken only of 'full withdrawal'.[14] By 12 November, when Rabin met Clinton again, the Jordanian track had also begun to show some prospect and Rabin told the president that his priorities were now to implement the Oslo accords and to move forward with Jordan. Discrete bilateral negotiations with the Palestinians and Jordan had proven effective and, in what may well have been an oblique criticism of Christopher's well-intentioned mediation, he stressed the importance he continued to attach to the opening of a direct channel with the Syrians.

For the United States, it was important to clarify whether Assad's interest in a settlement with Israel went beyond a general expression. Clinton decided to meet him in Geneva in January 1994, and Christopher visited Damascus to prepare for the meeting. As some public gesture by Assad would be helpful in Israel and could foster a more benign congressional attitude toward Syria, Christopher persuaded the Syrians to receive a delegation of staffers working for the congressional Committee on International Relations to seek information on the fate of Israeli servicemen missing in action, and exit authority for 800 Syrian Jews. Christopher also sought, but unsuccessfully, to persuade the Syrians to establish a discrete channel between Israeli and Syrian generals to discuss questions of security in some detail. In the absence of such a facility, security matters continued to be discussed at a more superficial level within the Washington forum.

Clinton's meeting with Assad convinced him of Assad's sincerity in seeking peace.[15] At their joint press conference on 16 January, Assad said: 'Syria seeks a just and comprehensive peace with Israel as a strategic choice that secures Arab rights, ends the Israeli occupation, and enables all peoples in the region to live in peace, security, and dignity'.[16] Clinton restated his view of Syria as 'the key to the achievement of an enduring and comprehensive peace'.[17] He said that he had discussed with Assad the possibility of American troops being deployed in the Golan Heights in the context of any peace agreement, but that no commitment could be made in the absence of an expressed decision by Israel and Syria, and that the matter would need to be discussed with the Congress.[18] He acknowledged the need to address problems in the US–Syria bilateral relationship and said that the two foreign ministers had been instructed to do so in detail. The two leaders had also discussed the question of Lebanon and the application of the Taif agreement to that country, which America supported. Assad had 'agreed that there should be a successful conclusion of the peace process which left Lebanon free and independent as a nation'.[19]

Rabin, who had watched the press conference live on television, was briefed on the content of the meeting by American officials immediately after the summit. He was disappointed with the outcome, feeling that Clinton had tilted too far in Assad's favour, and was concerned about the impact that would have on Israeli opinion. Assad's general commitment to 'peace' was an insufficient guarantee.

Rabin was to tell the Administration that, when the 'self-interest, goodwill, friendly persuasion, and gentlemanly mediation'[20] of the United States failed to produce results with the Syrians, recourse to more persuasive diplomatic instruments might be necessary. There was never a serious discussion of resorting to that alternative and Rabinovich understood that the United States was not attracted to the option. For its part, the United States was conscious that its role in the negotiating process was changing. As Christopher and Ross shuttled between Washington, Damascus and Jerusalem, they became fully-fledged partners in the negotiation. Such discomfiture as Israel felt about this was related to timing as well as to role change. While Rabin accepted that the United States would make its own judgements, he did not want it to play a mediatory role prematurely: its authority ought to be reserved to assist in resolving difficult issues at the end of the process.

Clinton's reference to the possibility of US troops being stationed in the Golan region provoked an orchestrated campaign within the United States against such an eventuality, fanned by those members of the pro-Israel lobby who favoured Israel's opposition Likud Party. It began in May 1994, but gained greater significance when the Republicans took charge of both houses of Congress and all committee chairs after the mid-term elections in November. American forces participated in the Multinational Force and Observers (MFO) in the Sinai Peninsula. The MFO worked well, but those Americans opposed to the creation of a comparable force for the Golan Heights were not persuaded by its example and conducted a particularly dirty campaign.[21] The subject was dropped.

If Clinton was encountering domestic difficulties, so was Rabin, whose political support declined as the peace process progressed. The Golan was not just a matter of security. If it were returned to Syria, what would be the future of some 12 000 Israeli settlers in the territory? Unlike the settlers in the West Bank, those in the Golan region were predominantly Labor supporters who had been encouraged to establish themselves in occupied territory by the party that, under Rabin, was now entertaining the question of withdrawal. The religious party of Sephardic Israelis (Shas) withdrew from the coalition government, resulting in a reduction of the government's majority to five Knesset seats. In 1994 an effort was made in the Knesset to pass a 'Golan entrenchment law' that would have made cession of that territory extremely difficult by requiring a special majority of some 70 or 80 of the 120 members of the Knesset. It was defeated, and another attempt was made to adopt it in 1995, by which time two members of the Golan lobby were talking of leaving the Labor party. A vote on 26 July 1995 ended in a draw, which meant that the motion failed to pass.

Assad, too, was under some constraint, though of a very different order. He adhered to the Arab position of the 1970s, which included: no negotiations with Israel before its withdrawal from occupied territory; no face-to-face negotiations with Israel; and no separate deals. He was critical of Sadat, Arafat and later, King Hussein for their accommodations with Israel. It was important to his self-image as an Arab nationalist that he demonstrate an ability to recover Syrian territory without compromise or impairment of Syrian 'dignity'. He had shown every indication since 1974 of a preparedness to hold out until he got back what he believed was rightfully Syrian, and seems to have hoped that Christopher's mediation signalled that the United States could eventually persuade Israel to meet his demands. Assad also had a domestic constituency to satisfy. The 100 000 Syrians expelled from the Golan area in 1967, and their descendants, now numbered over 400 000 due to natural increase.

After being briefed on the Clinton–Assad summit by Ross, Rabin co-opted him to tell the media in Jerusalem that Assad was ready for peace and had demanded full withdrawal from Golan in return. Simultaneously, the Israeli deputy defence minister was instructed to inform the Knesset that, if an agreement involving significant territorial concessions was envisaged, the government would submit it to a popular referendum. By bringing the notion of a referendum into the open in January 1994, Rabin sought both to calm down the Israeli political system and, while underlining to the United States and Syria the seriousness of the negotiation with Syria, to confront Assad with the need to appreciate that an Israeli government would require popular endorsement of so significant a matter.

Although the United States was aware of Israel's concerns, it may not have appreciated the strength with which they were held. When Israeli and Syrian ambassadors in Washington returned to their bilateral negotiations in February 1994, Christopher invited them to his office. He heard a reiteration of their well-worn positions, but saw no sign of movement. Three days later, an 'angry and bitter' secretary of state called in the Israeli ambassador. Rabinovich reported the encounter. Rabin was not impressed by it: these were existential issues for Israel, not a matter of 'credibility'. Rabin would insist on his position even at the risk of derailing the whole Israeli–Syrian track.[22] In the light of this, the United States decided to change tack: if prodding was not working, perhaps enticement might be worth a try. It sought to redress Rabin's grievances during his visit to the White House in March 1994. Clinton asked him to put together two packages: one addressing the timetable, phasing and security issues that the Americans could convey to the Syrians; and the other covering the bilateral security aid that Israel might seek from the United States in the event of an Israel–Syria agreement. The implication that the United States would meet Israel's shopping list could not, however, address Israeli susceptibilities. Israel's insecurity was not solely an externally induced phenomenon that could be assuaged by the provision of hardware and peace keepers. All that Clinton could do was to try to ameliorate Israeli concerns by holding out the prospect of meeting Israel's tangible needs. Rabin ceded to American persuasion, providing the Administration with a statement of Israel's position that could be put to the Syrians. He suspected, however, that Assad would probably respond with a lower counter-offer that the United States would then try to bridge.

Armed with Rabin's package, Christopher returned to Damascus. During the course of that meeting Assad made explicit his demand that 'full withdrawal' meant to the line of 4 June 1967. The Israelis felt that Assad had indulged in a sleight of hand in declining, until then, to define his objective. Rabin, who had also been less than explicit, said that he had intended the phrase to mean the 1923 border. Given the extremely small area of territory in question, Christopher was not greatly impressed by either the Israeli or Syrian claim to it. After digesting Assad's claim, Rabin agreed to Christopher discussing the matter during his next meeting with Assad on 21 July 1994, on the basis that it was Christopher's 'impression' that Israel would be prepared to consider the 4 June line in the context of the hypothetical 'assumption' floated the previous August. Assad responded more sympathetically this time, clearly delighted that the Israeli government was signalling its preparedness to negotiate on the basis of all occupied Syrian territory, and perhaps also jolted by the imminent signing of the Israel–Jordan Washington Declaration on 25 July. He told Christopher that he was prepared to proceed to negotiation on the basis of this 'clarification'; and that he was willing to have any deal implemented over two phases of six months each, a faster timetable than that envisaged by the Israelis. But he wanted to defer the establishment of diplomatic relations until after the conclusion of a comprehensive settlement. A further significant change in his position was that he now agreed to direct negotiation through the countries' ambassadors in Washington. Secret talks began on 29 July 1994 and continued for about a year, the parties' leaders often meeting at Dennis Ross's home.

While the ambassadorial negotiation was in progress, substantive movement toward a comprehensive settlement of the Arab–Israel dispute was in train elsewhere. The Washington Declaration was quickly followed by the Israel–Jordan peace treaty on 26 October, and the first Middle East and North Africa Economic Conference in Morocco on 30 October 1994. The Israelis and Palestinians were moving haltingly toward an Interim Agreement, and it was clear that Syria was becoming marginalised. The United States hoped that in the context of these developments Assad would become receptive to reaching some accommodation with Israel, but Assad showed no sign of moderating his demands. Clinton attached importance to Syria catching the tide. There would be general elections in Israel and the United States in 1996 and if the substance of the Israeli–Syrian negotiation were not to become caught up in the two countries' electoral processes, agreement ought to be reached during 1995. The United States pressed Syria for some gesture that would engage the Israeli people, but despite incremental movement on matters such as the timetable for any withdrawal, there was still nothing from the Syrian side to reassure the Israeli public.

The United States tried again to encourage Syria to engage in public diplomacy in October 1994 when Clinton visited the Middle East to attend the signing of the Israel–Jordan peace treaty. To assuage Americans who opposed his also visiting a place on their country's terrorism list, it was agreed that Clinton would travel to Damascus on the condition that Assad would employ, at their joint press conference, previously agreed language taking exception to terrorism. Assad did not do so and, again, failed to make any impact with Israelis on an issue that was at least as significant to them as to American opinion. He did, however, spell out Syria's commitment to peace and the establishment of normal relations with Israel 'in return for Israel's full withdrawal from the Golan to the line of June 4, 1967, and from the south of Lebanon';[23] and in their private discussion Assad offered Clinton some sign of flexibility on points of detail. One reporter at the joint press conference pointedly questioned Assad on the genuineness of his commitment to peace, drawing attention to the fact that Assad had not visited Israel, had never met Rabin, and that Syria supported Hezbollah and the rejectionist groups in Damascus. This elicited the viduous response: 'There's nothing we have that proves our desire for peace except our saying that we want peace'.[24]

During Christopher's visit to Damascus preparatory to that of his president, Christopher obtained Assad's agreement to another procedural milestone, a meeting between Israeli and Syrian high-ranking military officers. The chiefs of staff of the two countries visited Washington separately in November 1994, and met together there in December. Israel's representative was Lt General Ehud Barak. By agreement, Ross prepared a record of the aims and principles explored by the two sides at the meeting, which was designed to provide a framework for ensuing discussions. A further meeting of the military chiefs in June 1995 addressed such questions as the demilitarisation of zones on either side of any agreed border, and the placement, or retention, of early warning stations. Although the negotiation among the military advisers was limited, significant agreement seems to have been reached. Ross prepared a summary record of the discussion – a 'non-paper' – but unlike the aims and principles document, its text did not prove acceptable to either the Israeli or Syrian leaderships.

The widening circle of Israeli participants in negotiation with the Syrians, and the concomitant preparation of position papers, led to a leak at the Israeli end of the aims and principles paper and criticism of it. Syria responded to the leak with Radio Damascus broadcasting a commentary that carried a Syrian view of the negotiation. These developments sparked the fears of the Golan lobby and prompted the proposed 'Golan entrenchment law'.

The Israeli–Palestinian Interim Agreement had been signed in September 1995, and the United States believed that with the passing of that marker an opportunity now existed to focus on the Syrian track. It interpreted an expression of resentment by Assad of Israel's growing acceptance in the Arab world as indicating a fear of isolation. Assad had, however, said to an interviewer that 'peace is our strategic choice, but not at any price'.[25] Christopher had been told by Rabin that his own electoral timetable required that any agreement be completed by April 1996. Rabin's assassination in November 1995 required that it be rethought. Clinton informed Peres at Rabin's funeral that, from an American perspective, he would be available to help with negotiations until July 1996. But the issue was not so clear-cut for Peres, who had to decide whether to seek an immediate mandate as Rabin's successor, to hold elections on the due date on 29 October, or to test his mandate in May after six months in the premiership. He decided to give the negotiation with Syria a chance before naming a date for the elections, settling on this course after learning of the progress that had been made.

Peres floated an idea with the United States that very considerably embellished any prospective settlement with the Syrians. In December 1995 he proposed that any such settlement be integrated into a larger scheme that would include a bilateral United States–Israel treaty and a regional security pact. Clinton reacted cautiously: the relationship between the United States and Israel was accepted within the Arab world as a fact of life, but its formalisation in a treaty could only be seen by Arab states as provocative. It would impair the ability of the United States to lead the peace process. For the time being, he preferred to proceed along already established lines, and Christopher resumed his shuttle in mid-December. On this occasion he carried a message from Peres warning Assad that, notwithstanding Peres's disposition to go 'fast or slow, broad or narrow' according to Assad's preference, the situation in south Lebanon and Syria's support for Hezbollah was unacceptable to Israel and that Peres would have to react forcefully if violence continued. Assad had previously intimated to Ross a preparedness to try to restrain Hezbollah.[26]

Formal negotiations

Christopher was able, however, to persuade Assad to show flexibility on a number of issues of importance in the context of the ongoing negotiation. The United States was sufficiently encouraged by this to invite Israel and Syria to a conference at the Wye River Plantation, where detailed negotiations were undertaken in December 1995 and January and February 1996. The agreed cyclical framework was that discussion would be held over two weeks, after which Christopher would travel to Israel and Syria to encourage movement on 'sticky' issues.[27] The delegations at Wye seemed to have been genuinely seeking agreement. At the conclusion of the first round, Ross declared that more was accomplished during these six days than in the previous four years of negotiation. His summary of the discussion was endorsed by both parties and served as the agenda for Christopher's journey.

The United States was now to face another timing problem. During Christopher's visit to Jerusalem in January 1996, he was told that the Israeli political calendar required that Peres had to decide by early February whether to go for a May election. The second round of Wye talks began on 24 January, but even before its scheduled ending Peres had decided to seek a mandate in May. The United States had hoped that Peres would opt for the October date, and it is probable that Assad's negotiating tactic was predicated on the United States pressuring Israel to conclude an agreement by October. The announcement of an early election, and the conclusion in February 1996 of a defence cooperation agreement between Israel and Turkey, complicated Syria's position. Nevertheless, the United States continued to press ahead: a third round of negotiations began on 28 February. As that round opened, Palestinian rejectionists launched a series of bomb attacks in Ashkelon, Jerusalem and Tel Aviv designed to frustrate the whole peace process. The attacks put Peres on the defensive politically, Syria did not denounce them, and Peres suspended the Wye negotiations on 4 March.

With the peace process stymied on both the Palestinian and Syrian fronts, the United States had to employ countermeasures to arrest its further decline. It was powerless to prevent sporadic terrorist attacks, but it could marshal international condemnation of them. The United States obtained the assistance of Egypt in organising a summit at Sharm el-Sheikh on 13–14 March to enhance the peace process, to promote security and to combat terror. Its secondary objective was to enhance the prospects of Peres's re-election. Netanyahu, his principal challenger, had already signalled his disagreement with the peace process, with implications for Syria no less than for the Palestinians. Syria and Lebanon did not attend the meeting.

Iran was a particular subject of criticism at the summit for its assistance to the two actors whose activities had proven the most threatening to the peace process, Palestinian Hamas and Lebanese Hezbollah. Clinton was careful to draw a distinction between the policies of Syria and Iran.[28] This did not mollify the Syrians, who saw the prospect of concluding a peace treaty in 1996 slipping away from them. They had been able while negotiating with the Israelis at the Wye River Plantation, and without publicity, to restrain Hezbollah's activity in Lebanon. Israel's suspension of the Wye talks, and the carefully stage-managed criticism voiced at Sharm el-Sheikh, gave Syria an excuse to look the other way while Hezbollah undertook resurgent activity. Having conveyed Peres's warning to the Syrians, Christopher was well aware that incidents in southern Lebanon could jeopardise any future discussion between Israel and Syria. Conversely, the United States was also aware that the impact of Hezbollah's activity upon Israeli citizens in the north of the country, while destructive, was clearly marginal.[29] The impact was borne principally by the quisling South Lebanon Army, and to a lesser extent by the IDF, operating in the Israel-imposed security zone within southern Lebanon. No occupying force could expect to be totally immune from attack by activists of a host nation.

The United States advised Peres to avoid a military operation in south Lebanon, and urged Assad to do what he could to restore calm.[30] These representations proved ineffectual. Peres was determined to demonstrate to the Israeli electorate that he could be tough when necessary. Israel launched Operation Grapes of Wrath against southern Lebanon on 11 April 1996. Israeli shells struck a UN compound at Qana where hundreds of Lebanese villagers had taken refuge. The incident provoked international condemnation and caused many Arab Israelis to withhold their support for Peres in the general election in May. Once again, Christopher found himself negotiating the terms of a ceasefire agreement rather than pursuing a peace settlement.

Following Netanyahu's electoral victory in May, the United States had to deal with an Israeli leader who was implacably opposed to withdrawal from Syrian territory. Not only had he criticized Rabin's and Peres's policies, he had contributed materially to the building of the Golan lobby that had sought to pass the 'Golan entrenchment law' in 1994 and 1995. A third attempt to adopt such a law was made in July 1997.[31] Later, the Knesset passed a law requiring a 61-member affirmative vote, and a national referendum, to approve the return of any part of the Golan Heights to Syria.[32] For Assad the signs of Israeli obstinacy were clear, and it was important that he move to protect what he believed he had already won. He asserted publicly that he had secured an Israeli commitment to the return of territory to the 4 June 1967 line, and United States endorsement of the commitment, and demanded that negotiations be resumed at the point at which they had been interrupted. Netanyahu rejected the claim and was not prepared to do other than resume negotiation without prior conditions.

Nevertheless, Clinton explored with Netanyahu the question of how to revive negotiations between Israel and Syria, and how to deal with Lebanon. Netanyahu expressed a willingness to discuss an Israeli withdrawal from southern Lebanon with the Lebanese and Syrian authorities on the basis that 'somebody dismantle the Hezbollah military capacity'.[33] When asked whether it would be possible to reach a settlement in Lebanon without first reaching an overall settlement with Syria, Clinton responded that it would be a lot easier to do if there were also an agreement with Syria. Netanyahu's preference for pursuing peace with Lebanon before Syria, were it achievable, might honour the spirit, but not the letter, of UN Security Council Resolution 425 of 1978 which called for Israel's *immediate* withdrawal of its forces from Lebanese territory. His proposition made no reference to the Golan, and Syria was not disposed to acquiesce in negotiations over Lebanon without its own major territorial claim being addressed. It was evident to the United States from Netanyahu's position, and also from complications between Israelis and Palestinians, that conditions for movement toward a peace agreement with Syria were not propitious. Rather than risk an unwinding of the informal understandings tentatively reached between the Israelis and Syrians, the United States decided to wait it out.

If, as Assad claimed with some justification, his fundamental objective of securing 'full withdrawal' had been attained,[34] why was United States engagement in the negotiation unable to produce a settlement prior to Netanyahu's premiership? Christopher believed that despite the advances made, notably at Wye, there was no real possibility of concluding an agreement during Peres's brief tenure. Rabinovich on the Israeli side, and Assad's biographer, Patrick Seale, agreed. It would be difficult to convince Israeli public opinion of the advantages of peace with Syria, particularly in the context of Palestinian terrorism. The timing was tight, whether the Israeli election was to be held in May or October 1996; and the United States saw the need to keep the negotiation from becoming entangled in the politics of an Israeli election campaign. For Clinton, the substance of the negotiation with Syria was less of a consideration as he campaigned for re-election in November. Although a comprehensive Middle East peace settlement still proved elusive, he could point to Israel's agreements with the Palestinians and with Jordan, and to the Middle East and North Africa Economic Conferences, as achievements of his first term. Not only was the timing tight, there were still important differences to be overcome. Syria's concept of 'total peace for total withdrawal' was susceptible of varying interpretations, despite United States probing. The Israelis found the imprecision disturbing. For their part, the Syrians saw in Peres's vision of economic integration flowing from a peace, a threat to Syria's and the Arab world's socio-economic fabric. There was a fundamental dissonance between Assad's inclination 'to shrink [Israel's] influence to more modest and less aggressive proportions, which the Arab players in the Middle East could accept and live with' and Israel's ambition for 'peace as a means to extend its influence to every corner of the Arab world'.[35]

This profound conceptual difference went to the nub of United States objectives. Peres's view of an increasingly interconnected global economy resonated with Clinton's vision for the advancement of democracy and market economics. While an Israel–Syria settlement might contribute to its realisation, were American ideals including democracy, human rights and market economics ever to be incorporated into the Syrian polity, it would probably be through an extended process that would flow, at some remove, from acceptance of Syria as a cooperative member of the international community after conclusion of a settlement with Israel. There is little doubt that the United States saw attainment of its liberal agenda as sequential to the immediate peace objective. Syria's identification of the conceptual difference highlighted a tactical consideration. For so long as the broader strategic dimension remained in the background, the United States need not prosecute it while the two parties addressed tactical issues related to land and security and normalisation of relations. The Syrians knew, however, that no American Administration could be enlisted to help 'shrink' the ambitions of the only country in the region that broadly shared its democratic and human rights values. In the event, they were not sufficiently disturbed by the implications of Israeli regional economic expansion to decline United States overtures to negotiate further with the Israelis.

Resumption of negotiations

The United States saw an opportunity to resume its attempt to effect a peace settlement after Netanyahu's electoral defeat by former general Ehud Barak in May 1999. In June, Barak and Assad exchanged compliments through Patrick Seale;[36] in July, Vice-President Khaddam told radical Palestinian groups to end their armed struggle against Israel, and Syria prevented Hezbollah from firing rockets into Israel, but not from targeting Israeli forces in the security zone. Encouraged by this apparent atmospheric change, the United States once again facilitated intensive negotiation between the two parties, first secretly between officials at Bern, Switzerland, and later outside Washington at Bethesda. Barak, who had negotiated with the Syrians in December 1994, was more attracted to dealing with Assad than with Arafat.[37] The Syrian president sensed this, and sent his foreign minister to Washington in December 1999 to meet with Barak. This was the first time that senior officials of the two countries had engaged directly. Their talks were to continue at Shepherdstown in January 2000. They were to prove inconclusive.

Clinton paid a number of visits to Shepherdstown during the negotiation and was an active participant. This seems to have engendered an expectation within both parties that the president would intervene to force concessions upon the other. During the meeting the United States presented a summary of points of accord and discord. It was an American paper and the Administration was determined that it should be seen as such. Barak might see it before its formal presentation, but negotiation on the draft would be ruled out. An Israeli newspaper, working from a leaked copy of the document, said that it revealed Israel's apparent success in delaying discussion of borders while winning concessions on security that Syria was supposedly willing to make.[38] This second embarrassing leakage, and the newspaper's characterisation of the document, angered the Syrians, and the talks were postponed indefinitely.

Despite this setback, Clinton's Administration remained determined to reverse the situation. Substantial progress had been achieved at Shepherdstown, with the Syrians showing uncharacteristic flexibility. They got nothing in return from Barak.[39] Even after the failure of the Shepherdstown talks, Clinton and his officials worked hard to keep the lines open to both parties, urging that to the extent that tactical considerations allowed, Barak reveal his bottom lines, especially on delimitation of the border, security issues, water resources and diplomatic representation. This would give the United States a basis for further negotiation with the Syrians. Barak oscillated between wanting a dramatic and urgent breakthrough, and hesitation to intimate flexibility. He pressed for a meeting between Clinton and Assad to break the logjam. Clinton eventually arranged to meet Assad on 26 March 2000 in Geneva. The meeting was held in the context of Barak's having by then endorsed Rabin's 'commitment' of July 1994 provided Israel's security needs were met. Barak had told his cabinet that Rabin had given guarantees that Israel would fully withdraw from the Golan Heights in exchange for a security commitment by Syria, and that he would not 'erase the past'.[40] For their part, the Syrians had revealed at Shepherdstown a preparedness to entertain arrangements for the deployment of forces and the manning of early warning stations that went some way to accommodating Israel's security concerns.

The border was not solely a question of security, however. Access to water was also a factor. Some 50 years earlier the Syrian government had offered on two separate occasions to make peace with Israel on the basis that Israel agree to half of the Sea of Galilee being ceded to Syria in exchange for peace.[41] This was declined because the Sea provides about 40 per cent of Israel's water supply. Syria was prepared to agree not to draw drinking water from the Sea in exchange for Barak's acceptance of the 4 June line,[42] while the United States undertook to explore the possibility of Syria's water supply being met from Turkey. Syria's commitment would seem to be credible, given its responsible behaviour in relation to the Sea during the 19 years that it had enjoyed access to the waterfront. Also, Syria would be well aware of its vulnerability to Israel if it were ever to renege on such an undertaking. Population pressure, drought and poor water management had turned the Galilee/Jordan basin into a rapidly wasting asset, and the future needs of the riparian peoples might more effectively be met by building desalination plants, a thought that the United States was prepared to entertain.

Security and water are vital issues and Barak was facing continuing domestic resistance to withdrawal from the Golan lobby while simultaneously addressing the question of a more extensive withdrawal from the West Bank and Gaza. Three of the six parties in Barak's coalition government joined forces with the opposition to approve a preliminary bill that would make a future referendum on peace with Syria extremely difficult to pass.[43] Barak was unwilling to risk putting more or less concurrent withdrawals on both the Palestinian and Syrian fronts to the test of Israeli public opinion. He briefed Clinton to tell Assad that he wished to retain the Sea's entire waterfront in Israeli hands, but in compensation for the strip along the waterfront Israel would exchange a parcel of inland territory that had not previously been in Syrian hands.

By the time of Clinton's meeting with the Syrian president, Assad was clearly terminally ill. His preparedness to meet with Clinton may be read as indicative of an interest in concluding an agreement. Indeed, Clinton had told him over the 'phone that he had something 'you're going to like to hear'.[44] It would be Clinton's final opportunity to secure an agreement before a change of Syrian leadership. No incoming leader would inherit Assad's authority: if acquired, it would need to be earned over a period of time. Barak provided Clinton with a script for his meeting, insisting that the description of Israel's needs had to be recited word for word.[45] Albright records that the president was prepared to work from Barak's script for several reasons:

> He had more hope than the rest of us that the initiative would succeed, and certainly Barak's offer was more forthcoming than any other the Syrians were likely to receive. The President had also promised to support those in the Middle East who were willing to run risks for peace; astute diplomatic strategist or not, Barak led the region in this category. Finally, the President's inherent optimism encouraged him to believe that a concentrated push couldn't help but produce movement.

The reservations held by the president's advisers may have been due to their knowledge that Clinton had sent a message to Assad in June 1995 assuring him that 'he had in his pocket a commitment from Rabin that Israel was ready to withdraw to the 4 June 1967 borders'[46] on which he would now have to resile. The 4 June 1967 line had never been demarcated. Syria claimed to have been in occupation of territory to the Sea's north-eastern edge and to the west of the Jordan River for some distance before it flowed into the Sea. In Syria's view, it had thus enjoyed access to both the waters of the Sea and its principal tributary on 4 June. Israel countered that on that date some 60 per cent of Syria's positions were east of the 1923 line.[47] Clinton presented Barak's position: the 4 June line was acceptable to Barak, but Barak 'needed to make sure that Israel retained sovereignty over the water of the Sea of Galilee and the Jordan River and therefore the borderline should not touch either one'.[48]

Assad would not admit to Israeli sovereignty over what he considered to be Syrian territory. Clinton's public comments make it clear that he chose to put the onus on Assad to respond to Barak's position.[49] In doing so he seems to have hoped to deflect criticism of Barak for any breakdown in the negotiation. Clinton's failure even to keep the door ajar sealed its fate. Barak has been blamed for having failed to seize the moment,[50] but Clinton was complicit.

Hafez Al-Assad was succeeded by his son, Bashar, who announced that he would continue his father's policy of seeking reclamation of all of the Golan territory from Israel in return for peace. But Bashar's first priority was to consolidate his rule. This, and the failure of the summit in Geneva to produce a breakthrough, meant that in effect the US-mediated negotiation between Israel and Syria was ended.[51] The *al-Aqsa intifada* broke out in September 2000, further discouraging Israelis from possible accommodation with their Arab neighbours. Then Ariel Sharon was elected prime minister of Israel in February 2001 and vowed to retain the Golan Heights.

LEBANON

The United States had, on several occasions, to broker ceasefire agreements between Israel and Lebanon. Lebanese territory provided a base for the launching of Arab attacks against Israel. Because of this, sites in Lebanon became targets for the IDF. Israel seized control of southern Lebanon for the first time in 1978. It invaded Lebanon in 1982, and decided to create a security zone in Lebanese territory immediately to the north of the common border in 1985. Complementary to the ceasefire arrangements, the UN Security Council repeatedly called for Israel's withdrawal from all Lebanese territory. Islamist extremists were never much of a factor in Lebanon before 1982, but the more moderate Islamist groups were destroyed during Israel's invasion, creating a vacuum that came to be filled by Hezbollah. Hezbollah did not exist when Israel began the occupation and bombardment of southern Lebanon,[52] but it grew to become a major irritant to Israel's security. Conflict made Lebanon an important element in the Arab–Israel dispute, and the United States search for a comprehensive settlement of the dispute had to include a settlement between Israel and Lebanon.

Syria exercises considerable influence over Lebanon. It maintains a large military presence in the country. No settlement between Israel and Lebanon can be effected without Syrian concurrence. Israel and Lebanon had agreed to a peace settlement in May 1983, but Lebanon later abrogated it under Syrian pressure. The expressed commitment of the United States to Lebanon's unity, sovereignty, independence, territorial integrity and continued adherence to democratic principles reflected its desire to diminish Syrian hegemony over Lebanon. It sought an end to the targeting of Israel by Islamist militias and the support extended to them by, or through, Syria. The United States has generally seen Syria as controlling and supporting Hezbollah, with assistance from Iran, but Stephen Zunes claims that American officials have greatly exaggerated Syria's role: 'Syria has historically backed the rival Amal militia'.[53] While the extent of militias' dependence on Syria may be disputed, there is no doubting that they have received support from their eastern neighbour. If a comprehensive peace were to be concluded, the United States would have to persuade Israel to withdraw from southern Lebanon, and Syria to exercise such influence as it could over Hezbollah, in particular, to stop it from cross-border attacks on Israel.

While engaged in the task of bringing Middle Eastern states to the conference table at Madrid, Baker addressed the question of getting both Israeli and Syrian forces out of Lebanon. His letter of assurances to Lebanon on the eve of the Madrid conference recognised that although the withdrawal of Israeli troops and the withdrawal of Syrian troops from Lebanon were separate issues, both were covered by legal instruments. UN Security Council Resolution 425 applied to Israeli forces only, but the Taif agreement of October 1989 calls for the withdrawal of *all* non-Lebanese forces from Lebanon.[54] Baker also drew an explicit distinction between Resolution 425, which calls for Israel's withdrawal from 'all Lebanese territory', and the less precise terminology of Resolution 242 on withdrawal from 'territory'.

Although Lebanon participated in the Madrid conference, Washington 'understood that Lebanon and Israel would not sign a peace agreement unless and until Syria and Israel had resolved their differences'.[55] Barak's election to government in 1999 introduced a significant change of circumstance. A survey had shown that the majority of Israelis believed that Israel should pull out of Lebanon unconditionally. The expected gain would be an indirect one: by withdrawing from southern Lebanon, the cause of Hezbollah resistance would be removed and so would Syria's need to assist that group. In office, Barak repeated a campaign pledge that within a year Israeli troops would be out of the south Lebanon security zone. Albright believed that he wanted to have an agreement with Syria in place to ensure an orderly withdrawal and secure aftermath, and the United States clearly hoped that Israel's intention to withdraw could be traded for some significant gain in relation to Syria.

The withdrawal was completed in May 2000 from all save a small area known as the Shaba farms.[56] Israel's decision to withdraw was known to both Assad and Clinton, but Barak's brief for their meeting in March did not offer Clinton scope to use Israel's proposed withdrawal as a bargaining chip with Syria. The expectation of a cessation of hostilities along the northern border was not to be realised. Significant though the withdrawal was, it was not sufficient to sever the organic link that Syria had forged with Lebanon.

CONCLUSION

The United States viewed a peace agreement between Israel and Syria as the key to a comprehensive settlement of the Arab–Israel dispute and to a new geopolitical order in the Middle East. Clinton engaged personally in the search for a peaceful settlement between Israel and Syria. He established personal contact with his Syrian counterpart, and his senior officials shuttled between Washington, Damascus and Jerusalem. Notwithstanding these communication channels, the United States underestimated Assad's suspicion of the America–Israel alliance and was slow to offer reassurance when it would have been appropriate to do so.[57]

The Congress was not only sceptical about Syrian intentions, but concerned to restrain the Administration's links with that country. Neither the Administration nor the Congress would entertain the provision of US aid to Syria during the 1990s, although Syria seems to have harboured an expectation that it might become eligible for United States aid if a settlement with Israel could be concluded. The only incentive that the Clinton Administration dangled before both the Israelis and Syrians was the possibility of an international force or monitors being stationed on the Golan Heights in the event of an Israeli withdrawal from the area. This option, however, provoked a spirited campaign within the United States against American participation in any such peace-keeping force and Clinton dropped it.

Assad's refusal to enter into direct negotiation with Israel prior to December 1999 enabled the United States to become the intermediary and, in time, a full participant in the negotiation. Circumstances placed the United States in an exceptional position from which to exercise its influence. Why, then was it unable to effect a settlement? There were a number of reasons. First, the lack of United States leverage over Syria and Assad's obduracy complicated its task. Assad's inflexibility on the question of direct negotiation, his ineptitude in public diplomacy, and the lack of trust between Israel and Syria on territorial questions, were significant factors.[58]

Second, and also from an Arab perspective, the efforts of Palestinian insurgents to set back the peace process, and those of Hezbollah in the southern Lebanon security zone, presented difficulties. Clinton secured condemnation of terrorism, and was able to proclaim to terrorist groups that they were acting contrary to regional opinion that supported the peace process, but that outcome was obtained in the absence of Iran, Lebanon and Syria, which abetted terrorist activity.

Third, and from an Israeli perspective, although Clinton had urged Rabin to start preparing Israelis for the need to make concessions in order to achieve peace, he stopped short of encouraging the Israelis to determine an order of priority. The consequence of not prioritising the process was that Rabin appeared undecided in August 1993 whether to back the United States preference for the Syrian track, or the Palestinian one. His eventual opting for 'Oslo' was taken not on an analysis of which track would make the more important contribution to a comprehensive settlement, but on the basis that one offered a more immediate prospect than the other. Such a decision need not, in itself, prevent the achievement of a comprehensive settlement, but it threw up the conundrum of how to handle a demand for concurrent withdrawals from the Golan Heights, the West Bank and the Gaza Strip. Another opportunity to address prioritisation arose in 1999 when at a press conference Barak announced an intention to move forward 'simultaneously on all tracks',[59] but Clinton seems again not to have taken it up.

Finally, neither Peres nor Barak felt sufficiently secure politically to make the necessary accommodations to bring about a settlement with Syria, and Clinton declined to pressure them into doing so. He would generally defer to the judgement of Israeli premiers, especially after Rabin's assassination, which had affected him greatly.[60] Despite having encouraged Assad to believe that Israel would be prepared to withdraw to the 4 June 1967 line, and Barak having briefed his cabinet in those terms, Clinton carried a brief to his meeting with Assad in March 2000 designed to ensure Israel's continued sovereignty over the waters of the Sea of Galilee and the Jordan River, and accordingly the border line should not encroach on either. Assad rejected it flatly. After the meeting, Clinton chose tactically to put the onus on Syria to move on the border issue in an attempt to protect Barak and himself from having fumbled the negotiation.

It is not clear why Clinton should have agreed to carry Barak's brief without requiring that some concession be extracted from Syria in return for Israel's preparedness to withdraw from southern Lebanon. Neither Clinton nor Barak seems to have been concerned to maximise the leverage inherent in Israel's withdrawal. From the United States perspective, the explanation seems to lie in Clinton's tendency to defer to the Israeli leadership, and his expectations of Barak in relation to the Palestinians.[61] Perhaps, by then, he had also come to share Uri Savir's impression that both sides could go on living without peace,[62] given that they had existed in a state of dormant hostility since 1974.

Constrained in the use of positive sanctions, and unwilling to employ negative ones, the United States ability to effect its desired outcome in the negotiation between Israel and Syria depended upon its persuasive skills. These were insufficient to overcome the entrenched positions of the two parties.

NOTES

1 Rabinovich (1998) pp.41–3. Notwithstanding Shamir's interpretation of UN Security Council Resolution 242, which he sustained during eight rounds of Washington talks, he had secretly conveyed to the Syrians in 1992 that he did not rule out the possibility of some territorial concessions in the Golan as part of an Israeli–Syrian settlement.
2 Ibid. Cited at p.78.
3 Ford (1975).
4 Baker (1992a) pp.119–20.
5 Rabinovich (1998) pp.141–2. The border had been set by the British ten metres east of the shoreline of the Sea of Galilee. The 1948 war ended with Syria in control of some territories west of the international border, only to lose them to Israel in 1967; Slater (2002) pp.84–6. There is a history of customary Syrian usage of the Sea of Galilee. Both Britain and France allowed the Syrian government to have a pier on the lake, and Syrian villagers to use the lake for fishing, to feed their cattle, and for drinking water. The legitimacy of the Israeli claim is confused by its insistence on the one hand that the armistice lines must reflect the military outcome of the 1948 war, which resulted in Israeli territorial gains going well beyond the UN partition plan boundaries, while on the other demanding that Syria withdraw to the 1923 international boundary.
6 Prados (2002) pp.3–4.
7 Rabinovich (1998) p.92.
8 Butler (1997) pp.83–4.
9 Rabinovich (1998) pp.104–5.
10 Ibid. p.105.
11 Ibid. p.118.
12 Strindberg (2003) p.27. Damascus became the exile headquarters for the Alliance of Palestinian Forces, a cross-factional umbrella organisation established in order to reject the Oslo process and challenge Arafat's leadership.
13 Rabinovich (1998) p.125.
14 Ross (2004) p.113.
15 Clinton, W.J. *Public Papers, 1994*, p.86.
16 Ibid. pp.81–2.
17 Ibid. p.82.
18 Ibid. p.89.
19 Ibid. p.84.
20 Rabinovich (1998) p.188.
21 Ibid. p.166. An organised letter-writing campaign claimed that: 'Any such deployment of U.S. troops will begin with good intentions and end with American body bags and vehement American protest demonstrations. This will no doubt lead to a rise in anti-Semitism in the U.S.'
22 Ibid. p.134.
23 Clinton, W.J. *Public Papers, 1994*, p.1882.
24 Ibid. pp.1883–4.
25 Heikal (1996) p.547.
26 Ross (2004) p.233.
27 Christopher (1996) p.3.
28 Clinton, W.J. *Public Papers, 1996*, pp. 449–50.
29 Seale and Butler (1996) p.29. From 1982 to 1996, a period that included the Israeli invasion of Lebanon, not more than ten Israeli civilians in northern Israel were killed by Arab attacks. Only one Israeli civilian was seriously wounded during Operation Grapes of Wrath, while several dozen suffered minor cuts or were 'treated for shock'; Luft (2000). Luft states that more than 4000 Katyusha rockets landed in the Galilee region in the years 1985 to 2000, but remarkably, only seven civilians were killed by this weapon.
30 Cobban (1999) p.157; Ross (2004) p.251.
31 Rabinovich (1998) p.262. Although it passed by a slender majority of 43 to 40, as this was the first of three readings the vote as such had no operative significance.

32 Migdalovitz (2002) p.10. The law was adopted on 26 January 1999. Sixty-one members would be a simple majority if all 120 members of the Knesset were present and voting.
33 Clinton, W.J. *Public Papers, 1997*, pp.152, 154–5.
34 Butler (1997); Cobban (1999) p.73; Sontag (2000a).
35 Seale and Butler (1996) pp.36–7; Pelletreau (1996) p.336.
36 Delaney (1999).
37 Ross (2004) p.509.
38 Perlez (2000).
39 Ross (2004) p.561.
40 Sontag (2000a). It was the first time that an Israeli prime minister had ever admitted that Israel had agreed, conditionally, to complete withdrawal.
41 Ma'oz (2003b). Assurance of water supply was one of the factors in the 1967 war.
42 Slater (2002) p.96.
43 The bill would have required that a referendum pass by a simple majority of the electorate. The government would have to win about 65 per cent of the votes cast in order to satisfy the requirement. Sontag (2000b).
44 Bregman (2005) p.55. Bregman cited Clinton's national security advisers.
45 Albright (2003) p.480; Clinton, W.J. *Public Papers, 2000*, Appendix A. Clinton rang Barak on 26 March, prior to and following his meeting with Assad.
46 Sid-Ahmed (1999).
47 Bregman (2005) p.24. Bregman cites retired Israeli General Uri Saguie.
48 Ross (2004) p.584.
49 Clinton, W.J. *Public Papers, 2000*, p.648.
50 Slater (2002) pp.99–100.
51 Malley (2001a).
52 Zunes (2000) p.1.
53 Zunes (2000).
54 Baker (1992b) p.120.
55 Mark (2002) p.1.
56 Eldar (2002). The Lebanese claim that the area – a strip 14 km long and 2 km wide – belongs to Lebanon, while Israel contends that it is Syrian territory and subject to whatever agreement may be reached between Israel and Syria. An official of the French mandatory noted in 1920 that the demarcated border between Lebanon and Syria on an Ottoman map did not correspond to customary usage. While the Shaba farms were shown as Syrian territory, persons living in the area were under Lebanese regulation and paid Lebanese taxes. He characterised the situation as a Lebanese enclave within Syrian territory. Syria took over the area in 1950 and its population was counted in the Syrian census of 1960. The UN Secretary General has supported the Lebanese claim to the territory on the basis of modern maps.
57 Cobban (1999) p.150.
58 Muslih (1994). Muslih records Syrian officials as having indicated Assad's preparedness to engage in public diplomacy and to prepare his people for peaceful relations with Israel once Rabin committed himself to a return to the 4 June 1967 line.
59 Clinton, W.J. *Public Papers, 1999*, p.1407. Barak said: 'It is our intention to move the process forward simultaneously on all tracks – bilateral, the Palestinians, the Syrians, and the Lebanese, as well as the multilateral'.
60 Cobban (1999) pp.193–4.
61 Clinton, W.J. *Public Papers, 1999*, p.1203.
62 Savir (1998) p.271.

6. Frustration and failure: the United States, Israel and the Palestinians, 1996–2001

During the second phase of negotiation between Israel and the Palestinians, from 1996 until the expiration of Clinton's presidency in 2001, the United States made serious endeavours to secure a resolution of the parties' differences, but was unable to effect a peace settlement.

1996 was a significant year for the United States. It had to adjust to the transformation of the PLO into the Palestinian Authority in January 1996 and the defeat of Peres by Netanyahu in May, and Clinton had to secure his own re-election in November. His second-term agenda accorded primacy to a need to build the first undivided democratic Europe in history, reflecting the United States concern to create a new European architecture following the Cold War. The search for peace in the Middle East occupied second place on his agenda, followed by the need to meet the threat of terrorism. A resolution of the Arab–Israel dispute was thus juxtaposed with the factor most likely to frustrate its attainment. The United States intervened more actively in the prosecution of a settlement during this period than was the case before 1996, with the president advancing his own proposals in his final weeks in office.

THE LIKUD APPROACH

Clinton received Netanyahu on his first visit to Washington as prime minister in July 1996. Netanyahu's disenchantment with the peace process was public knowledge. The Likud Party platform for the election offered little encouragement to Palestinians and others who sought an accommodation between Israel and the Palestinians. The party's assertion of the right of the Jewish people to *Eretz Yisrael* as 'an eternal right, not subject to dispute'[1] was reinforced by a declaration that Israel's permanent eastern border lay along the Jordan River. The establishment of an independent Palestinian state was explicitly opposed; and institutions of the Palestinian Authority in Jerusalem such as Orient House, an important symbol of the Palestinian presence in the city, were to be closed because it was claimed that they undermined the status of Jerusalem as the united and undivided capital of the State of Israel. Settlement activity would be strengthened, and 'Jewish settlement, security areas, water resources, state land and road intersections in Judea, Samaria and the Gaza Strip shall remain under full Israeli control'. The Palestinians would be enabled 'to manage their lives freely, within the framework of self-government ... [but] ... foreign affairs and defence ... [would] ... remain the responsibility of the State of Israel'. The possibility of some form of partnership between Palestinian self-government areas and Jordan was not ruled out, although its form was not specified.

Clinton found some encouragement in Netanyahu's statement that he would work closely with the Palestinian Authority on full implementation by both parties of the Declaration of Principles and the Interim Agreement, and on easing economic conditions on the Palestinians.[2] Netanyahu believed that the United States, Russia and the European Union should play only a limited role in the negotiations between the Arabs and Israel: only the parties that bore the consequences had the right to decide. Clinton could draw limited satisfaction from hearing him say: 'We inherited two agreements, Oslo I and Oslo II, not to our liking ... But I inherited them as prime minister. And governments keep agreements'. In Netanyahu's view the obligation was on the Palestinian Authority to fulfil its commitments first, which would then put the Authority in a 'moral position to ask us to fulfil the remaining of our obligations'. He instanced two matters that he had promised during the election campaign to prosecute if elected and that he looked to the Palestinian Authority to undertake. These were that the Palestinian Authority desist from maintaining an official presence, including that of security personnel, in Jerusalem; and that Hamas and Islamic Jihad be disarmed. He acknowledged that the Palestinian Authority had shown a capacity to curb terrorist activity during the Israeli election campaign, and encouraged the Authority to continue doing so.

Violence erupted in September 1996, provoked by Israel's desire to renegotiate the terms of redeployment from Hebron; Israel's easing of restrictions on settlement building in the West Bank; and its plans to open a tunnel in Jerusalem that bordered the Dome of the Rock. Clinton responded, inviting Netanyahu and Arafat to attend a meeting in Washington with King Hussein and himself to clarify points of difference and to lower the temperature between the two parties. He secured an important commitment from Arafat and Netanyahu 'not to renegotiate agreements by which both sides are bound, but instead to talk about the ... steps necessary to implement those agreements'.[3] Implementation of the Hebron agreement, deferred by Peres and Arafat until after the Israeli election, would be top priority, backed by recognition of the need to improve cooperation between the two sides' security forces. Negotiation on these matters would resume in Israel in October 1996, with Ross as a participant. On 14 January 1997 the president announced that agreement had been reached on the Hebron redeployment and a roadmap for further redeployment by Israel over the period to mid-1998, and that this brought his Washington summit to a successful conclusion.

The Hebron agreement was not achieved without difficulty, and Ross had been about to give up when King Hussein intervened and persuaded Arafat and Netanyahu to accept the completion date for a three-stage redeployment that Ross had been pushing. The original agreement with Peres had allocated the Palestinians about 88 per cent of the city. The 'Netanyahu agreement' divided Hebron into a Palestinian zone, covering 80 per cent of the city, and an Israeli one whose 20 per cent included the town's commercial centre. The Jewish settlers, who constituted only 0.3 per cent of the town's population, were favourably endowed under it. Netanyahu was also insisting on 'reciprocity' by the Palestinians as a condition for further concessions. Neither Israelis nor Palestinians were in full compliance with all of the detail of the Oslo accords, but only Israel would gain from using that term to justify any suspension of negotiations. The term was employed in Ross's Note for the Record prepared in connection with the new Hebron agreement. Christopher, who in a letter to Netanyahu[4] accepted his insistence on 'reciprocity', expressed a 'belief' that Israel would proceed with the three-stage withdrawal plan, rather than an assertion of it as an Israeli commitment. He accepted that Israel would decide the extent and location of further withdrawals, which would not be subject to negotiation with the Palestinians. And he employed the language of Israeli hawks in referring to Israel's entitlement to 'secure and defensible' borders, which was a significant variation of the UN Security Council Resolution 242 formula of 'secure and recognised boundaries' on which the peace process was based. The United States brokered an agreement, but at considerable cost to the Palestinians.

THE COMPLICATION OF ISRAELI SETTLEMENTS

Even as the Israelis and Palestinians were negotiating IDF redeployments, the Israeli government was expanding its holding in parts of the West Bank through settlement and road building. Clinton underestimated the depth of Arab resentment, despite an Arab summit having been held in Cairo in June 1996 that sent a clear message to the United States and Israel that unless Israel honoured the ground rule of land for peace on which the peace process was predicated, it would collapse. He had to decide, once again, how to handle the settlements question within the United Nations when Israel's decision to open an entrance to the Hasmonean tunnel under the western wall of the al-Aqsa Mosque in East Jerusalem, and the shooting of Palestinians demonstrating against that action, was brought before the Security Council in September 1996. The United States was able to persuade the Council not to criticise Israel by name in a resolution and abstained during its adoption.

The next such issue before the Security Council flowed from Israel's decision in March 1997 to build a settlement in Jebel Abu Ghneim/Har Homa. Clinton has recorded that '[e]very time Netanyahu took a step forward, as with the Hebron agreement, his governing coalition made him do something that drove a wedge between Israel and the Palestinians'.[5] The housing settlement would isolate Palestinian neighbourhoods in East Jerusalem from the rest of the West Bank, and was viewed by Arabs as a continuation of an Israeli policy of 'Judaisation' of Jerusalem. Other grievances subsumed in this matter included charges by the Palestinians of the withdrawal of the identity cards of Palestinian residents of East Jerusalem, and of lengthy delays to shipments of food and medical supplies at international crossing points and in the ports. Also, European companies were prevented from starting work on the construction of the Gaza seaport, to be financed mainly from French and Dutch aid. In addressing this matter, the United States was confronted by a cleavage within the Security Council between itself and the Council's other Western European members. Britain and France co-sponsored an ill-fated draft resolution with Portugal and Sweden that would have called on Israel to refrain from all actions or measures, including settlement activities, which altered the facts on the ground.[6] Clinton held to the position subscribed to by American Administrations ever since Reagan characterised Israeli activity in the occupied territories as an obstacle to peace, and had argued strongly with Netanyahu against the project. The United States would have preferred that there be no draft resolution, and tried to have the Security Council issue a strong presidential statement instead, but failed. Nor was it able to persuade the co-sponsors to employ language that would enable an abstention. The United States vetoed it. Questioned about the veto, Clinton and President Mubarak, who was visiting Washington at the time, made clear that they had registered with the Israelis their concerns about the Har Homa project. They had been unable to persuade Netanyahu to stop it. Explaining the veto, Clinton said that peace could never be achieved through UN Security Council resolutions; that the draft contained language that the United States had vetoed in the past; and that the matter should properly be part of the final status negotiations.

The exercise of the United States veto power did not end consideration of this matter within the United Nations. Frustrated by it, Arab states and their supporters requested a meeting of the UN General Assembly to consider the settlement question. On 13 March the General Assembly adopted a resolution that called for Israel to refrain from all actions or measures that pre-empted the final status negotiations, and to abide by its legal obligations and responsibilities under the Fourth Geneva Convention. It was opposed by the United States and Israel.[7]

The Palestinians were to complain to the Secretary General that Israel had reaffirmed its decision to proceed with the construction of the Har Homa project less than 24 hours after the resolution's passage. Accordingly, the Arab members of the Security Council took the matter back to the Council on 21 March. Once again, the United States vetoed a draft resolution, explaining that controversy over the project would not be resolved by interference from the Security Council or the General Assembly, and should be left to the parties concerned, which had demonstrated since the Madrid conference that they could overcome the problems and differences that separated them. Russia, which voted for the draft, was unequivocal: the situation had continued to deteriorate and was becoming increasingly confrontational because of Israel's acts of provocation. The Palestinians found it difficult to accept either that the US veto had been employed to protect the peace process or that bilateral negotiations offered the prospect of a solution when one of the parties was changing the demography of Jerusalem by settling some 20 000 Jews on land that the Palestinians claimed.

The Arab states were irritated by the action of the United States and decided once again to circumvent the Security Council. They mustered a majority in support of the convening of an emergency special session of the UN General Assembly. It met in April, July and November 1997. The proponents focussed on the Israeli settlement project, which they addressed in terms of the principles of the Fourth Geneva Convention. Their intent was to apply the pressure of international opinion to the United States as much as to Israel, knowing that the United States would be unable either to persuade the General Assembly to its position or to shield Israel from the force of international criticism. Because the General Assembly lacked mandatory authority, the United States could tolerate the international community's venting of steam. It was unlikely to have other than an atmospheric affect on the peace process.

At its April meeting the special session recommended that the High Contracting Parties to the Fourth Geneva Convention, which include Israel, 'take measures, on a national or regional level, in fulfilment of their obligations under … the Convention'.[8] This resolution was endorsed by an overwhelming majority, with only Israel, Micronesia and the United States voting against it. The American representative at the special session said that the United States shared the concern expressed by other representatives about Israel's decision to begin construction of the project, but then diverted to address jurisdictional matters.[9] The Secretary-General, who had been authorised to monitor the situation, reported to the UN membership in June that Israel had imposed unacceptable restrictions on a proposed on-the-ground investigation into the building project by his special envoy; and that Israel had not accepted *de jure* applicability of the Fourth Geneva Convention to all occupied territories. This provoked a tougher resolution from the special session in July. The new resolution recommended that the High Contracting Parties 'convene a conference on measures to enforce the Convention in the occupied Palestinian territory, including Jerusalem'.[10] It attracted the same three negative votes. The United States objected that a conference of the contracting parties to the Convention was not the proper forum to address the situation, and was troubled by the ostensible goal of such a conference. Russia, which had voted in favour of the April resolution, shared this concern and abstained: what enforcement agency would be used, and how would enforcement be effected?

The General Assembly's action did little to ease tension between Israel and the Palestinians. Clinton's Administration would have read the report of the Israeli human rights organisation, B'tselem,[11] which recorded that between the beginning of the *intifada* on 9 December 1987 and 30 November 1997 some 1479 Palestinians had been killed by the IDF, security forces and settlers, and 383 Israelis had been killed by Palestinians. While Israel was proceeding with settlement construction, during the decade some 447 Palestinians' houses had been demolished and 294 sealed off as punishment for violent offences committed by a suspected or convicted family member, some 106 demolished by artillery fire, and another 1800 demolished on the ground that they were built without a permit. Security and settlements were therefore high on Madeleine Albright's agenda when, as secretary of state, she visited Israel on 10 September 1997. She tried to persuade Netanyahu to commit to limiting settlement construction if the Palestinian Authority were able to win its battle against Palestinian terrorist elements, suggesting 'time-out' on the building programme, but he refused to comply.

The Israelis went ahead with their programme, announcing on 24 September that they would put up a further 300 housing units at another site south of Bethlehem. The Administration called again for a freeze on settlement expansion in the West Bank. Netanyahu rejected it on 26 September. The efforts of the United States were backed from an unlikely source: Sheikh Ahmed Yassin, the founder of Hamas, told reporters on 7 October that Hamas would stop targeting Israeli civilians if Israel stopped killing Palestinians, confiscating land, demolishing houses and building settlements. Undaunted by appeals from the United States, Netanyahu produced a map of Israel on 27 November which showed the Jordan Valley, the coastline of the Gaza Strip, Jerusalem (within enlarged municipal boundaries), and a narrow 'security zone' east of the 4 June 1967 line as falling within Israeli territory.

Although the General Assembly was unaware of this detail at the time, it remained concerned about Israel's continuing practices in the occupied territories. It requested Switzerland, depository of the Fourth Geneva Convention, to assist in convening a Conference of its High Contracting Parties. The United States was unable to prevent the Conference from reaffirming the normative value of the Convention and declaring its applicability to occupied Palestinian territory, including East Jerusalem. In a direct reference to Israeli practices, the participating Parties recalled that no Contracting Party 'shall be allowed to absolve itself of any liability incurred by itself in respect to ... wilful killing, torture, unlawful deportation, wilful depriving of the rights of fair and regular trial, extensive destruction and appropriation of property not justified by military necessity and carried out unlawfully and wantonly'.[12]

Clinton clearly recognised that Likud's settlements policy was inimical to the peace process and tried to persuade Netanyahu to drop it. Albright was later to conclude that the United States should have pushed harder to halt the expansion of settlements.[13] But the Administration refrained from exercising leverage to prevent construction. United States tax law permits transfers to Israeli settlements and settlers by non-profitable charitable organisations funded through tax-deductible contributions. None of the principal United States actors – Clinton, Albright or Ross – had given any indication of having considered the possible application of negative sanctions to reinforce their argument that settlement construction be halted. They relied on the strength of their verbal presentations. Clinton, who was not attracted to punitive or coercive measures, may have calculated that their employment would have alienated Netanyahu, whose interest in the Oslo process was tenuous. Nothing could be gained if Netanyahu broke with the process, and Clinton would not wish to provide him with an excuse to resile from his commitment to keep agreements. Netanyahu was later to explain to Clinton the political imperative of his proceeding with the Har Homa project, and the president understood the prime minister's needs.[14] In one sense, Clinton was exceptionally well-placed to exert leverage had he wished to do so. He had been re-elected in November 1996 with the backing of American Jewry, and for at least the next 12 months need not be unduly concerned about Netanyahu appealing to an American constituency over his head.

A re-elected president usually enjoys a measure of independence at the beginning of his second term. But Clinton faced constraints of a different order. The Republicans had pursued him throughout his presidency about alleged personal indiscretions, some of which pre-dated his election to that office. Eleven possible grounds of impeachment were advanced in a report lodged with the House Judiciary Committee in September 1998. He would need the help of his congressional supporters if the Congress were to proceed with impeachment, and he was careful not to alienate them. Also, his wife had been approached about standing for the Senate in the interest of the State of New York[15] and would be courting the vote of its influential Jewish community. Moreover, he had pledged when first running for the presidency never to criticise Israel publicly[16] and true to this confined criticism to private conversations. Accordingly, his position on the world stage was seen as one of public protection for Israel and preservation of the Oslo process, leading many in the Arab world and beyond to question America's professed role in the peace process as an honest broker.

Clinton hoped that some amelioration in the level of violence would encourage Netanyahu to advance the peace process. He proscribed access by designated Middle Eastern terrorist organisations to sources of financial support in the United States through an Executive Order in January 1995, and announced in March 1996 the stationing of American specialists in Israel to work with and to improve antiterrorism cooperation among Israeli, Palestinian and regional governments. The commitment was backed by a two-year $100 million programme for Israel, supplemented by intelligence sharing arrangements with the CIA. He reviewed progress under the programme with Netanyahu in February 1997 and announced that delivery would begin that year of F-15-1 fighters to strengthen Israel's air defences. But he was dealing with a prime minister who had rejected the assessment of his General Security Service and his director of military intelligence that Arafat had no incentive to cooperate with Israel in the fight against Islamic terror as long as he believed that Israel was not complying with the Oslo accords.

By mid-1997 it was clear that the peace process had stalled.[17] Clinton was challenged about avoiding the implications of Netanyahu's refusal to bargain land for Palestinian peace and asked whether he preferred to minimise short-run frictions with the Israeli government or reach for a long-term peace.[18] The president defended his position, stating that 'there is no foreign policy problem to which I have given more of my personal time since I became president in 1993'. He added that 'until the parties trust each other and until the Israelis believe that the Palestinian Authority is making 100 per cent effort, which is different from 100 per cent results ... it is impossible for peace to proceed'.

REINVIGORATING THE PEACE PROCESS

During her first six months as secretary of state, Albright concentrated on European affairs, a reflection of Clinton's second-term priorities. She believed that Christopher had squandered time and political capital in visiting the Middle East two dozen times in his four years, often to no apparent effect. By August 1997 she had decided that if the peace process were to be reactivated, a more energetic United States role was necessary.[19] She suggested that, instead of using the gradual confidence-building approach of the Oslo accords, momentum might be restored by getting the parties to focus on their ultimate goal. Netanyahu had made a similar proposal in April, but it had been rejected by Arafat and other Arab leaders.

Although reinvigoration of the peace process was the ostensible reason for Albright's involvement, there was a strong sense of its being an exercise in damage control. She reminded both parties of their mutual responsibilities, conscious in doing so that she was working against a preference in the Congress that her message should be confined solely to a denunciation of Palestinian terrorism. Arafat found her appeal to mutual responsibility more persuasive than Netanyahu, and offered some new and encouraging counter-terrorism initiatives. This had prompted her to advance her unsuccessful 'time-out' proposal.

Albright met Netanyahu again in London and Arafat in Bern in November 1997, where she discussed ideas that the United States believed were necessary to get the two parties started on accelerated negotiations leading to permanent status, but Albright was irritated by Netanyahu's now apparent lack of interest in faster movement. At the Middle East and North Africa Economic Conference in Doha, itself an embarrassment because Arab states had decided not to participate, she stated bluntly that the peace process was 'in danger ... because leaders have failed to take the actions required to realise the possibilities of peace'[20] and that 'there will be no peace if the leaders of [the] region sit on the sidelines and wait for others to take the risks'. Exasperation with the unravelling process was evident: the secretary had other urgent matters to worry about and she threatened that she was not inclined to return to the Middle East unless there was enough happening for her participation to make a difference.[21]

Notwithstanding her frustration, the United States continued to explore the prospect of moving negotiations more quickly into the final status stage. When Netanyahu had originally advanced this, he had expressed concern that a lot of the issues to be resolved were highly contentious and it would ease his domestic difficulties to put them all into the one package and to have as few ratification votes as possible.[22] Subsequent American diplomacy helped the parties to agree on an agenda. The United States worked with both sides in accordance with the agenda and planned that its efforts would result in the final status talks being launched in Washington on 11 May 1998, but the gap between the two parties' positions remained too wide to offer any prospect of movement. Arafat was seeking a transfer of a further 30 per cent of the remaining territory to the Palestinian Authority, while Netanyahu had intimated to Clinton that he might only be able to go as high as 11 per cent. Also, Netanyahu was insisting on Arafat applying measures to protect Israelis from attacks by Palestinians. Netanyahu interpreted these measures broadly as encompassing incitement to anti-Israel action and incarceration of activists.

Clinton was obliged to issue a statement that day saying that the meeting would not take place.

In the course of its dialogue with Israel and the Palestinians, the United States developed its own appreciation of the parties' positions and of a possible way forward. Albright articulated this on 12 May. She stressed the urgency of launching the permanent status talks because the interim period under the Oslo accords was due to expire in a year's time, on 4 May 1999. She suggested that the only way of achieving a settlement by that date was if Israel were to undertake a further force redeployment. Albright was, of course, aware that her predecessor had written to Netanyahu in 1997 saying that the extent and location of any further withdrawal was a matter for Israel alone, but she argued that it was 'in the nature of partnership that Israel should take Palestinian concerns into account, while following the terms of its agreement'.[23] While she did not define the area from which Israel should redeploy, it was known that the United States was thinking of withdrawal from about a further 13 per cent of West Bank and Gaza territory. Although less than Arafat's claim, this was acceptable to him.

In Albright's appreciation, there was little prospect of going directly to the final status negotiations without an Israeli redeployment. Ross explored with Netanyahu and Arafat separately the possibility of their accepting such an arrangement, and whether they might meet each other when they visited New York in September 1998 for the UN General Assembly meeting. Albright brought the two leaders together and left them alone. That was sufficient to break the ice after more than a year's estrangement. The president met with them on 28 September and announced after their meeting that there had been 'a significant narrowing of the gaps between the two parties across a wide range of issues that were in the American initiative that we've been working on for months'.[24]

The president tasked Albright to gauge the prospect for success if he were to invite the two leaders to a detailed negotiating conference. She was concerned that any summit should succeed because failure would leave the United States looking impotent.[25] She visited Gaza in October and reported that a new spirit pervaded the resumed Israel–Palestinian dialogue. Clinton then invited the parties to the Wye River Plantation later that month. With only months remaining to May 1999, the final status deadline would be impossible to meet, but to walk away from it without at least the appearance of an effort was to invite a new cycle of despair, extremism and violence. Netanyahu accepted the logic, conscious that participation in negotiations did not commit him in advance to any particular outcome. Throughout the discussions leading to his attendance, Albright had maintained pressure on him to acquiesce in her interpretation of the way forward. She enjoyed Clinton's backing in this. The task of the United States at Wye would be to convince Netanyahu to concede without breaching the tradition of US support for Israel.

WYE RIVER PLANTATION NEGOTIATIONS

The negotiations[26] appeared to meet the objective of the United States in opening the way toward further progress. An agreed Memorandum [27] provided for the transfer of land to the Palestinians in two tranches – 13 per cent in the first and 14.2 per cent in the second – and the establishment of a committee to consider any subsequent tranche. To assist the economic development of the Palestinian Authority, the timely opening of the Gaza industrial estate and port were agreed. Israel's security concerns were addressed, with the United States agreeing to be a full partner with the Palestinians in the systematic and effective combat of terrorist organisations and their infrastructure, for which purpose they would meet biweekly. Concurrently, a US–Palestinian–Israel committee would be established to enhance cooperation to prevent arms smuggling and to monitor cases of possible incitement to violence or terror, and 'a high-ranking US–Palestinian–Israel committee will meet ... not less than biweekly to assess current threats, deal with any impediments to effective security cooperation and address the steps being taken to combat terror and terrorist organisations'. In a further concession, as important to American domestic opinion as to Israeli sensibilities, the Palestine National Council would, at a meeting of the Council to be attended by President Clinton, reaffirm the nullification of those provisions of the Palestine National Charter that were inconsistent with the peace process, and reaffirm its support for the peace process. Finally, the two sides agreed to negotiate continuously and without interruption on permanent status issues with a view to reaching an agreement by 4 May 1999.

The United States was strongly opposed to the Har Homa project, for which tenders were about to be called, seeing it as pre-empting the negotiations on permanent status with new facts on the ground, and Ross told Netanyahu so. Perhaps international criticism of the project in 1997 had stiffened United States resolve. Netanyahu made it clear that politically he had no choice but to proceed with it. Clinton used this admission to extract agreement on the transfer of land to the Palestinians. Having achieved that, and Arafat not having challenged the trade-off when Clinton explained the situation to him, the president did not feel that he could fight Netanyahu further over the project.[28]

Within a week of the Memorandum's signing Clinton had to address what the United States could do to prevent its unravelling. Netanyahu had run into difficulties with his government: the right fearing that Netanyahu would implement Wye, handing over territory to the Palestinians, while the left feared that he would halt implementation of the agreement as soon as possible on one pretext or another. And a Palestinian suicide bomber launched an attack on 29 October. Eight members of the Israeli cabinet approved the agreement, four voted against it and five ministers abstained. The uncertainty within the cabinet did not reflect Israeli public opinion. A newspaper poll showed that 74 per cent of Israelis supported the terms of the Wye River Memorandum. The Knesset overwhelmingly approved the agreement by 75 votes to 19, with nine abstentions. In order to give sceptical Israelis some reassurance, Clinton concluded an agreement with Netanyahu on the potential threat to Israel posed by the proliferation of ballistic missiles and weapons of mass destruction in the region, and intimated the possibility of additional aid to Israel.[29] To convince Palestinians of the value of the agreement, Albright convened a pledging conference on 30 November. She brought Arafat together with the European Union, Norway and the World Bank, and the European Union promised a significant additional amount for the West Bank and Gaza.[30]

Netanyahu greeted Clinton on his arrival in Israel on 13 December 1998, complaining that the Palestinians were saying they would unilaterally declare statehood, with East Jerusalem as their capital, on 4 May 1999. Clinton responded in an address to the people of Israel, reassuring them that 'Palestinian leaders must ... avoid the impression that unilateral actions can replace agreed-upon negotiations'.[31] He stressed the importance of the Wye agreement and explained that the prime minister had succeeded in obtaining a set of systematic Palestinian security commitments and a structure for carrying them out. And he challenged Israelis to define their vision for the future, pointing out that Israelis and Palestinians are 'bound to be neighbours. The question is not whether you will live side by side, but how you will live side by side.'

The next day he attended a meeting of the Palestine National Council and witnessed the vote to amend the Palestine National Charter. He applauded the Council's rejection of the passages of the Charter calling for the destruction of Israel and said that it sent a powerful message not to the Government but to the people of Israel.[32] While enjoining Palestinians to recognise the right of Israel and its people to live safe and secure lives today, tomorrow and forever, he said that Israel must recognise the right of Palestinians to aspire to live free, today, tomorrow and forever. The president acknowledged the Palestinians' high unemployment level; grief as a result of losses from violence and the separation of families; hardship due to restrictions on the movement of people and goods; and concerns about settlement activity, land confiscation and home demolitions. His empathy was well received by his audience, but less favourably so in Israel.

United States expectations from the signing of the Wye memorandum were rapidly confounded. Although the Knesset had endorsed the agreement, Netanyahu's government continued to find it highly divisive. He suspended the Wye process on 20 December, and in doing so broke his own commitment to observe all of his country's agreements. The reason for his doing so are unclear: perhaps divisions within his cabinet made progress impossible; perhaps he could not bring it upon himself to surrender any part of *Eretz Yisrael* to which he was ideologically committed; or perhaps he never really believed in it, having signed it under American pressure. Three days later the Knesset decided to dissolve itself and to hold new elections for the parliament and premiership.

Netanyahu's premiership had not only set back the development of constructive relations with the Palestinians, it had eroded hard-won recognition of Israel within the Arab world and North Africa. The Clinton Administration had found him an exasperating 'partner'.[33] The Administration's achievement in keeping the peace process afloat during Netanyahu's term in office was a considerable one. During most of the Netanyahu years the president was preoccupied with other issues, including from January 1998 with domestic difficulties flowing from his dalliance with a White House intern. Counsel with connections to the Republican Party inquired into his conduct. Netanyahu may well have concluded that the president's authority was on the wane, and that the Israeli government need only make minimal concessions to him until such time as his star was eclipsed. Despite Clinton's preoccupations, he and his Middle East negotiators had been able to preserve for the longer-term the intimate character of the United States relationship with Israel, while contending with Israeli policies to which they were clearly opposed; at the same time, they had been able to retain a working relationship with the Palestinians. They were clearly frustrated by Netanyahu's flagrant breach of agreements and his policy of building Jewish settlements in the vicinity of Jerusalem. Netanyahu's policies contributed to a lowering of living standards in Palestinian territory and resulted in a growing attraction among Palestinian youth for direct action against Israelis. Unable to persuade Netanyahu to desist from policies that fuelled anti-Israeli behaviour, the United States brokered agreement at Wye on measures that might restrain Palestinian rejectionists. But Netanyahu declined to give these measures a chance to prove their effectiveness, notwithstanding public support for them. His actions suggest that he believed that he could ignore United States importuning and inducement, and that Israel could impose its own settlement terms on the Palestinians.[34]

ISRAEL'S RETURN TO LABOR

The election of 17 May produced a decisive victory for Ehud Barak, who won 56 per cent of the votes for the premiership. But in the concurrent parliamentary vote, not only did support for his Labor Party decline, but the centrist parties together could only muster 50 seats in the 120-seat Knesset. He put together a coalition, adding the 27 seats of the three religious factions to his centrist core. Barak had pledged to the electorate that he would implement the Wye River accord and resume negotiations with the Palestinian Authority, but that Israel would not withdraw to the 1967 'border' or from large blocs of Jewish settlements in the West Bank and Gaza Strip. Israel would control all of Jerusalem. The Palestinians were not certain how to view this change of guard. While Netanyahu's departure was a relief, his policies had produced a gradual cooling of America's relations with Israel and a concomitant warming of its relations with the Palestinian Authority.[35]

Clinton saw Barak as a helpful actor, and one who would enable a different approach to be taken. Barak met a number of Middle East leaders before visiting Washington in July. He said that he had assured them that Israel would work with them in a spirit of mutual trust; and that Israel would abide by all previous agreements, including the Wye accords.[36] Barak had his own perception of an appropriate United States role in the peace process: he was looking to the United States to contribute to the process more as facilitator than as a kind of policeman, judge and arbitrator. Clinton agreed. But Barak seemed less certain whether to focus on the Palestinian or Syrian tracks and, in relation to the Palestinian one, how to subsume the previously agreed phased withdrawals into final status issues.[37] On the matter of Israeli settlements, he declared that he was not going to build new ones, but neither was he going to dismantle any of them. He envisioned the permanent status negotiation resulting in an Israel that incorporated a strong block of settlements that will include most of the settlers in Judeo–Samaria and the Gaza Strip.

Clinton was satisfied that Barak was sincere in pressing ahead with the peace process. Suggestive of their having agreed to test first the receptiveness of the Palestinians, Clinton rang Arafat after Barak's visit and urged him to meet with the prime minister and to hear him out. And to shore up Barak's support, inducements were offered that ranged well beyond the assistance promised for implementation of the Wye River accord. By mutual agreement, the United States would increase incrementally its annual military aid to Israel over the next decade to a level of $2.4 billion, while phasing out economic aid over a comparable period, and the United States pledged to work with Israel and regional partners in two areas addressed by the multinational working groups – tourism and water. In respect of the latter, the United States would promote the development of new and additional sources of water, including desalination, and examine ways to transfer water to arid lands.[38]

Clinton had evidently convinced Arafat to treat with Barak. A decision to integrate the Wye commitments with final status negotiations was expressed in a memorandum concluded by Arafat and Barak at Sharm el-Sheikh on 4 September 1999, witnessed by President Mubarak, King Abdullah and Albright. The memorandum provided for a determined effort to conclude a

Framework Agreement on all permanent status issues within five months, and the conclusion of a comprehensive settlement within one year from the resumption of the permanent status negotiations on the basis of Security Council Resolutions 242 and 338. Further territory would be transferred to the Palestinian Authority in three bites in September and November 1999 and January 2000; Palestinian prisoners who had committed offences prior to the signing of the Declaration of Principles in 1993 would be released; and work would begin on safe passage for the movement of persons, vehicles and goods between the Gaza Strip and the West Bank.[39] After the first withdrawal and the release of the prisoners, arguments erupted over how much and which territory was to be handed over to the Palestinians in the second stage in November. Barak offered withdrawal from territory that was virtually unpopulated. His practice of permitting the expansion of existing settlements led the Palestinians to suspend negotiations in December, and destroyed any prospect of the conclusion of a Framework Agreement by the February 2000 deadline.

Nabil Sha'ath, a minister in the Palestinian Authority and a prominent member of the Palestinian negotiating team, reminiscing about the Oslo process, has said that from the Palestinian perspective the settlement issue was the main factor that destroyed any kind of agreement. Tables 6.1 and 6.2 show the extent of Israeli settlement in the West Bank and East Jerusalem.

Table 6.1 Israeli settler population in the West Bank (excl. East Jerusalem)

(*a*) 1992	(*b*) 1996	*b*/*a* %	(*c*) 2000	*c*/*b* %	(*d*) 2002	*d*/*c* %	(*e*) 2004	*e*/*d* %
101 100	142 700	41.2	192 976	35.2	214 722	11.3	234 487	9.2

Note: Percentages are percentage increase for each time period.

Source: Foundation for Middle East Peace (2005a).

Table 6.2 Israeli and Palestinian populations in East Jerusalem

	(*a*) 1992	(*b*) 1996	*b*/*a* %	(*c*) 2000	*c*/*b* %	(*d*) 2002	*d*/*c* %
Israeli	124 400	160 400	28.9	172 250	7.4	175 620	2.0
Palestinian	130 700	173 200	32.5	172 900	(0.2)	184 630	6.8

Note: Percentages are percentage increase/decrease for each time period.

Source: Foundation for Middle East Peace (2005b).

During the currency of the peace process that began at Madrid in 1991 and metamorphosed after Clinton's departure from office in January 2001, the number of Israeli settlers in the West Bank (excluding East Jerusalem) increased by 91 per cent from 101 000 to 193 000 (Table 6.1). Over the same period, the number of Israeli settlers in East Jerusalem increased by 38.5 per cent to almost equal the number of Palestinians resident in that area (Table 6.2). By 2004, the settler population of the West Bank had grown to 235 000, an increase over the period from 1992 of 132 per cent. Data for 2004 are not available for East Jerusalem, but by 2002 the number of Israelis in that area had shown an overall increase of 41.2 per cent to 176 000, while the number of Palestinians had increased by a comparable percentage to 185 000.

Although a precise correlation between these data and the periods in office of various Israeli governments is not possible, the data show that the major period of Israeli settler expansion, in both the West Bank and East Jerusalem, occurred during the Shamir and Rabin premierships as Israel absorbed Jewish immigrants from the former Soviet Union. During the Netanyahu and Barak premierships the rate of increase of settler population in the West Bank fell to 35.2 per cent, and in East Jerusalem to 7.4 per cent. Sharon's prime ministership, too, saw a further decline in the rate of Israeli occupation in the West Bank to 9.2 per cent, and in East Jerusalem to 2.0 per cent. Internal migration from other parts of Israel accounted for some 94 per cent of those who settled in the West Bank (excluding East Jerusalem) and the Gaza Strip during the three years 1999–2001.[40] The Palestinians were aggrieved that Israeli settlement activity should continue in the occupied territories even as they were engaged in a negotiation whose end product was the shape and future of those territories. A particular irritant was the apparent 'Judaisation' of the area surrounding East Jerusalem – 'Greater Jerusalem' – impacting upon the demographic character of the city's immediate neighbourhood and cutting it off from its Palestinian hinterland. The United States urged Rabin and Netanyahu to moderate settlement activity, with limited success. Edward S. Walker Jr, former ambassador to Israel and Assistant Secretary of State for Near East Affairs, explaining why the US did not argue more strongly against Israel's practices, has recollected that once Barak settled into negotiations with the Palestinians after the ill-fated Syrian exercise, the Administration assumed that the negotiation would override other considerations and that the settlements would not be an issue.[41] They were taking their cue from Barak, who assured reporters that a final status agreement with the Palestinians was within reach and in the meantime, he was bound as prime minister to uphold Israeli law.

Concurrent with these developments, Barak had been making overtures to Syria. In mid-December 1999, the United States judged the prospect of movement between Israel and Syria as sufficiently attractive to warrant the convening of meetings at Shepherdstown. David Makovsky, a former executive director of *The Jerusalem Post*, has recorded that Barak figured that his best chance to get the Palestinians to compromise while neutralising the last military threat on Israel's borders was to cut a separate deal with Syria.[42] The failure of negotiations with Syria has been discussed in Chapter 5, as has Barak's unilateral withdrawal of forces from southern Lebanon. United States and Israeli preoccupations with those matters effectively constrained further development on the Palestinian track for some months. Negotiation of a Palestinian final status agreement was resumed in March 2000.

The Israelis agreed to transfer land around Jericho, Ramallah and Jenin to the Palestinians, and Clinton was mandated by Barak to tell Arafat that three Arab villages in the neighbourhood of East Jerusalem would also be transferred to the Palestinian Authority. But the fragile nature of Barak's coalition was exposed when its right-wing members prevented his transferring the villages. Clinton was furious at having been made out to be a 'false prophet' to a foreign leader.[43] Ministers from three of the coalition parties resigned in July, and the Knesset voted 54 to 52 in favour of a no-confidence motion that fell short of the 61 votes needed by law to topple a government. Barak claimed with some justification that the party structure of the Knesset no longer reflected the popular will, which was in favour of peace and supported major concessions to achieve it.

Nevertheless, Clinton continued to explore prospects of movement between the Israelis and Palestinians with key actors. For his part, domestic difficulties suggested to Barak that if he were to secure agreement to the terms of any settlement, all concessions and all rewards would have to be presented to a national referendum in one comprehensive package that would show the Israeli public the shape of any final settlement. In coming to this conclusion he was, in fact, building upon an idea first floated by Netanyahu in 1997, rejected at that time by Arafat, and later investigated by Albright.

Israeli and Palestinian negotiators met officially during the first part of 2000 with a view to drafting a Framework Agreement for Permanent Settlement by 23 May, but did not make much progress. So the formula of secret meetings that had proven productive at Oslo in 1993 was tried again. A back channel had also been used in 1995 when some Israelis and Palestinians had met unofficially in Stockholm. Their outline had been rejected by Peres when it was presented to him shortly after Rabin's death. The parties met in Sweden again from March to May 2000. A major issue was the area of West Bank land that should, eventually, be transferred to the Palestinians. The Israeli delegation was empowered to discuss also security matters and the question of Palestinian refugees, but it was not to broach Jerusalem. The Israelis advanced propositions on matters that had been taboo for half a century, but the Palestinians found their offers inadequate and were frustrated that they could not engage the Israelis in discussion on the emotional and symbolic issue of Jerusalem. 'Israelis and Palestinians who took part say ... that the discussions were groundbreaking ... They made progress on the issues of territory, borders, security, and even refugees, although there were both advances and retreats on every issue.'[44] Constructive negotiation was frustrated by leaks about the secret meeting and the content of the agenda, placing the leaderships of both parties under pressure. Ross was encouraged by the progress achieved by the negotiation, but it was terminated as Barak mounted a case for the convening of a summit.

Barak insisted on the holding of a summit, judging that without it he would be unable to keep his government together. From the perspective of the United States, Barak's determination to reach a final deal and the risks he was prepared to take to get there contrasted favourably with Arafat's perceived inflexibility and insistence that Israel implement interim commitments, notwithstanding the fact that it must have been apparent to Arafat that the longer the negotiating process was stretched out, the more Israel took advantage of its unconstrained power to pre-empt the outcome by renegotiating interim agreements and creating new facts on the ground. Consequently, Clinton acquiesced in Barak's request for a summit against the advice of Arabs, Europeans and Palestinians.[45] Arafat had expressed his reservations directly to Clinton at their meeting on 15 June.[46] He was also talking about unilaterally declaring statehood on 13 September 2000, seven years from the signing of the Declaration of Principles. The United States viewed this as unhelpful to the peace process, and decided that the convening of an early summit might forestall it. That decision was made even as the two parties were holding to maximalist positions.

Any summit had to be out of the way before the Democratic National Convention met to select its candidate for the 2000 presidential election. Vice President Al Gore was a candidate, and the White House did not want to see meetings at Camp David at a time when the focus should be on the Convention and Clinton's former running mate. Arafat had asked for more time to prepare for a meeting. The Administration shared his perception of the need for adequate preparation, but was constrained by the domestic political timetable.

Arafat posed several conditions for agreeing to participate,[47] seeking additional preparatory talks to ensure that Camp David would not fail, and that the third Israeli redeployment be implemented before any summit. The latter request was clearly incompatible with the purposes of a summit to resolve all permanent status issues and was turned down by the United States. Arafat modified it, seeking a safety net in the form of a US guarantee that the third withdrawal would take place even if Camp David did not yield an agreement. Clinton extracted Barak's agreement to this, and thus secured Arafat's participation. US officials believed that the Palestinians' reservations would evaporate in the face of an appealing final deal; and officials having accepted Barak's argument for a final status summit, chose to use their leverage with the Israelis to obtain movement on the issues that had to be dealt with in a permanent agreement rather than expend it on interim ones. On the eve of the summit Clinton also volunteered that the United States would remain neutral in the event that it failed and that Arafat would not be blamed, but the United States proceeded to disregard each of these undertakings.

THE CAMP DAVID SUMMIT

The summit was held in July 2000. There were no formal drafting or position papers in circulation, no party was bound by any proposal discussed at the summit, and nothing was to be taken as agreed until everything was agreed.

Despite having sought the meeting, Barak refused to negotiate directly with Arafat. The Administration became the intermediary, proposing 'ideas, suggestions, even language'.[48] Barak's strategy was that Israel ought not to reveal its final positions, not even to the United States.[49] He feared that if he put forward concessions he would have to pay the price domestically; that the Palestinians would use any concession as a point of departure for further concessions; and that the United States would reveal his positions to the Palestinians. He therefore conveyed his positions through the United States as 'immovable', asking the United States to present the Palestinians with a choice between propositions that he judged would be sufficiently attractive to command their support, and unattractive alternatives, only to modify them when rejected. Not only were the propositions conveyed orally, but they were generally presented as US concepts, not Israeli ones. Barak and the Americans insisted that Arafat accept the propositions as general 'bases for negotiations' before launching into detailed discussion.

While Israel and the Palestinians were clear about their objectives, and the Israelis had prepared diligently for the summit, the United States was unprepared for it.[50] A US non-paper that drew heavily on the work done at the supposedly secret talks in Sweden in May was drafted for circulation to the two parties, despite the fact that neither Barak nor Arafat had accepted the outcome of the Swedish negotiation. An advance copy of the draft was shown to the Israelis on 11 July. Barak, who had arrived at Camp David after having on the previous day been unable to muster sufficient votes to outnumber the 54 Knesset members who expressed a lack of confidence in his government, demanded considerable modification to the draft. Clinton's pollsters were also Barak's, and he was aware of Barak's political realities and accommodated him.

The effect was to undermine, from the outset of the summit, Palestinian credence in United States brokerage.

After three days at Camp David the situation was that the Israelis had rejected the first draft presented by the United States and Arafat had rejected the second. Clinton then proposed on 14 July that four groups be set up to address the core issues – borders and settlements, refugees, security, and Jerusalem. That initiative also failed. So the president pushed for a meeting of two Israeli and two Palestinian negotiators, whose existence should be known to only the leaders of the two sides. He hoped that this secret conclave would lead to a breakthrough. The two teams reported to Clinton on 16 July, and it was clear that the Israeli delegates had moved on both Jerusalem and on territory, but Barak refused to countenance his negotiators' concessions as they had not been matched by concessions from the other side.

On 18 July Clinton threatened to call off the summit if he did not hear something new from the parties within two hours. This provoked an Israeli initiative that addressed the issues of Palestinian territory, Israel's security needs and the prospect of a 'satisfactory solution' to the refugee question. Its element on Jerusalem caught the Palestinians off-guard. Refugees and Jerusalem were highly emotional topics that, because of their sensitivity to both sides, had been conspicuously left to the end of the Oslo process. The introduction of these issues at Camp David without comprehensive exploration lent credence to Arafat's expressed concern about the need for adequate preparation. Both the Oslo agreements were the product of protracted negotiations, conducted away from the glare of publicity. On Jerusalem, Barak advanced the possibility of Palestinian sovereignty over seven of the nine outer neighbourhoods of Jerusalem and the Muslim and Christian Quarters of the Old City. The Haram al-Sharif/Temple Mount area would be the subject of a UN Security Council resolution to hand joint custodianship of the disputed sacred area to Palestine and Morocco, the chair of the Organization of the Islamic Conference's Al-Quds Jerusalem Committee. Barak wanted this to be presented as an 'American initiative': if Arafat accepted it, Barak would submit to United States blandishments and concede.[51] There was no possibility that Arafat could, in accepting shared custodianship, effectively cede sovereignty over the site of the third most significant Islamic shrine to Israel. This was not solely a Palestinian matter: it affected the whole Muslim world and Arafat had no mandate to negotiate on its behalf. The refugee issue, too, involved the interests of other governments that had been hosting Palestinian refugees for many decades and on which they ought properly to be given an opportunity to have their say.

The role of go-between was not a comfortable one for the United States. Clinton found himself in an untenable position as Barak shifted his ground and expostulated about his treatment.[52] The Palestinians, too, were unaccommodating. Unaware of what the Israelis would present to him, Arafat had little opportunity to prepare a considered response. Worse, his delegation lacked coordination. This may suggest why the Palestinians did not advance propositions of their own. Whatever may have been the reason, Arafat's obduracy provoked the president: 'Let's let hell break loose and live with the consequences'.[53]

Clinton was not, however, entirely a victim of circumstance. On the eve of his departure for Okinawa to attend a meeting of the Group of Eight industrialised countries, he misrepresented Barak's condition for continued negotiation during his absence. Barak had told Clinton that he would be prepared to continue negotiation on Jerusalem provided Arafat accepted the other elements of the so-called 'American initiative'. The president suggested to Arafat that negotiations proceed on Jerusalem and the Haram, and all other matters. He then told Barak that he had secured Arafat's agreement to remain at Camp David and to continue the negotiation process. The two leaders were left with differing understandings of their terms of reference when Clinton flew overseas on 20 July. The situation was further confused when Albright, in an attempt to clarify the ambiguity, said that the president's ideas were 'off'. She clearly intended her remarks to refer to the terms under which the two parties had agreed to remain at Camp David. Barak was fearful that he had gone too far in seeking an accommodation with the Palestinians, especially on Jerusalem. He exploited the secretary's statement, interpreting it as nullifying and voiding the 'American initiative', thus cocooning his own proposals from further debate until after the president returned on 23 July.[54] Both Clinton and Albright had been careless in their use of language on a vital issue and at a critical stage in the negotiation. The ensuing confusion was apparent to all. It fuelled Arafat's and Barak's suspicions that their opponent – and perhaps the United States too – was resorting to trickery, which for Barak was sufficient reason to resile from his original propositions.

The United States was dealing with a Palestinian leader who seemed more anxious to survive the Camp David summit than to benefit from it.[55] It dangled various inducements before him in order to secure agreement. Statehood, involving recognition by the United States, Israel and the international community, was one prospect; another was financial assistance from the world's major industrial countries. Arafat acknowledged the Palestinians' need for aid, but said that he would not exchange Jerusalem for a state.[56] Clinton then rang Arab leaders and urged them to advise Arafat to accept the offers under discussion or, failing that, to encourage him to sign an agreement postponing the Jerusalem issue. But Arafat had taken care to keep Arab and international leaders regularly informed about developments, and few responded to the president's appeal. Another line taken by the United States was that a solution for Jerusalem would open the doors to solving all the other issues, but Arafat held to his position that he would not 'sell' Jerusalem. Some days later, Clinton employed the threat of a congressional freeze on aid to the Palestinian Authority. Arafat was unfazed. A new tack was tried, with Clinton suggesting that a 'sovereign presidential compound' be established for the *ra'is* and his state adjacent to the al-Aqsa Mosque. Arafat envisioned the situation – not so much a Holy See within the Italian capital as a small island surrounded by Israeli soldiers who controlled the entrances – and again demanded full Palestinian sovereignty over the territory of Jerusalem occupied in 1967. On 25 July Clinton drew upon Barak's proposals and set forth four points that he said was the final offer on Jerusalem: a committee made up of the UN Security Council and Morocco would grant the Palestinian state 'sovereign custody' of the Haram, while Israel would retain 'residual sovereignty'; the Muslim and Christian quarters of the Old City would come under Palestinian sovereignty, while the Jewish and Armenian quarters would fall under Israeli sovereignty; the Palestinians would have functional jurisdiction over some 'inner' neighbourhoods; Jerusalem's 'outer' neighbourhoods would be under Palestinian sovereignty. If the 'inner' neighbourhoods were also to come under Palestinian sovereignty, a special regime would have to be agreed upon that would apply to the Old City.[57] The Palestinians responded in the early hours of 26 July that the proposals on Jerusalem were in contradiction with international law, which had to be the basis for any agreement. With that, the summit ended.

Malley and Agha have drawn attention to the complex and often contradictory roles of the United States at Camp David:[58] as principal broker of the putative peace deal; as guardian of the peace process; as Israel's strategic ally; and as its cultural and political partner. They believed that America's ability to be an effective broker was hamstrung by its political and cultural affinity with Israel and its strategic relationship with that country. Such was the cultural affinity between the United States and Israel that members of the American delegation were taken aback when Barak indicated that he could accept a division of the Old City of Jerusalem and they wondered whether he could sell such a proposal to his people. The question was rarely, if ever, asked about Arafat's ability to sell accommodations to the Palestinians. The strategic relationship was governed by a broad interpretation of Kissinger's 'no-surprise rule' under which America had committed to share in advance each of its ideas with Israel, but Barak felt under no compunction to behave correspondingly. The more corrosive effect of the multiple roles played by the United States, including that of go-between, was that they hid from the Palestinians Clinton's many attempts to persuade Barak.

A reported comment by Barak about Clinton being closer to the Palestinian position than to Israel's challenges Malley and Agha's argument that the United States strategic partnership with Israel impaired its effectiveness as a peace broker. The strength, and at times the emotion, with which the Administration argued with the Israelis in private in support of some accommodation with the Palestinians is a reflection both of its appreciation of various Palestinian positions and of the close and indissoluble relationship between the United States and Israel, which could take the strain without irreparable damage. Arab and Muslim states were in no doubt about the sustained effort of the United States to keep the parties engaged in negotiation, albeit in its self-designated role as broker and guardian of the peace process. Malley and Agha's reference to the political partnership is telling. Clinton's predisposition neither to coerce Israel nor to criticise it publicly has been addressed earlier. His willingness to convey an Israeli brief at his final meeting with Assad has also been discussed. At Camp David he again agreed to become the conduit, allowing Israel to hide behind the fiction of its proposals being presented as 'American'. The proprietorial attitude of the United States toward the whole process since its inception in 1991 denied a significant managerial and intellectual role to other states. There is no telling whether external influences might have helped reshape and advance the peace process. A different constellation of forces might have produced an alternative approach. The relevance of such speculation is questionable.

After the summit, Clinton was interviewed for Israeli television and praised Barak's courage.[59] He countered leaks that Barak had offered up part of Jerusalem, challenging any thought that Barak might have compromised the vital interest of the people of Israel and Jerusalem. In praising Caesar, Clinton effectively buried Arafat.[60] A mythology has developed that Arafat turned down the best offer any Israeli government had ever made. In fact, because of the manner in which ideas were advanced orally through American mediation, possibly later to be amended, there never was an Israeli 'offer', as such, on the table. The myth also conveniently skirts the fact that Arafat had no mandate from third parties to negotiate accommodations that affected their interests.

POST-CAMP DAVID NEGOTIATIONS AND CLINTON'S 'PLAN'

Although disappointed by the failure at Camp David, Clinton remained determined to press for a peace settlement. Palestinian negotiators began talking about the need for the United States to be an honest broker and to put forward compromise proposals of its own, not just re-worked Israeli ideas, while Barak spoke of the need for United States proposals if there was to be a final agreement. This represented a reversal of the position he had advanced in 1999 when he asked America to restrict its role to that of a facilitator. Clinton agreed to present ideas, but only if the parties resumed talks and made initial headway on their own. Israeli and Palestinian negotiators conducted more than 50 negotiating sessions in August and September, and produced two draft chapters of a permanent peace agreement that were kept secret from all but the leaders. Toward the end of September, there seemed to be a glimmer of hope that the negotiation might get back on track. Barak and Arafat came together for what both sides described as an unusually cordial meeting.[61]

The United States began preparation of a proposal during August and September.[62] Any hope that it might contribute toward a final settlement received a major setback when on 28 September 2000, the leader of the opposition Likud Party, Ariel Sharon, visited the Haram al-Sharif/Temple Mount area on which the al-Aqsa Mosque stands. The provocative nature of such a visit was clearly foreseen by the Israeli government, which had provided a large security escort. Although Sharon did not enter Islamic places of worship, Muslims interpreted the visit as a flaunting of Israel's claim to authority over the holy sites. After noon prayers the next day, large numbers of young Muslims poured out of the mosques and began throwing stones at Jews praying at the Western Wall below the compound. The Jews had gathered in some numbers on the eve of their New Year. The Israeli police fired at the Palestinian crowd, killing several and wounding many others. By 10 October, some 90 Palestinians had been killed and some 2000 injured in the ensuing conflagration. There were only a handful of Israeli casualties.[63] On 12 October two Israeli soldiers were seized and murdered at a police station at Ramallah and the body of one was paraded through the streets.[64] The UN Security Council condemned the violence, 'especially the excessive use of force against Palestinians',[65] and again called upon Israel to abide by its legal obligations under the Fourth Geneva Convention. The United States abstained.

The United States recognised that a truce would have to be arranged if the peace process were again to be rescued. Albright met Barak and Arafat in Paris to try to secure it. Arafat was reluctant to issue a call for an end to the fighting unless Israel agreed to an international inquiry into the origins of the clashes. Clinton, too, interceded in the matter. He telephoned Arafat and Barak on 30 September and 10 October, and persuaded them to accept an invitation from President Mubarak, whose services he had again co-opted, to attend another meeting at Sharm el-Sheikh. The agreement reached there on an early redeployment of Israeli forces, and a lifting of the blockade imposed on the Palestinians, including a reopening of entry ports and crossing points 'in order to pacify the Palestinian streets and bring matters back to normal', owed much to Clinton's personal efforts.[66] The United States undertook to work with the Israelis, Palestinians and the UN on establishing the facts of the al-Aqsa incident, and Clinton secured the agreement of Barak and Arafat to consult with the Administration over the next two weeks on how to move forward. During that period he spoke with the two leaders several times a week in an effort to have the violence halted. His interventions, however, had little impact upon the *al-Aqsa intifada*.

While doing what he could to encourage a cessation of violence, Clinton worked over the proposal that he would submit to the two parties. He announced on 28 November that he had put some ideas on the table.[67] Over the following weeks, his Administration sought to convince the Israelis and Palestinians to negotiate within the president's parameters. Clinton was certain that if a peace agreement were possible, it would be within the context of his initiative, and that if it could be achieved at all, it could be resolved within a matter of weeks. Circumstances were unlikely to get better; in all probability they would become more difficult.

That remark was prescient. By the end of 2000 the three principals were virtually *hors de combat.* Al Gore had won the popular vote for the US presidency, but the Electoral College vote came down to a contest for the Floridian vote that was resolved in the courts, resulting in the swearing in as president on 20 January 2001 of George W. Bush. Barak's shaky government was on the verge of collapse and he decided to pre-empt his rivals by forcing new elections for the premiership on 6 February 2001. Arafat's position at the time was also uncertain because he could not gain control over the *al-Aqsa intifada*. Israel's withdrawal of the IDF from Lebanon encouraged some Palestinians to believe that they could eventually force Israel to offer more accommodating terms than those advanced at Camp David. They had seen the Palestinian leadership commit to negotiation with Israel in 1993. Seven years of negotiation had resulted in the recovery of limited territory while daily humiliation persisted. Hezbollah's armed confrontation in southern Lebanon had resulted in the return of occupied territory to the state. Jerome Slater has concluded, however, that 'there is no evidence and no Israeli intelligence consensus on whether Arafat ordered, acquiesced in, or was powerless to control the ... wave of Palestinian bombings inside Israel'[68] at the time. 'The most plausible interpretation is that the *al-Aqsa intifada* began as a largely spontaneous eruption, but one over which Arafat and the Palestinian Authority ... gained some but by no means complete control'.

Clinton was motivated to press on, partly because his place in history would be assured if he were able to effect a peace between Israelis and Palestinians. He brought the negotiators together again at the White House on 23 December, where he advanced five parameters for negotiation.[69] They were that:

- there could be no genuine resolution to the conflict without a sovereign, viable Palestinian state that accommodated Israel's security requirements and the demographic realities. That suggested Palestinian sovereignty over Gaza and the vast majority of the West Bank, and the incorporation into Israel of settlement blocks with the goal of maximising the number of Jewish settlers in Israel while minimising the area of annexed land. To be viable, Palestine would need to be a geographically contiguous state, and the land annexed into Israeli settlement blocks should include as few Palestinians as possible consistent with the logic of two separate homelands. To make the agreement durable, there would have to be some territorial swaps and other arrangements;

- a solution would have to be found for the Palestinian refugees that allowed them to return to a Palestinian state. All refugees should receive compensation from the international community for their losses and assistance in building new lives. Israel could not be expected to acknowledge an unlimited right of return as that would threaten the very foundation of the State of Israel;
- there will be no peace and no peace agreement unless the Israeli people have lasting security guarantees. These need not come at the expense of Palestinian sovereignty. An international presence could be positioned in Palestine to provide border security along the Jordan Valley and to monitor implementation of a final agreement;
- Jerusalem should be an open and undivided city with assured freedom of access and worship for all. What is Arab should be Palestinian, and what is Jewish should be Israeli; and
- any agreement would have to mark the decision to end the conflict.[70]

Clinton's resolve, fuelled by exasperation, was clear: 'it was time – past time – to put up or shut up'.[71] He had concluded that unless the United States narrowed the range of debate, in effect forcing the big compromises up front, there could never be an agreement. His first point was the nearest any American president had come to endorsing a two-state solution. The immediate reaction of the Palestinians to his ideas was that the proposal divided a Palestinian state into three separate cantons connected and divided by Israeli-only roads that jeopardised the state's viability; divided Palestinian Jerusalem into a number of unconnected islands separate from each other and from the rest of Palestine; and obliged Palestinian refugees to surrender their right of return.[72] As no map had been presented, it was difficult to determine the extent of the territorial exchanges envisaged, but the parameters seemed to suggest that Israel would annex 4 to 6 per cent of the West Bank with the Palestinians being compensated through a land swap of 1 to 3 per cent. A particular concern for the Palestinians was that the United States had adopted the Israeli practice of excluding the areas of East Jerusalem, 'no-man's land' and the Dead Sea from the base figure from which the transfer percentages were calculated.

On the vexed question of the right of return of refugees, Clinton had proposed to Arafat at Camp David that as he knew that all Palestinians in the diaspora could not be resettled in Israel, he should acknowledge this.[73] Israel could not be expected to accept an unrestricted right of return and the most realistic option for refugees would be return to the new state of Palestine, not their original homes. This was contrary to a provision of UN General Assembly Resolution 194, whose relevance to final status issues Albright had sought to expunge through her letter of 8 August 1994. It was an issue on which there was also a clear cleavage between the pragmatic accommodations entered into by the PLO/PA, and the refugees who perceived the Oslo accords 'as detrimental to their legal, national, and human rights, reinforcing their sense of dispossession and disenfranchisement'.[74] Ross worked with the Israelis to find a possible formula to cover the refugee question. Even if the Palestinian Authority discouraged Palestinians from exercising any right of return, the Israelis were concerned that acceptance of a 'right' would be open-ended in its time frame and would expose them to claims for compensation. Ross had sought to reframe the issue in terms of a 'right of application'. Again, the Israelis were concerned that it put the onus on them.[75]

Barak won his government's acceptance of Clinton's proposals, conditional on Arafat accepting them as the basis for negotiations. He was gambling on the hope that an agreement would ensure his re-election on 6 February 2001, while privately hoping that Arafat would reject them, thus putting him in a favourable light.[76] But on reflection he told Clinton that he would not sign any agreement until after the election. Arafat accepted the proposals, with qualifications, as a basis for negotiation after meeting with Clinton on 2 January. Officials from the two sides met at Taba, without their leaders and without the United States, which was effectively disempowered during the transition from Clinton's Administration to that of the President-elect.

The Palestinians claim that tangible steps were taken at Taba toward a final agreement, notably on territory, Palestinian sovereignty over all Arab neighbourhoods in Jerusalem, and the evolution of an 'agreed narrative' that would defuse the refugee issue and protect the Jewish identity of Israel.[77] Once again progress was halted when violence in the West Bank resulted in the deaths of Israelis. Barak said that the talks would be resumed after the elections, but was not in any position after the polls to honour the pledge. Arafat's position was that he did not want to be forced by artificial deadlines to make fateful decisions. He knew that Clinton would not be around after 19 January to assist with the remaining difficult negotiation before a final agreement could be reached, and may also have been hoping that the incoming president, with his well-known connections to the oil industry, would be more sympathetic to Arab concerns.[78] Clinton found himself at the end of his term with both parties reluctantly accepting his general framework, but without time to push for full agreement. The Palestinian negotiator Nabil Sha'ath summed up the situation: 'If Camp David was too little, Taba was too late'.[79]

CONCLUSION

It became evident within months of Clinton entering his second term that the Oslo process was stalled, if not in danger. The United States would have to become proactive if its peace settlement objective were to be realised. It exercised its power ideationally and through the application of positive sanctions.

The overriding concern of the United States was that the Oslo process be protected and sustained because despite its shortcomings, it offered the best prospect for achievement of a settlement of the core 'Palestinian' element of the Arab–Israel dispute. The ideational power of the United States was invested heavily in preventing a collapse of the process, sometimes expressed in a somewhat naive belief that resolution of differences was possible once protagonists engaged in face-to-face negotiation. A higher premium was attached to maintenance of the process than to normative behaviour. This was particularly evident in the Administration's handling of Israel's settlement activity. The United States objected to Israel's policy, but declined either to join other states in seeking to bring Israel to account for its breach of the Fourth Geneva Convention or unilaterally to impose sanctions. Clinton's concern to achieve outcomes within the Oslo context at the expense of principle was evident also in relation to an agreement of January 1997 on the redeployment of Israeli forces from Hebron.

The United States extended many positive sanctions to Israel, some to the Palestinians, and some for the benefit of both parties. The United States sent American specialists to the region to participate in antiterrorism arrangements among Israeli, Palestinian and regional governments; authorised an anti-terrorism programme for Israel, supplemented by intelligence sharing with the CIA; announced the provision of fighter aircraft to Israel; concluded a memorandum of understanding addressing the challenges of weapons of mass destruction, counter-proliferation and theatre missile defence and Israel's acquisition of an Arrow anti-missile battery; and facilitated pledges of additional economic assistance to the Palestinians. United States inducements may have encouraged Netanyahu to keep the dialogue open, but were insufficient to dissuade him from building settlements. It cannot be shown whether he would have been susceptible to United States coercion because it was never tried. Nor were positive sanctions sufficient to assure Israel's implementation of the Wye River agreement. The agreement exposed the schism within Netanyahu's government between those who wanted a peace settlement and those who wanted the West Bank incorporated into an *Eretz Yisrael.* The offer of positive sanctions could not coax an accommodation on Jerusalem from Arafat because he had no mandate to negotiate on a matter of such sensitivity to the Islamic world. They did, however, secure nullification within the Palestinian legislature of the provisions of the Palestine National Charter calling for the destruction of Israel.

Domestic considerations constrained the projection of United States power. Clinton was aware of congressional opposition to Bush I's deferral of Israel's request for loan guarantees as a means of coercion. He had a particular need to assure congressional support in the event of his impeachment, and to assist his wife's Senate candidacy. He was aware of the gradual cooling of United States relations with Israel during Netanyahu's premiership and of a concomitant warming of its relations with the Palestinian Authority. The provision of substantial inducements to Israel may have had the auxiliary purpose of reassuring both the people of Israel and their supporters within the United States of America's enduring commitment.

Israel's return to a Labor-led government in May 1999 offered the prospect of movement toward the peace objective, but the incoming premier was also to face difficulty in holding together a coalition prepared to transfer land and powers to the Palestinian Authority in exchange for peace. The United States was receptive to Barak's argument that his difficulties would be eased if a summit were to be held at which all concessions and all rewards could be wrapped up in one comprehensive package to be presented to a national referendum. The president convened a summit at Camp David in July 2000. It was timed with an eye to the electoral calendar in the United States rather than to the preparedness of the two parties. The United States was not well-prepared for the Camp David summit, its contribution often emphasised process over content, and its diplomacy was not always astute. Significantly, it failed to advance proposals that addressed the parties' bottom lines. The negotiation was largely determined by what Barak thought the Palestinians might accept. Clinton threw himself into it, permitting the office of President and the authority of the United States to be used as instruments of Israeli diplomacy without knowing whether Israel's proposals represented a negotiating position or its bottom line. In so doing, he placed himself in an untenable position as Barak shifted his ground. Although Clinton expostulated against the prime minister's tactics, the fact that he should have permitted the world's superpower to be subjugated in this way can only be explained in terms of an expectation that the authority of the President of the United States would be sufficient to persuade or entice Arafat to accept an Israel-designed peace settlement, whatever its shape may be; and the attraction of a legacy that might include his contribution to resolving the Israel–Palestinian dispute.

The ideational power of the United States was expressed when Clinton presented an outline for a settlement in December 2000, endorsing a two-state solution. Barak tactically accepted it as a basis for negotiation, and Arafat was to follow suit after being persuaded to do so by the president. But the initiative having been launched within Clinton's last month in office, his Administration was in no position to influence the direction of the ensuing negotiation.

President Clinton had made the search for a comprehensive settlement of the Arab–Israel dispute a major objective of his two-term presidency. He was emotionally committed to the objective and devoted considerable personal effort toward its accomplishment. For much of his presidency, he was convinced of the sincerity of his Israeli partners (although Netanyahu's contribution was a qualified one) in pursuing a peaceful settlement with the Palestinians. There were limits as to how far all four Israeli prime ministers during that period would go toward accommodating fundamental Palestinian demands. There were some among both Israelis and Palestinians who were opposed to the Oslo process in principle and sought to frustrate its realisation. The extremists' actions, and the reprisals they provoked, contributed to an erosion of confidence among Palestinians that the process would lead to a betterment of their living conditions. As the standard of living of Palestinians fell, as their sense of dispossession rose due to continued settlement activity, and as they appealed to the international community for understanding, the United States devoted energy to damage limitation. The United States instruments were used effectively to protect the negotiation process, marshal international condemnation of terrorism, encourage donors to contribute development assistance to the Palestinians, create conditions for its participation in tripartite antiterrorist arrangements with Israel and the Palestinian Authority, and to bring the parties back to the negotiating table. In doing so, its address perforce focussed on the process rather than its desired outcome. Personal disinclination and political constraints inhibited Clinton's employment of coercive or punitive instruments to enhance the prospect of realising the United States objective. By the time that he was persuaded to employ the ideational power of the US to propose the 'non-negotiable' shape of an outcome, it was too late in his presidency for him to be able to attain the goal.

NOTES

1 Likud Party Platform (1996). Ch.1.
2 Clinton, W.J. *Public Papers, 1996*, pp.1089–94.
3 Ibid. p.1739.
4 Christopher wrote to Arafat and Netanyahu after the conclusion of the Hebron agreement. Only the letter to Netanyahu has been made public.
5 Clinton (2004) p.752.
6 United Nations (1997). The draft resolution was defeated: 14–1 (USA).
7 UN General Assembly Resolution 51/223 was adopted by recorded vote: 130–2 (Israel, USA)–2 (Marshall Islands, Micronesia).
8 UN General Assembly Resolution ES-10/2 was adopted by recorded vote: 134–3 (Israel, Micronesia, USA)–11.
9 United Nations. *Yearbook of the United Nations 1997*. The delegate referred to the General Assembly's 'infringing on the Security Council's authority and ... [the] ... dangerous

precedent … [set by] … the Assembly endorsing collective action against one of its Members'. p.397.

10 UN General Assembly Resolution ES-10/3 was adopted by recorded vote: 131–3 (Israel, Micronesia, United States of America)–14.

11 Kadman (1998).

12 Government of Switzerland (2001).

13 Albright (2003) p.507.

14 Ross (2004) p.452.

15 Clinton, H.R. (2003) p.483. The question of her candidature was first raised in December 1995. It gathered momentum when Democrat Senator Moynihan announced in November 1998 that he would not be seeking a further term.

16 Clinton, W.J. *Public Papers, 1999*, p.1238.

17 Group of Eight (1997). Para 84: 'The Peace Process faces a crisis, and we are determined to reinject momentum into it … Both sides must refrain from actions that impede the peace process by preempting permanent status negotiations'.

18 Clinton, W.J. *Public Papers, 1997*, p.1062–3.

19 Erlanger, S. (1997).

20 Albright, M.K. (1997) pp 7–8.

21 Lippman, T.W. (2000) p.203.

22 Clinton, W.J. *Public Papers, 1998*, p.747.

23 Albright, M.K. (1998).

24 Clinton, W.J. *Public Papers, 1998*, p.1698.

25 Albright (2003) p.303.

26 The Wye River Plantation talks began on 15 October and concluded with the signing of a memorandum on 23 October 1998; Albright (2003) Ch.19 and Ross (2004) Ch.17 record the trials and atmospherics of the negotiation.

27 Wye River Memorandum (1998).

28 Ross (2004) pp.329, 450–2467.

29 Clinton, W.J. *Public Papers, 1998*, p.2169. Clinton said that he would seek from Congress a $1.2 billion package to help Israel meet its security needs, including those growing out of the redeployments under the Wye agreement.

30 European Union (1998); Clinton, W.J. *Public Papers, 1998*, p.2194.

31 Clinton, W.J. *Public Papers, 1998*, p.2168–9.

32 Ibid. p.2176–7.

33 Ross (1999) p.3.

34 Hermann and Hagan (1998) p.133.

35 Malley and Agha (2001).

36 Clinton, W.J. *Public Papers, 1999*, p.1378.

37 Ibid. p.1380.

38 Ibid. pp.1413–4.

39 US Department of State (1999).

40 Foundation for Middle East Peace (2005b).

41 Swisher, C.E. (2004) p.152. Swisher cites an interview with former ambassador Edward S. Walker Jr.

42 Makovsky (2001) p.37.

43 Malley and Agha (2001); Sontag (2001) p.80. Sontag says that Barak had won the Knesset's consent to transfer the villages, but decided to defer the transfer indefinitely because violence had erupted in the West Bank.

44 Sontag (2001) p.80. At a public lecture in Canberra on 13 August 2003 the Palestinian negotiator, Ahmed Qurei, said that the Stockholm meeting had broken with convention and focussed on the eastern border of any Palestinian state. The critical question of its western border had not been addressed and was one of the matters that informed the Palestinian view that any summit needed further preparation.

45 Hedges (2001) p.135.

46 Malley and Agha (2001). Arafat argued that Barak had not implemented prior agreements; there had been no progress in the negotiations; and the prime minister was holding all the cards. He told Albright that the only outcome of a summit in these circumstances was to

have everything explode in the president's face; Hanieh (2001) p.76. Hanieh said that the Americans were warned not to get themselves into a situation such as the president encountered with President Assad in Geneva.

47 Hanieh (2001) p.84. Arafat is reported to have preferred not to clash with the United States on a procedural matter such as the convening of a summit, saving his energies for substantive issues.

48 Clinton, W.J. *Public Papers, 2000*, p.1855.

49 Albright (2003) p.485.

50 Swisher (2004) p.264. Swisher cites an interview with Aaron Miller, a member of America's negotiating team.

51 Bregman (2005) p.107.

52 Malley and Agha (2001).

53 Ibid.

54 Bregman (2005) pp.113–5.

55 Malley and Agha (2001).

56 Hanieh (2001) pp.89–95.

57 Ibid. p.96.

58 Malley and Agha (2001).

59 Clinton, W.J. *Public Papers, 2000*, pp.1709–15.

60 Ibid. pp.1674–5.

61 Sontag (2001) p.77.

62 Sontag (2001).

63 Morris (2001) p.665; Reinhart (2002) pp.112–6. 'More than seven thousand Palestinians were reported injured in the first five weeks of the uprising, many in the head, legs, or knees by carefully aimed shots, and, increasingly, live ammunition.'

64 On the same day USS *Cole* was holed by terrorists in Aden harbour and 17 sailors killed.

65 UN Security Council Resolution 1322, 7 October 2000. It was adopted by 14 votes – 0 – 1 (USA).

66 Clinton, W.J. *Public Papers, 2000*, p.2501.

67 Ibid. p.3205.

68 Slater (2001) p.191.

69 Ross, D.B. (2002b). Clinton presented his proposal orally. Ross ensured that both sides recorded each word accurately.

70 Clinton, W.J. *Public Papers, 2001*, pp.33–4; Ross (2002b). Ross asserts that this proposal 'would have resulted in a Palestinian state, with territory in over 97 per cent of the West Bank, Gaza, and Jerusalem; with Arab East Jerusalem as the capital of that state (including the holy place of the Haram al-Sharif, the Noble Sanctuary); with an international presence in place of the Israeli Defence Force in the Jordan Valley; and with the unlimited right of return for Palestinian refugees to their state but not to Israel'.

71 Clinton (2004) p.937.

72 Palestinian Negotiating Team (2001).

73 Interview with Dennis B. Ross at Washington DC on 20 April 2001.

74 Bowker (2003) p.160.

75 Interview with Dennis B. Ross at Washington DC on 20 April 2001.

76 Bregman (2005) p.145.

77 Sontag (2001) p.84.

78 Quandt (2001) p.372.

79 Sontag (2001) p.84.

7. Distrust and disengagement: the United States, Israel and the Palestinians, 2001–06

President Bush II and many within his Administration envisioned a role for the United States in international affairs different from that of President Clinton. They undertook an early reassessment of the part that the United States should play in seeking a resolution of the Israel–Palestinian conflict. This chapter will carry the United States contribution forward to early 2006 when both Israelis and Palestinians went to the polls.

Changes of government occurred in both the United States and Israel in 2001. A Republican Administration replaced Clinton's Democrat one, and the Israeli public preferred the leadership of the seasoned Likud Party hard-liner, Ariel Sharon, to that of Ehud Barak. Candidate George W. Bush undertook to promote and maintain peace throughout the Middle East region; ensure Israel's security; protect United States economic interests including the reliable flow of oil; and reduce the threat of weapons of mass destruction (WMD).[1] This summary of the national interests of the United States in the region included the same elements that had persuaded Bush I and Clinton to pursue a comprehensive settlement of the Arab–Israel dispute over the previous decade. While the policies were similar, Bush made it clear that if elected his objective and style would be different from Clinton's. He believed that Clinton had tried to make Israel conform to his own plans and timetables,[2] and attributed the outbreak of the *al-Aqsa intifada* to Clinton's policies. His perspective was influenced by a strong neoconservative element within his group of close advisers and the growing influence within the Republican Party of fundamentalist Christianity with its dispensationalist belief. At his first National Security Council meeting, ten days after his inauguration, Bush II announced that the United States was going to tilt back towards Israel. Secretary of State Colin Powell demurred, saying that the consequences could be dire, especially for the Palestinians, but the president suggested that there was not much that the United States could do in relation to the *al-Aqsa intifada* and that it was time that it pulled out of the situation. The remainder of the meeting then addressed the situation in Iraq,[3] indicative of the new president's marginalisation of the Israel–Palestinian dispute in favour of his interest in Iraq, a country that was to engage his attention over the ensuing years of his presidency.

THE *AL-AQSA INTIFADA*

An immediate task before the incoming Administration was to offer its good offices to help rein in the level of violence that began after Sharon's visit to the Haram al-Sharif, on which the al-Aqsa Mosque stands, on 28 September 2000. Militants from a newly constituted Al-Aqsa Martyrs' Brigade, an agency of Arafat's Fatah movement, had joined Hamas and Islamic Jihad insurgents in the *intifada* after 2000. Each provocation by Palestinian terrorists brought harsh retaliation by the Israelis, who targeted activist leaders and destroyed the homes of the families of the bombers. Just a month after taking office, Bush sent Powell to talk to Israel's prime minister-elect and Arafat. Powell told the Israeli and Palestinian leaders that Bush II's Administration believed that they must solve their own security problems. The United States would help, but that would be no substitute for action by the parties themselves. Sharon averred that he was committed to peace with the Palestinians, and to negotiation with the Palestinian Authority. An easing of the economic condition of the Palestinian population would take place upon cessation of hostilities. The level of fighting worsened, however, posing a risk of broader conflict. Hezbollah took advantage of the situation to attack Israeli soldiers at Shaba farms, an enclave in southern Lebanon claimed by both Lebanon and Syria that Israel had reserved for transfer to Syria in any peace settlement with that country.[4] In the confident belief that Syria supported Hezbollah, Israel responded targeting Syrian radar sites in Lebanon. In order to clamp down on Palestinian militants, in mid-April the IDF reoccupied part of the Gaza Strip that had been ceded to the Palestinian Authority. Powell urged maximum restraint on both sides, described Israel's actions as 'excessive and disproportionate', and called upon the Palestinians 'to exercise control over all elements of the PLO and the Palestinian Authority, and to discipline violators'.[5]

Former US Senator George Mitchell had been appointed to head the commission mandated at the Sharm el-Sheikh summit in October 2000 to investigate the cause of the *intifada*. The commission presented its report at the end of April. It postulated that the greatest danger was that the culture of peace, nurtured over the previous decade, was being shattered; and suggested a list of confidence-building measures, most of which had already been the subject of agreements between Israel and the Palestinians.[6] Specific recommendations included that: all settlement activity by the government of

Israel, including that characterised as 'natural growth', be frozen; the IDF adopt non-lethal responses to unarmed demonstrators; Israel should lift closures, transfer to the PA all tax revenues owed, and permit Palestinians who had been employed in Israel to return to their jobs; Israeli security forces and settlers refrain from the destruction of homes and roads, as well as trees and other agricultural property in Palestinian areas; and the IDF withdraw to the positions it had occupied on 28 September 2000. It criticised the lack of control exercised by the Palestinian Authority over its own security personnel and armed elements associated with the Palestinian leadership. The commission's efforts failed to take root, the parties preferring to use it as a basis for further political charges against each other.

The violence continued, and in May Powell sent a State Department official to urge the Israelis and Palestinians to declare an unconditional ceasefire and to endorse formally the recommendations of the Mitchell Commission. Even as the envoy prepared for his task, Islamic Jihad claimed responsibility for inflicting further injury on Israelis. The mounting death and injury toll occasioned by groups over which the PA had no authority registered with Arafat. He was fearful of Israel's retaliatory capacity and called for a ceasefire on 2 June. He also ordered his security forces to prevent attacks on Israeli targets from Palestinian-ruled territory. This engendered hope that dialogue, and perhaps cooperation, might be resumed between the two parties. To help cement this, Bush II announced on 5 June 2001 that he would be sending the Director of the CIA, George Tenet, to the area to draft a ceasefire plan. Tenet's plan sought reconfirmation of the parties' commitments to the security agreements forged at Sharm el-Sheikh in October 2000, and effectively a revitalisation of the security machinery created under the Wye Accord,[7] but neither side halted the exchange of blows.

The Palestinian Authority's attempt to impose central dominance over militant Palestinian organisations proved impossible. Hamas and Palestinian Islamic Jihad, with their militias, were the Authority's principal political rivals. Also, Fatah, at the core of the Authority, had militants who participated in Fatah Tanzim and the Al-Aqsa Martyrs Brigade, which operated independently and at times against the purposes of the Authority's 50 000 formal security forces. In addition, there were some minor Palestinian movements based outside Palestinian-claimed territory that impacted upon Palestinian relations with Israel.

As the Palestinian Authority was unable to control the extremists, Israel targeted the leaders of these movements, killing among others Sheikh Ahmed Yassin, the co-founder of Hamas, in March 2004. His death provided the basis for taking Israel's practice of 'extrajudicial execution' before the UN Security Council. The United States vetoed a draft resolution, because it was silent about terrorist atrocities committed by Hamas.[8]

It was only after the terrorist attacks on American soil of 11 September 2001, when al-Qaeda included the Palestinian cause among its rhetoric, that the United States began articulating its vision of an Israel–Palestinian settlement. To that point, the Administration's focus had been on constraining the *intifada*. The president needed the help of Islamic states in his war against terrorism and their support for the incursion of the United States into Afghanistan in October. Saudi Arabia and other Arab states asked Bush II in return to address the *intifada*. By November the Saudi foreign minister was publicly expressing frustration that Bush II's Administration had failed to present a promised new peace initiative, and charged that the president, who refused to meet with Arafat, could not establish himself as an honest broker when he met with only one of the parties. The foreign minister is reported to have said that the president's failure to commit personal prestige to forging a final peace settlement 'makes a sane man go mad'.[9] Bush II's Administration sought to de-escalate the rampant *al-Aqsa intifada* by publicly acknowledging the Palestinians' cause and conceding that if any permanent accommodation were to be found it would have to be within a two-state solution. In doing so, it took the first of Clinton's parameters of December 2000 and formalised it as an objective of American policy.[10] On 19 November 2001 Powell announced the outline, foreshadowing the eventual creation of a viable Palestinian state. In the meantime, the Palestinians were challenged to make a 100 per cent effort to end violence and terror and to prepare their people for the hard compromises ahead, and Israel was again called upon to stop building settlements in the West Bank.

In foreshadowing the eventual creation of a Palestinian state, Bush II gave primacy to United States foreign policy interests over domestic considerations. Only three days before Powell's announcement, the president had received a letter from 89 senators following consultations with American Jewish leaders and advice from the American Israel Public Affairs Committee, demanding that the United States not restrain Israel from retaliating against the Palestinians and insisting that his Administration state publicly that it stood steadfastly behind Israel.[11] Some senior members of Bush II's Administration have connections with the Project for the New American Century (PNAC). The PNAC wrote to the president urging that the United States support Israel's fight against terrorism.[12] A second letter from the PNAC conflated Israel's activity in rooting out terrorists with the efforts of the United States in its war on terrorism. In the PNAC's view, it was critical that negotiations between Israel and the Palestinians not be the product of terrorism or conducted under the threat of terrorist attack and that the United States should no longer urge Israel to negotiate with Arafat.[13] Bush II would persist with the peace process because a negotiated settlement remained a desirable objective and could assist the attainment of his Administration's goals in the region, but the United States would no longer feel challenged to produce this 'public good' in order to demonstrate the beneficence of US hegemony.

United States endorsement of a two-state solution was insufficient to persuade Palestinian extremists to halt the violence. According to Human Rights Watch, at least 1949 Palestinians and 637 Israelis had been killed between September 2000 and October 2002, the majority of whom were civilians. The indiscriminate nature of the conflict is revealed in the number of children killed – 292 Palestinians and 79 Israelis.[14] Bush II tasked a retired US Marine Corps General, Anthony Zinni, to go to Israel and get the parties to commit to the Tenet plan. This, like the Mitchell Commission's report, had been endorsed by both sides, but suffered the same fate. Sharon was content to go along with various American ceasefire initiatives, but Israelis looked for evidence of Palestinian compliance before they would act.

Any doubt whether the Palestinian Authority was tolerating, if not encouraging, Palestinian terrorism had to be dismissed in January 2002 when a Palestinian ship, carrying some 50 tons of arms supplies from Iran, was intercepted by the Israeli authorities. Arafat denied knowledge of the operation. While it is conceivable that the order may have been commissioned without his knowledge, his highly centralised management style and control of the purse strings leaves little doubt about the question of his involvement. The Israelis responded, utilising the full range of US-supplied materiel at their command. They entered both Ramallah, where they isolated Arafat's West Bank headquarters, and the Palestinian Authority's headquarters in Gaza. They also deployed forces into and around Bethlehem and other Palestinian cities, and targeted the Palestinian Authority's civilian infrastructure.[15] The Israelis again attacked the PA headquarters at Ramallah and Gaza City in February 2002, and invaded the Balata and Jenin refugee camps in the West Bank. The IDF saw the refugee camps as bases for Palestinian terrorists and was determined to send a clear message that there was no safe haven for terrorism.[16]

Bush II was dealing with two protagonists, in Arafat and Sharon, with a long history of personal enmity. Sharon chose to hold Arafat personally responsible for the assassination of Israel's tourism minister in October 2001.[17] All contact with the Palestinians would be frozen. The 'Oslo' ideal vanished as the combatants reduced the contest between Israel and the Palestinian leadership to the level of a personal duel in which the IDF was used to demonstrate Arafat's irrelevance. Marginalised, the best Bush II could achieve as Sharon cornered Arafat was to insist that he desist from exiling or killing the Palestinian leader. Bush believed that international opinion would be outraged if Sharon were to press for the coup de grâce.

THE US'S RE-ENGAGEMENT

Mitchell, Tenet and Zinni had each presented measures that the conflictual parties were encouraged to take. The measures having failed to take root, the United States decided to re-engage in the search for a negotiated settlement. The consequential flurry of diplomatic activity was a response to the severity of Israeli action in Palestinian-controlled territory and intense international criticism of Israel's action in the Jenin refugee camp; it was also a preparation for measures to remove Iraq's Saddam Hussain from office, for which the United States would need, at the very least, the tacit agreement of Arab states. The United States was able to divert the UN Security Council's attention to ascertaining the facts surrounding Israeli actions, rather than focussing on an immediate condemnation of Israel that it might have to veto. The Council acted upon a United States draft welcoming an inquiry by the UN Secretary-General, but the Israelis declared that they would not co-operate with it.[18]

Bush II proceeded to garner international support to effect a change in Israel's aggressive policies. The president spoke on 4 April 2002 of the need to restart negotiation. He also explored the desirability of an international conference being convened to help reactivate the negotiation process. The British Prime Minister (Tony Blair) had been pressing for a conference, in part to ameliorate his public's scepticism about his support for United States policy on Iraq. Sharon thought that Arab states represented at a conference might be able to restrain the Palestinians from further attacks against Israel.

Like several of his predecessors, the president was to be drawn personally into the Israel–Palestinian dispute. During March and April 2002 Bush II made some 16 telephone calls to the leaders of Middle Eastern and Western European countries, Russia and the United Nations to discuss the situation.[19] The United States also added the weight of international opinion to the Mitchell and Tenet recommendations, and earned approbation for its efforts. Within the UN Security Council, the United States supported a number of resolutions during those two months that addressed the IDF's incursion into territory ceded to the Palestinians under the Oslo process. The first, sponsored by the United States, affirmed a vision 'where two States, Israel and Palestine, live side-by-side within secure and recognised borders' and called for 'implementation of the Tenet work plan and Mitchell Report recommenddations with the aim of resuming negotiations on a political settlement'.[20] The second called for an immediate ceasefire, 'the withdrawal of Israeli troops from Palestinian cities, including Ramallah', and for the parties to cooperate with General Zinni to implement the Tenet and Mitchell plans.[21] On 4 April, the Council noted further deterioration on the ground and that its earlier resolution had not been implemented, and demanded that it be implemented 'without delay'. The resolution also welcomed a forthcoming mission of the US Secretary of State to the region and the efforts of others 'to bring about a comprehensive, just and lasting peace'.[22] Bush II called upon Israel to halt incursions into Palestinian-controlled areas. This uncharacteristic public rebuke of Israel by an American president provoked dissent within the Administration and Israel's American friends, including those of the Christian 'right'. Neoconservatives in the Administration felt that Sharon's fight against terrorism was justified, and they doubted the wisdom of Powell visiting the region under the prevailing circumstances, which they viewed as unpropitious.

Powell's visit went ahead, backed by a president who saw value in demonstrating American understanding of the position of the Palestinians as he pursued his foreign policy objectives in Iraq. There was plain talking on all sides. Sharon was insistent that Israel's requirement for withdrawal would be the handing over by the Palestinians of five persons implicated in the assassination of the tourism minister and a sixth man whom the Israelis believed to have been behind the financing of the shipload of arms. He also told Powell that he was now opposed to the holding of an international conference, as it would be seen as rewarding Arafat. Powell told Arafat that there was a real risk that the Bush Administration would soon reach a point where it would no longer deal with him at all,[23] and again urged Arafat to stop the killing and to restore cooperation on security matters with Israel. Even as he pleaded with Arafat to cooperate with the United States in the Palestinians' 'national' interest, the neoconservative element in the Administration was at work persuading the president to abandon thought of an international conference and to instruct Powell not to commit the president to any political process.[24]

By 21 April Israeli tanks had been withdrawn from all but Arafat's compound in Ramallah, in which the six persons most wanted by Israel were hiding, and Bethlehem's Church of the Nativity, where some Palestinian militants had taken refuge. Bush II demanded Israel's withdrawal from the vicinity of the church, concerned to protect the birthplace of Christianity from possible attack and damage. Israel responded that if the United States countered the UN inquiry into events at the Jenin camp, it would lift the siege on Arafat.[25] Bush II concurred: the Crown Prince of Saudi Arabia had already made it clear that he was prepared to jeopardise US–Saudi relations in order to secure the lifting of the siege of Arafat.[26] A way had to be found that would enable Sharon to back down. The British came to the rescue, proposing that they would ensure that the Palestinians set up a proper prison regime whose integrity they would guarantee and monitor.[27] Sharon agreed, and Britain made arrangements for the imprisonment of key Palestinians, and the deportation of others involved, that met Israel's desire to bring the perpetrators to account. On 2 May, the day that the siege of Arafat's headquarters ended, the UN Secretary-General announced that he was disbanding the Jenin inquiry. Israel's withdrawal did not last long, however: by mid-May every one of the towns evacuated had been reinvaded at least once. Reinvasion carried the message that Israel was now solely in charge of security.

In demanding Israel's withdrawal from Palestinian-controlled territory, Bush II had once again pursued a foreign policy objective in the face of domestic criticism. American Jewish leaders and Christian evangelicals told him not to pressure Sharon. The Congress also moved to back Sharon, both Houses passing resolutions reaffirming support for Israel; a bipartisan congressional delegation to Israel stated that Sharon should resist United States pressure to negotiate with Arafat; and the House appropriations committee considered the provision of an extra $200 million to Israel to fight terrorism, against the opposition of the secretary of state.[28]

Concurrent with the escalation of hostilities between the Israelis and Palestinians, Bush II had kept in touch with Crown Prince Abdullah of Saudi Arabia and other Arab leaders.[29] He had encouraged the Crown Prince to proceed with a Saudi proposal that the Arab Summit to be held on 27–28 March 2002 address a unanimous proposition to the UN Security Council offering an exchange of normal relations and security with Israel for full withdrawal from all occupied territories, recognition of an independent Palestinian state with al-Quds al-Sharif (East Jerusalem) as its capital, and the return of refugees. The Summit adopted the Saudi initiative, affirming that were Israel to implement the terms, the Arab countries would consider the Arab–Israel conflict ended and would enter into a peace agreement with Israel.[30] The Summit's declaration did not become a circuit breaker. Israelis were confused by the move, which offered the attraction of Arab recognition of the State of Israel within the 4 June 1967 borders in exchange for Israel's withdrawal from all territory occupied after that date, but the price was unacceptable to the Israeli right, and Sharon temporised. The proposal remains on the table.

After almost a year in office, Sharon met with Palestinian officials for the first time. That meeting, on 2 February 2002, saw the parties talk past one another as the prime minister emphasised that Israel's security was his main concern, while the Palestinians repeated their need for a Palestinian state and, in the prevailing circumstances, security from Israel's heavy-handed retaliatory measures. A trilateral security meeting among Israeli, Palestinian and American officials followed two days later. The meetings did not produce results, though they were significant for having been held at all. The timing of Sharon's meeting, one month after the capture of the Palestinian arms shipment, suggests that he may have concluded finally that Israel could never rely upon a divided Palestinian community, whose militias could challenge the legitimacy of the designated central authority, to contribute toward maintenance of Israel's security from its side of any negotiated border. That was the message he wished to convey to the Palestinians. The State of Israel had been born in violence and violence had attended its entire life. Most of Sharon's career had been spent in an elusive effort to assure his country's security. Israel's negotiators throughout the Oslo process had been similarly conditioned to treat security as paramount. Even as they worked toward a settlement predicated upon an assumption that a peace settlement would bring with it a concomitant obligation to preserve the peace, they were conscious of the fragility of any such compact. A two-state solution, posited on UN Security Council Resolution 242's 'secure and recognised boundaries free from threats or acts of force', could expose Israel to porous frontiers in either or both the West Bank and Gaza Strip and fell well short of a necessary security guarantee.

When Sharon met with the Palestinian officials he said that he was not against the Palestinian people, but was simply fighting terror. In discussion with the United States, he chose tactically to conflate the Palestinian insurgency with Bush II's war against terrorism, nudging the Administration toward accepting the Palestinian insurgency as part of a much larger problem. Vice President Cheney and some others in the Administration were receptive to this interpretation. This tactical manoeuvre enabled Sharon to position himself as an ally even as his country was coming under increasing United States pressure to moderate its actions against the Palestinians. His finesse worked, with Bush II declaring that the best way to 'get some meaningful dialogue going [between Israelis and Palestinians] ... is to help secure the region, in particular, Israel's homeland, by a united front against terror'.[31] The manoeuvre also enabled Sharon to mask his strategic objective behind the common cause of 'peace'. In the name of peace, Sharon would pursue his country's security: peace would be a product of security, not its precursor.

It is clear that Bush II did not fully appreciate the distinction between his vision of 'two states living in peace, side by side [as offering] the only solution to this conflict' and Sharon's interpretation of 'peace' as being predicated on absolute security. The president's characterisation of Sharon as a 'man of peace' demonstrates this.[32] So does the fact that when, months later and after considerable criticism of his epithet, Bush II heard Sharon talk again of peace and security, he persisted with the dichotomy saying that he knew Sharon to be a man of security, but wished him to work harder on the peace part.[33] Israel and the United States were pursuing different agendas.

REFORM OF THE PALESTINIAN AUTHORITY

A difference of Israeli and United States agendas had become evident in early March 2002. At a time when Bush II was trying to mobilise international support behind his efforts to re-establish conditions for negotiation toward a two-state solution, and suggesting that a regional ministerial peace summit might offer such a prospect, Sharon was declaring that it was premature to accept the notion of a Palestinian state as the outcome of the peace process.

An intermediate objective, common to both the United States and Israel, was reform of the Palestinian Authority.[34] The two leaders were distrustful of Arafat and sought for their own reasons to marginalise him. Sharon's antipathy toward Arafat was well established, while Bush II had argued that Arafat should exercise leadership in restraining Palestinian violence and had implied that his refusal to meet with the Palestinian leader was intended to signal his disapproval of Arafat's performance. Again, there was a divergence of view within the Administration. Cheney believed that the principal foreign policy objective of the United States was to pursue the war against terrorism and that Arafat should be written off because of his failure to rein in Palestinian militants. Powell recognised that while it was exceedingly difficult to work with Arafat, he was the elected leader of the Palestinians. Bush II bridged the issue, championing calls for reform of the PA's institutions that would constrain Arafat's power. Fortuitously, a desire for reform came also from Arafat and the Palestinian community, although various proponents of reform had differing reasons for it.[35]

In a landmark speech on 24 June 2002, Bush called on the Palestinians to elect new leaders not compromised by terror.[36] He had in mind the election of an executive prime minister who would serve under the titular leadership of the Palestinian *ra'is*. Bush identified a need for substantial change involving a Palestinian constitution, establishment of the rule of law, and governmental transparency including through a treasury capable of battling corruption. Although the Authority was widely believed by the international community to be corrupt, the allegation related more to Arafat's highly personalised and non-transparent manner of financial allocation and to waste and mismanagement than to widespread and endemic malpractice.[37] Arafat remained an iconic figure, but Bush II wanted to see him sidelined from management of the Palestinian Authority. In promoting change, Bush II was identifying with a push for fundamental reform that was also present within the Palestinian population.[38] For his part, Arafat favoured only minimal changes to his cabinet and to the upper echelon of the security service, but he was unable to counter the force of the reform movement and conceded, declaring in February 2003 his intention to appoint a prime minister. An attempt by Arafat's supporters to limit the premier's authority and to maintain day-to-day operational powers in Arafat's hands was defeated by the legislature. Arafat, as chairman of the PLO, would retain responsibility for negotiations with Israel and 'national security'. The Palestinian National Authority has declared that the PLO 'is the Palestinian government in exile and carries out the state functions of the Palestinian people', whereas the 'Palestinian Authority is a temporary administrative body (intended only to serve during the interim period prior to the establishment of a Palestinian state)'.[39] Confusion, and unresolved tension between the Palestinian *ra'is* and his prime minister, and between the prime minister and militant Palestinian groups, were among the factors that led Mahmoud Abbas to submit his resignation after six months in the premiership. After Arafat's death in November 2004, Abbas was endorsed by Fatah as its preferred candidate for the Palestinian presidency, securing election with 62 per cent of the vote in January 2005.

THE QUARTET'S ROADMAP

Bush II had planned to submit a new peace proposal in autumn 2001, but the attacks of 11 September prevented this. Then, in his speech of 24 June 2002, he announced that an initiative was in preparation. Although the United States had no desire to become embroiled in the protracted war between Israel and the Palestinians, it appreciated that its relationships with the wider Arab and Islamic world required an American initiative. Its decision was also a response to a European perception that the United States should attempt to heal the rifts its policies had caused in international institutions and in its alliances and relationships. Further violence played indirectly into Bush II's hands. Sharon retaliated against suicide attacks in September 2002 and resumed the siege of Arafat's headquarters, and the United States permitted the adoption of a UN Security Council resolution whose tilt was anti-Israel. The resolution demanded Israel's cessation of measures in and around Ramallah and expeditious withdrawal of occupying forces from Palestinian cities, while calling on the Palestinian Authority to ensure that those responsible for terrorist acts were brought to justice.[40] The president's national security adviser, Condoleeza Rice, told Israel that the United States expected a speedy resolution of the siege, because it did not help US efforts to muster support for the campaign against Iraq.[41]

The foreshadowed initiative was published on 30 April 2003, six weeks after the commencement of hostilities against Iraq. Release of the final document was withheld to pressure Arafat to agree to the appointment of a prime minister. The United States had worked in association with the European Union, Russia and the United Nations, and the Quartet produced a performance-based and goal-driven roadmap,[42] with clear phases, timelines, target dates and benchmarks aimed at progress through reciprocal steps by the two parties in the political, security, economic, humanitarian and institution-building fields. The objective would be a final and comprehensive settlement of the Israel–Palestinian conflict by mid-2005. The plan established what the co-authors believed to be a realistic timeline for implementation. Progress would require and depend upon the good faith efforts of the parties, and their compliance with each of the obligations outlined. In each phase, the parties would be expected to perform their obligations in parallel, unless otherwise indicated. Should the parties perform their obligations rapidly, progress within and through the phases could come sooner than indicated in the plan: non-compliance with obligations would impede progress. The Quartet undertook to meet regularly at senior levels to evaluate the parties' performance on implementation of the plan. A precondition of acceptance of the plan was that the Palestinians undertake an unconditional cessation of violence.

Bush II met with the leaders of Bahrain, Egypt, Jordan and Saudi Arabia and the Palestinian prime minister on 2 June 2003 to garner support for the roadmap and its provision for constitutional reform leading to a strong parliamentary democracy in an eventual Palestinian state. The Arab states undertook to use all lawful means to prevent support from their countries reaching illegal organizations, and to channel all financial assistance directly to the Palestinian Authority. The following day the president met with the Israeli and Palestinian prime ministers at Aqaba and secured their formal agreement to the plan. The Palestinians had accepted the roadmap upon its release. Israel was not attracted to its terms and submitted 14 amendments. Its concurrence was obtained after securing an acknowledgement from Powell and Rice that Israel's concerns were 'real concerns ... [and that the Administration] ... will address them fully and seriously in the implementation of the roadmap'.[43] The integrity of the roadmap was thus unilaterally diminished by one of its signatories in order to accommodate Israel on the eve of its formal adoption. To make matters worse for the Palestinians, Abbas performed at the launching ceremony to United States choreography, while Sharon departed from it. Abbas was disparaged on the Palestinian street for having toed the Americans' line; and felt that the Americans and Israelis had betrayed him.

The Palestinian Authority was conscious of the roadmap's precondition on violence from an early draft. It had, with Egyptian assistance, sought Hamas's commitment to halt suicide bombings for three months prior to the Aqaba summit,[44] but Hamas refused to accept the plan and launched further terrorist attacks after the plan's adoption. Israel retaliated, killing four of the militants' political leaders, including Hamas's second-in-command. As the violence continued over ensuing months, Arafat called the plan 'dead'; the Israeli government, continuing to impute responsibility to Arafat personally, announced on 11 September 2003 that 'Yasser Arafat is a complete obstacle to any process of reconciliation between Israel and the Palestinians. Israel will work to remove this obstacle (*sic*) in a manner, and at a time, of its choosing.'[45] Despite the plan's provenance, involving the co-sponsors of the

1991 Madrid Conference, and including the European Union as the principal donor to the Palestinian Authority, and the legitimacy conferred by the United Nations Secretary-General, the roadmap attracted little more than lip service. Its release in the wake of the United States-commanded invasion of Iraq, led many to view it as a sop to Arab opinion. One of its few positive outcomes was an agreement on 27 June, brokered by the United States, for Israeli disengagement from the Gaza Strip and Bethlehem areas.

Attempts by the Quartet to stimulate progress in accordance with the roadmap had little more success overall than Zinni's or Tenet's efforts. Every attack by Hamas and other militant groups elicited an Israeli response, sometimes targeting Hamas's activists but often the Palestinian Authority's infrastructure. One observer has concluded that Israeli retaliation, in the aggregate, actually weakened the Palestinian Authority, its infrastructure and its Fatah tributary, more than Hamas.[46] Given so tangible a reward, Hamas had no reason to desist. Further, Hamas operated as a quasi-government, providing an extensive service network that included hospitals and schools, as well as a military arm, and possessed some of the infrastructure needed to step in as an alternative if the Palestinian Authority were eventually to collapse. Hamas was able to draw upon charitable donations to fund its social services, while the Palestinian Authority slowly reduced the range of services that it provided due to a weakened infrastructure, financial constraints, corruption and poor leadership. As early as 2003, Hamas began talking publicly of taking over from Fatah as the governing party within the Palestinian Authority through the electoral process.

The address of the first phase of the roadmap was the ending of terror and violence, the normalising of Palestinian life and the building of Palestinian institutions. The co-authors looked to the legitimate government of the Palestinian Authority to constrain dissidents within the Palestinian community. They expected that the Authority's security forces, which numbered some 35 000 in 2000 but which may have exceeded that figure, would be able to exert control over the activities of militants, whose combined forces they greatly outnumbered.[47] Events showed that the Palestinian Authority was unable to command groups whose philosophical approach toward Israel was different from its own. The roadmap's insistence on a cessation of violence conferred, in effect, a negative veto upon radicals whose independent acts could, and did, frustrate the Authority's cause. Also, while the roadmap calls for an end to Israeli 'incitement against the Palestinians' it does not – and possibly could not – take into account provocation by Israel to which the Palestinians would feel bound to respond. The erection of a barrier around much of the West Bank was to become a prime example of such an eventuality. Finally, insistence on a cessation of violence as a precondition for dialogue and subsequent activity constrains the possibility of further progress. The refusal to negotiate with terrorist agencies is understood, but Israeli citizens were not the only victims of violence. Palestinians whose homes were destroyed or whose lands were sequestered also harbour grievances, and find it hard to accept that the obligation to move first falls on their community. Communication becomes particularly important when matters are at their most parlous.

Bush II was not alone in seeking to keep the objective of a negotiated two-state solution alive. The influence of Clinton's parameters of December 2000 extended to an unofficial Israeli and Palestinian peace group that included former ministers of the Palestinian Authority and Israel's Labor government and retired high-ranking officers of the IDF, as well as members of the two legislatures. They finalised an 'accord' in Geneva in October 2003, and comparable discussions were under way elsewhere.[48] The Geneva 'accord' addressed such issues as the border between the two sovereign states, Israel's responsibility for resettling Israelis residing in Palestinian sovereign territory, security, compensation to refugees for refugeehood and loss of property, remuneration to states that hosted refugees, recognition of Israeli and Palestinian sovereignty over different parts of Jerusalem, and transfer of the Haram al-Sharif/Temple Mount compound to Palestinian sovereignty. The 'accord' thus anticipated a possible resolution of several final status issues that the government and many Israelis would have preferred to leave for deliberation to a much later stage. Its crafting showed, however, that a negotiated peace agreement that addressed contentious issues was possible, albeit by actors without political responsibility for its implementation. The United States paid attention to it, but neither Sharon nor Arafat endorsed it. For Sharon, it pointed in a direction that he wished to bypass.

SHARON'S DISENGAGEMENT POLICY

With Arafat sidelined and Abbas and the Authority under increasing challenge from Hamas and other groups that had rejected the Oslo process, Sharon was free to entertain alternative solutions. Henceforth his principal constraints would come from within his own government. He considered the implications of separation from the Palestinians, rather than a compact with them. The Labor Party had floated the idea of separation at the general elections in 2001 and 2003,[49] and had lost both to Sharon. In June 2002, as Bush was foreshadowing a United States initiative, Sharon turned to the idea of building a security barrier around the West Bank in order to keep Palestinian suicide bombers and militants out of Israel. He seems to have decided subsequently that if the barrier were effective, Israel would be able to withdraw from such occupied territory as it chose (Map 7.1). He would present this to the

Palestinians as a down payment toward statehood. Finally, he concluded that in order to secure the necessary domestic support for withdrawal, the two elements had to be linked. This was not a spontaneously conceived concept: the policy was announced progressively over the space of three years.

Israel began building the barrier in June 2002. Its action attracted criticism from the Palestinians and the international community.[50] A report of the UN Commission on Human Rights[51] acknowledged that Israel's security concerns could not be denied, but that a balance must be struck between respect for human rights and the interests of security. It recommended that construction of the wall and the annexation of territory incorporated within it be condemned as unlawful. An emergency Special Session of the UN General Assembly sought a non-binding advisory opinion on the matter from the International Court of Justice (ICJ), which was issued on 9 July 2004. Israel informed the Court that Palestinian attacks against Israeli civilians over a 40-month period had claimed 916 dead and over 5000 injured, many critically. Referral of the matter to the ICJ revealed differences among the co-authors of the roadmap. The United States and the EU submitted that as a matter of judicial propriety the Court should not offend the principle that advisory proceedings were not the means to address disputes of states without their consent. Russia argued that all efforts should be focussed on stopping and reversing the construction of the wall.[52] Acting on the advisory opinion, the resumed Special Session of the UN General Assembly demanded that Israel heed it and halt construction on the security barrier, tear down portions built on Palestinian land, and provide reparations to Palestinians whose lives had been harmed by the wall.[53] Israel and the United States opposed the resolution, with the United States delegation expressing reservation about some of the legal conclusions in the Court's opinion. While the protracted procedures of the United Nations were taking their course, some Palestinians petitioned Israel's Supreme Court about official orders issued in relation to construction of the wall. The Court found in favour of the petitioners in seven of the eight matters before it, ruling that sections of the wall violated Palestinian rights by separating Palestinians from their towns, villages, farms and fields.[54] The government modified its route, reducing the amount of land to be annexed by Israel to 40 000 hectares, or about 8.5 per cent of the total West Bank area including the disputed territory of East Jerusalem. Settlers and religious-nationalist Israelis oppose the fence, fearing that it will preclude Israel from eventually acquiring all or most of the West Bank. Most Israelis, however, favour the structure as a means of protection against terrorist infiltrators. It has already produced a decline in the number of attacks from places bounded by the barrier. Bush II told Sharon that the barrier should be a security, rather than political instrument, temporary rather than permanent, and therefore, not prejudicial to any final status issues, including final borders. Its route should take into account, consistent with security needs, its impact on Palestinians not engaged in terrorist activities.[55] While he hoped that the barrier's existence would be temporary, it is debatable whether a construction that is estimated to cost $1.3 billion is likely to be dismantled. In all probability, it will come to demark the border of any Palestinian 'state'.

The fence was the first of Sharon's two pillars. The second was his decision in December 2003 that Israel should withdraw unilaterally from parts of the occupied territories. Division within the Palestinian community meant that, in Sharon's view, the PA could no longer be relied upon to represent the Palestinians. The cost of years of conflict between Israelis and Palestinians, and Israel's vulnerability to insurgents prepared to risk all in challenging the might of the IDF, led him to the conclusion that 'the idea of keeping 3.5 million Palestinians under occupation is the worst thing for Israel, for the Palestinians and also for the Israeli economy'.[56] His exceptional use of 'occupation' to refer to Israel's presence in the West Bank and Gaza Strip suggests that Sharon had come to realise that *Eretz Yisrael* could not be achieved by the two practices he had pursued throughout his working life. His military and political careers had focussed on national security and settlement building in the occupied territories under the IDF's shield, but he must now concentrate pragmatically on what part of the vision of his past that he could salvage.

Anticipating domestic opposition to his plan, Sharon took it first to Washington on 14 April 2004 to secure Bush II's endorsement and to obtain written reassurance of the United States's commitment to Israel's security. With these in hand, he announced that he would be submitting his proposal to the Likud Party for its approval. In essence, he would disengage from the peace process until there was evidence on the Palestinian side of a willingness, ability and actual realisation of a need to fight terrorism and to implement the reforms stipulated in the roadmap.[57] Confident that these terms would not be met, he announced that Israel would withdraw completely from Gaza, while reserving a right to supervise and guard 'the external envelope on land' and to exclusive control of Gaza's airspace and coastal zone. Israel's withdrawal from the West Bank would be less comprehensive. Civilian settlements, military zones and places where Israel had additional interests would remain part of the State of Israel. Palestinian territorial contiguity would be assured only in the northern parts of the West Bank from whence four small Israeli settlements would be withdrawn. Finally, there would be no right of return for Palestinian refugees to land held by the Israelis. Bush II recognised that the situation in the West Bank had changed since the passage of UN Security Council Resolutions 242 and 338: 'In the light of new realities on the ground, including already existing major Israeli population centres, it is unrealistic to expect that the outcome of final status negotiations will be a full and complete return to the armistice lines of 1949 … all previous efforts to negotiate a two-state solution have reached the same conclusion'.[58]

MAP 7.1 PALESTINIAN SOVEREIGN AREAS (BARAK AND SHARON PROPOSALS)

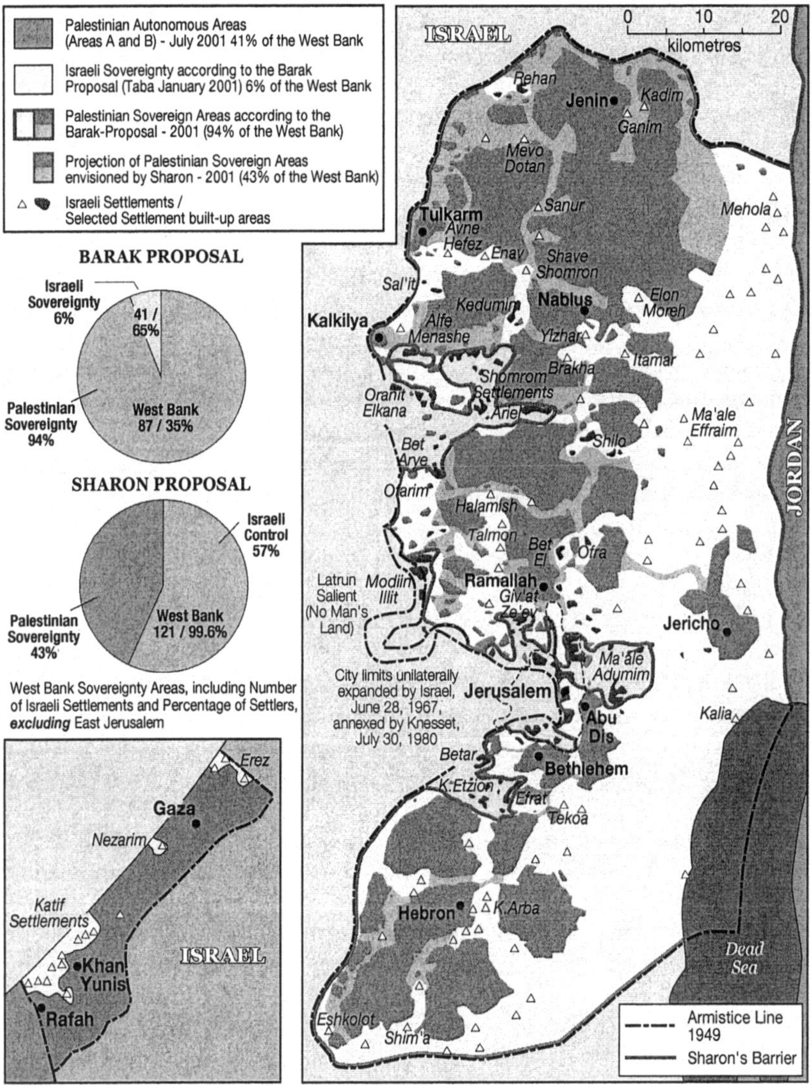

The British Prime Minister and the Secretary-General of the United Nations, who were meeting in New York at the time, were more reserved, stressing that the proposed withdrawal should be seen as a step toward reactivation of the Quartet's roadmap.[59] The Group of Eight industrialised countries also placed the move in the context of the realisation of two states, and pledged to work with the international community in providing humanitarian and economic assistance to the Palestinians, and in building 'democratic, transparent and accountable Palestinian institutions'.[60] The Palestinian leadership reacted angrily to Bush II's endorsement of Sharon's plan. They characterised the plan as 'an illegitimate land grab by Israelis, and a unilateral attempt by Sharon to set the borders between Israel and a Palestinian state rather than negotiating them as part of a final settlement'.[61] Arafat warned that Israel could not gain security until there was an independent Palestinian state free from Israeli occupation, settlements and siege.[62]

When submitted to a referendum of Sharon's Likud Party, more than 60 per cent of voters opposed the plan. Sharon undertook to submit a revision, while the Quartet urged Israel to proceed with full withdrawal from the Gaza Strip. After reshuffling his cabinet to assure passage of his plan, Sharon presented his ministry with an amended version that delayed all withdrawals until September 2005. He secured cabinet approval in June 2004, after two National Union ministers were dismissed from the cabinet. Some Likud members also expressed dissatisfaction with his proposal, and two ministers from another small party left the coalition. Sharon would have had insufficient backing to secure Knesset approval of his plan, but for the Labor Party deciding to support it and to join him in a National Unity government in December 2004. The Knesset passed the plan in February 2005 by a healthy majority.[63] Withdrawal was effected in Gaza between 15 August and 12 September. The process involved the relocation into Israel of the Gaza industrial zone, causing a considerable increase in unemployment in the Gaza Strip. Withdrawal from the four villages in the north of the West Bank was completed ten days later.

The third element of Sharon's disengagement plan involved the Palestinians. With the participation of Mubarak and King Abdullah of Jordan, Sharon met Abbas at Sharm el-Sheikh on 8 February 2005. The Israeli and Palestinian leaders agreed to a cessation of Palestinian acts of violence against Israelis, and Israeli military activity against Palestinians. Security responsibility for Palestinian areas would be transferred back to the Palestinians, and Israel would release 'hundreds of Palestinian prisoners'.[64] Sharon announced that the plan could pave the way to the implementation of the roadmap. Although sporadic Palestinian acts of violence were to continue, constrained in part by the barrier, this agreement effectively brought the mass *al-Aqsa* uprising to an end.

Sharon had achieved greater security for Israelis at some cost to his own party: the right wing element, which incorporated the religious Zionist–nationalist movement whose members he had once encouraged to settle in the occupied territories, was implacably opposed to his agenda. He was able, however, to tap into the general mood of a public tired of decades of war against the Palestinians. He launched a new party, Kadima (meaning 'Forward') in November 2005, whose popularity came largely, but not exclusively, at the expense of Likud. Much of its attraction to those politicians who left their parties to join him, and to the public, focussed on Sharon's leadership, but he was to become incapacitated through illness in January 2006.

Ehud Olmert, Sharon's deputy, took Kadima to the polls in March 2006. The party won 29 seats in the 120-seat Knesset, and formed a government in coalition with Labor (19 seats) and other minor parties. Because of the breakaway of Sharon and his supporters from Likud, its representation (once again under Netanyahu's leadership) shrank from 38 seats in the former legislature to 12 in the new. Prior to his incapacitation, Sharon had pledged that Kadima would abandon the unilateralist approach employed in 2005 and adopt the staged processes of the Quartet's roadmap. The roadmap's transitional provisions provide for 'an independent Palestinian state with provisional borders and attributes of sovereignty ... as a way station to a permanent status settlement'. This goal was dependent upon the Palestinian leadership 'acting against terror [and] willing and able to build a practicing democracy based on tolerance and liberty'. When Sharon made his pledge, the Palestinian leadership possessed in President Mahmoud Abbas and Prime Minister Ahmed Qurei the two persons most influential in the PLO's conclusion of the original Oslo agreement. The Palestinian election in January changed the situation, and Olmert has declared that he, not the Palestinians, will determine the agenda of any negotiation with them.

The Palestinians went to the polls on 25 January 2006 to elect a new legislature. Hamas secured a solid but not resounding victory,[65] in spite of America's promotion of the credentials of candidates in favour of negotiations, and efforts by Abbas to gerrymander a Fatah victory. Hamas secured a majority in the legislature, with 76 of the 132 seats, displacing the governing Fatah party, which won 43 seats. A number of factors contributed to the swing: Arafat, Fatah's founder, was no longer alive and able to project his iconic personality in his party's favour; Israel's impediments to Palestinian electioneering and voting were less obstructive than they were at the 1996 election, which permitted Hamas to campaign; public frustration with the maladministration of the Fatah-dominated Palestinian Authority, and its seeming inability to secure adequate accommodations from Israel; dissatisfaction with the 'old guard' that had returned from exile and assumed the leadership of the Palestinian community to the detriment of the younger home-grown generation that had launched the 1987 *intifada* and which was at the forefront of the continuing insurrection; and the fact that Hamas, contesting the election in its own right for the first time, was able to draw upon its record as both a service provider and a party prepared to challenge Israel's occupation of 'Palestine'. Despite its reputation as a service provider, Hamas has had no experience in public administration. The prospect of a coalition with Fatah was briefly entertained, but Fatah and all the other Palestinian political groups rejected the notion. The new cabinet of the Palestinian Authority, under Prime Minister Ismail Haniyeh, is composed only of members of Hamas and some technocrats. Abbas, as both *ra'is* and the head of Fatah, has advocated that Hamas recognise Israel's right to exist and adopt his vision of a two-state solution.

The election result has posed problems for Israel and the United States. Hamas is committed to the overthrow of Israel and the realisation of an Islamic state, although it would be prepared to accept the formation of a Palestinian state within the territories occupied in 1967 as a means of assessing Israel's long-term intentions.[66] Anticipating the formation of a Hamas government, Israel, which collects around $50 million a month in tax and other revenues on behalf of the Palestinian Authority, announced that it would suspend the money transfers. Olmert was later to declare the severance of all links with both Abbas and the Hamas government. Bush II's initial public position was subtler, pointing to the impossibility of achieving the two-state solution to which the United States is committed when one party's objective is the destruction of the other. His Administration had championed reform of the Palestinian Authority and democratic values, and the president held to this philosophy in his State of the Union address on 31 January,[67] but he made it clear that his Administration would not deal with an entity determined to challenge Israel's existence. The paymasters of the European Union echoed this. The United States has sought also to persuade other states to withhold financial assistance, or to become a conduit for financial transfers to a Hamas government, employing negative sanctions in order to coerce Hamas to adopt a more accommodating policy. Egypt has declined to do so, and a question mark hangs over Iran, which has supported Hamas in the past. Abbas has sought support for the Palestinian Authority from Jordan and Morocco against the Israeli siege, which he has characterised as illegal.[68] He has also challenged the Hamas-led government to accept a proposal by a group of Palestinians in Israeli gaols that implicitly recognises Israel, or he would hold a referendum on it.[69] It remains to be seen whether Abbas's predilections, the responsibilities of office and financial constraints will induce the new government to deal constructively with Israel, or whether Olmert will be able to persuade his government to follow Sharon's example and deal with Palestinian issues unilaterally.

CONCLUSION

The decision of President Bush II to confine the US role in relation to Israel and the Palestinians to that of facilitating negotiations was a deliberate departure from the policy of his predecessor. Under Bush United States power was employed sparingly, and then primarily in its ideational form such as when declaring support for a two-state solution, articulating a need for improved governance within the Palestinian Authority, and co-authorship of the Quartet's roadmap.

Israel had made it clear that there could be no negotiation leading to a Palestinian settlement for so long as the *al-Aqsa intifada* persisted. Bush II shared that interpretation. As the United States pursued its war against terrorism, Sharon conflated the Palestinian insurgency with terrorism and found a receptive audience in Washington. From an Israeli perspective, the possibility of resuming negotiation with the Palestinians during conflict was viewed as indicative of weakness. The need for a complete cessation of violence became the unquestioned precondition of both the United States and Israel for high-level contact with the Palestinian leadership and the reactivation of negotiations, effectively according a veto to any agency determined for its own purposes to frustrate the process.

The consequences of US failure to exert greater authority over the parties in conflict were an escalation in the level of violence perpetrated by both sides, and the destruction of trust between the parties. In the ensuing asymmetrical warfare the Palestinians made the most of what little they had, including of persons willing to commit suicide bombings for their cause. The Israelis responded with the arsenal at their command, largely ignoring international concern about the heavy-handed nature of their actions until Bush II felt compelled to intervene, demanding Israel's withdrawal from Arafat's compound and other areas previously transferred to the Palestinian Authority. The US policy of leaving matters to Israel and the Palestinians had achieved little. When, like several American presidents before him, Bush II was drawn into the machinations of the Israel–Palestinian dispute and became engaged, he exercised the authority of the United States and was able to attain a desired, albeit limited, outcome against domestic opposition.

Re-engagement occurred within the context of America's ambition to topple Saddam Hussain, and Bush II formally committed to a two-state solution to the Israel–Palestinian dispute. A need to assure the support of Arab states for the Iraq policy of the United States does not wholly explain the president's change in direction, for there were differences of opinion within his Administration. Some senior figures believed that primacy ought to be accorded to the commonality between Israeli action in the occupied territories and the war against terrorism, while Bush II's domestic constituency was critical of aspects of his policy that appeared to diminish the wholehearted commitment of the United States to Israel. Although he was prepared to apply pressure to Israel *in extremis*, particularly to protect the Church of the Nativity and to ensure that Arafat was not sent into exile or killed, cooperation with Israel was his generally preferred choice.

The United States identified with a general view of the need to improve the Palestinian Authority's system of governance and transparency and its power was employed to help achieve that. The inducement of a further United States initiative to resolve the dispute was offered, but kept beyond reach until Arafat's involvement in the management of the PA had been circumscribed.

The United States participation in the Quartet's production of the roadmap shows that Bush II had concluded that his predecessor's proprietary attitude to the peace process was limiting. Even as it was being made public, the Administration was resiling from some of its provisions in order to accommodate Israeli objections, diminishing its probable contribution to the peace process. This may yet prove to be academic, as rejectionist Palestinian organisations were no more persuaded of its value than that of any other instrument of the peace process. Also, considerable scepticism has been entertained about the intention of the United States in launching the roadmap, coming as it did only six weeks after its invasion of Iraq.

The cycle of violence and retribution between the Palestinians and Israel inhibited Bush II, as it had his predecessor. He was confronted with differing agendas by the Palestinian Authority and the militant Palestinian organisations active in the field, and the Authority's inability to impose its dominance. The multiplicity of targets confused the situation, and the relational nature of American power in respect of each became diffused. Bush II judged that he would be unable to command acquiescence and backed off. After Arafat's death, the United States supported moves by Abbas to bring some measure of unity to the Palestinian forces and a ceasefire between them and the IDF, but the attempt failed because of continuing differences among the Palestinian elements.

The United States recitation of the 'cease hostilities' mantra came to be confounded with Sharon's insistence on the primacy of Israel's security from Palestinian attacks. Sharon concluded that no agency within the Palestinian community had the necessary power to assure his country's security and that Israel should embark upon a policy of unilateral disengagement from the Palestinians. When he began to do so, he seems to have taken the United States by surprise, and the United States was left to make the most of the situation. It criticised the ICJ's departure from established principle when considering the validity of the West Bank barrier, but Bush II temporised on its construction. He equivocated, expressing a hope that its existence would prove temporary while recognising a requirement for excisions beyond the 1967 'green line' if major Israeli settlements were to be incorporated into the State of Israel. Israel's withdrawal from the Gaza Strip and northern parts of the West Bank were somewhat lamely received by the Quartet as a step in the direction of the roadmap's destination, and they hoped that it would lead there.

Although at times irritated by Israeli policies, Bush II's support for Israel was certain. Clinton was hailed as the best friend Israel had ever had, but he was concerned that the Palestinian claim should be fairly considered. Bush II's position has been more pragmatic. His support for Israel has to be read within a regional context. He has been prepared to criticise Israel publicly, and in doing so to go against the grain of his supporters. But in acquiescing in Sharon's unilateral disengagement he has shown that in politics, as in the market place, rewards belong to the strongest.

NOTES

1 Republican National Convention (2000).
2 Bush, G.W. (2000).
3 Suskind (2004) pp.70–2.
4 See note 56 at the end of Chapter 5.
5 US Department of State (2001).
6 Report of the Sharm el-Sheikh Fact-Finding Committee (Mitchell Report).
7 Government of Israel, Ministry of Foreign Affairs (2001).
8 United Nations (2004a).
9 Sciolino and Tyler (2001).
10 Powell (2001).
11 Mearsheimer and Walt (2006).
12 Project for the New American Century (2001).
13 Project for the New American Century (2002).
14 Human Rights Watch (2004).
15 Hammami (2002).
16 Government of Israel (2002); United Nations (2002) para.56 cites 23 Israelis and 52 Palestinians as having been killed in the battle, adding that '[a] senior Palestinian Authority official alleged in mid-April that some 500 were killed, a figure that has not been substantiated in the light of the evidence that has emerged'; Bregman (2005) p.205 states that '[t]en per cent of [Jenin] camp was totally destroyed, with approximately 150 buildings razed to the ground and many others left structurally unsound. Some 4000 Palestinians became homeless.' He quotes the same number of persons killed as in the UN Secretary General's Report.
17 The Popular Front for the Liberation of Palestine had claimed responsibility for the assassination and the Palestinian Authority had condemned it.
18 UN Security Council Resolution 1405, adopted 19 April 2002.
19 Bush, G.W. *Public Papers, 2002*, Appendix A. pp.1094–1103.
20 UN Security Council Resolution 1397, adopted 12 March 2002 14–0 (with Syria abstaining).
21 UN Security Council Resolution 1402, adopted 30 March 2002 14–0.
22 UN Security Council Resolution 1403, adopted 4 April 2002 unanimously.
23 Bregman (2005) p.198.
24 Ibid. p.202.
25 Ibid. p.211.
26 Ibid. p.209. This emerged during a visit by Crown Prince Abdullah to President Bush's ranch in Texas on 25 April 2002.

27 Ibid. p.213.
28 Mearsheimer and Walt (2006).
29 Bush, G.W. *Public Papers, 2002*, Appendix A. pp.1094–1103.
30 Council of Arab States (2002).
31 Bush, G.W. *Public Papers, 2002*, p.528.
32 Ibid. pp.632–3.
33 Kesler (2006); Bush, G.W. *Public Papers, 2002*, p.360. Bush made a similar point when he said that 'there's got to be a vision for peace. There's got to be more than security.'
34 Bush, G.W. *Public Papers, 2002*, p.733.
35 Klein (2003) pp.194–212.
36 Bush, G.W. (2002).
37 Khalidi and Butler (2002); Dunn (2004).
38 Klein (2003) pp.204–5.
39 Palestinian National Authority (2003).
40 UN Security Council Resolution 1435, adopted 24 September 2002 14–0 (with USA abstaining).
41 Benn, A. (2002).
42 A Performance-based Roadmap to a Permanent Two-State Solution to the Israeli–Palestinian Conflict 2003. The roadmap seeks an end to the Israeli occupation that began in 1967, and includes an agreed, just, fair and realistic solution to the refugee issue, and a negotiated resolution on the status of Jerusalem that takes into account the political and religious concerns of both sides, and protects the religious interests of Jews, Christians and Muslims worldwide; that fulfils the vision of two states, Israel and a sovereign, independent, democratic and viable Palestine, living side-by-side in peace and security; and that attracts Arab state acceptance of full normal relations with Israel and security for all the states of the region in the context of a comprehensive Arab–Israel peace.
43 Washington File (2003).
44 Schanzer (2003).
45 Palestine Facts (2003).
46 Schanzer (2003); Laub (2002) states that 'Israel has destroyed most of the 150 security buildings, including prisons, in the West Bank and Gaza Strip. Without bases, the roughly 50 000 security agents and police officers roam the streets, stay at home or work from tents.'
47 Cordesman (2005) pp.166–7. The approximate figures for the Palestinian forces operating in the West Bank and Gaza Strip in 2000: (*pro-PLO*) Palestinian Authority – 35 000; Fatah Tanzim – 3500; Al-Aqsa Martyrs' Brigade – unknown; and (*anti-PLO*) Palestinian Islamic Jihad – 350; Hamas – 300; Popular Front for the Liberation of Palestine-Special Command – 100.
48 Geneva Accord 2003; *The New York Times on the Web* (2003); statement by Hanan Ashrawi on *7.30 Report*, Australian Broadcasting Corporation, 4 November 2003.
49 Bregman (2005) p.280.
50 United Nations (2003a). Only 11 per cent of the wall's length will run along the 1949 armistice line. It will be 687 km long and is estimated to cost $4.7 million per kilometre to build. It will annex 14.5 per cent of West Bank land into Israel. Approximately 680 000 Palestinians, or close to 30 per cent of the Palestinian population in the West Bank, will be directly affected by the wall; Said (2003); Sheehan (2003).
51 United Nations (2003b).
52 *Guardian* (2004); *BBC News* (2004).
53 United Nations (2004b). Adopted 20 July, 150–6–10.
54 Israeli Supreme Court (2004).
55 Bush (2004).
56 *BBC News* (2003).
57 *CNN.com* (2004b).
58 Bush (2004).
59 *CNN.com* (2004c).
60 Group of Eight (2004).
61 *CNN.com* (2004b).

62 *CNN.com* (2004a).
63 The vote was 59 in favour, 40 against with 5 abstentions.
64 Government of Israel (2005).
65 Hamas secured 60 per cent of the seats in the Palestinian Legislative Assembly, but only 70 per cent of the population of registered voters cast their ballots, and only 40 per cent of them voted for Hamas.
66 *CNN.com* (2006).
67 Bush (2006). The president said: 'Elections are vital, but they are only the beginning. Raising up democracy requires the rule of law, and protection of minorities, and strong, accountable institutions that last longer than a single vote'.
68 International Press Center (2006).
69 *Economist* (2006c). Advocates of the proposition include members of Hamas and Fatah. At its core is a suggestion that Hamas become a member of the PLO, the umbrella body that includes the PA and which officially recognises Israel. Hamas has been trying to become a member of the PLO, though it wants changes to the PLO first.

8. Vision and reality: a *post hoc* evaluation

The power of the United States was projected over some 15 years, with varying degrees of engagement, to effect a peaceful settlement of the Arab–Israel dispute. There was a widespread hope in the early 1990s that the authority and incomparable resources of the United States would be employed to good effect. Its failure to achieve its objective suggests a need to examine the efficacy of the projection of United States power. The *post hoc* evaluation undertaken in this chapter addresses the acts by which one actor influences another; the capabilities utilised for that purpose; and the responses solicited.[1] The methodology starts with an analysis of the objective of the United States and the relevance of the negotiating structure it devised in order to achieve it. It then notes any constraints upon the ability of the United States to attain its objective. This will be followed by an analysis of the effectiveness with which the instruments of statecraft discussed in Chapter 1 were employed by Bush I, Clinton and Bush II, noting their disinclination to use all of them. That analysis includes also an appreciation of how unintended consequences were addressed where they arose.

This evaluation is a preparatory contribution to the discussion in the Conclusion to this work whether the study reveals limits to the power of the United States, and whether the evaluation technique presented in this study might be more generally applicable.

THE OBJECTIVE

The salience of the Arab–Israel dispute in relation to the Middle Eastern interests of the United States was established in Chapter 1. An objective common to Bush I and Clinton was that a Middle East peace should mean a good deal more than simply the absence of hostilities. They sought a peace that would legitimate Israel's place in the region and facilitate the development of friendly relations between Israel and its neighbours.

The desirability of achieving such a peace is incontestable. What is more problematic are questions about how it might be attained, and its terms. The negotiating process was prolonged and dynamic and the United States contribution cannot be assessed solely in terms of a pre-embarkation statement of how peace might be achieved. A *post hoc* evaluation of the effectiveness of United States power must necessarily recognise that the contribution of the United States extended to both how peace might be attained and the terms of any settlement.

The negotiation structure

The United States launched a framework for bilateral and multilateral negotiations at Madrid in 1991 that was designed to facilitate the conclusion of a comprehensive settlement. It proved capable of producing a peace agreement between Israel and Jordan in 1994, and one with Syria seemed within reach in 2000. The structure could not, of itself, assure a satisfactory outcome. Arab suspicions that the multilateral channel might legitimise Israeli economic and nuclear hegemony in the region led to its disbandment in 1997. Tensions emerged during the course of the bilateral negotiations between Israel and the Palestinians and Syrians respectively, leading to periodic suspension of negotiations and their eventual demise in 2000. Under Clinton, absolute priority was accorded to protection of the Madrid process, the United States veto being employed in the UN Security Council when necessary. The United States did so principally to advance the negotiation process, not to further the interests of individual parties, although that was a collateral outcome of its action. The United States brought the parties back to the negotiating table too many times for doubt to be entertained about its commitment to the process.

A new framework was launched in 2003 by Bush II and other co-authors of the roadmap, who undertook to monitor progress toward a resolution of the dispute. The effectiveness of its mechanisms is unlikely to be tested, because it has not been possible to put a stop to conflict between the Palestinians and Israel, Bush II does not share Clinton's commitment to the cause, and Israel has decided to pursue independent policies.

The terms of any comprehensive settlement

The United States objective was both overly ambitious and imprecisely defined. Bush I launched it with a broad statement of objectives. A precise definition would have had to address the particular concerns of five different entities – Israel, Jordan, Lebanon, Syria and the Palestinians. This may have seemed prescriptive. It was ambitious in that a comprehensive settlement would involve conclusion of, at a minimum, a number of different bilateral treaties, and probably also international agreements covering regional or sub-regional issues.

Imprecision about objectives and strategies was reflected in the United States lofty claim at the outset of the process to act as an honest broker. Its confidence in bringing the parties together at Madrid was not to be matched by intent to propose a *pax americana*. Clinton implicitly endorsed Bush I's undertaking to accept whatever the parties' leaders decided would be in their national interest.[2] Bush II explicitly concurred in that approach. As the process proceeded, the partiality of the United States to Israel became increasingly evident, notwithstanding Clinton's *sotto voce* criticism of that country and Bush II's more assertive tone in the context of his pursuit of a higher regional priority.

Central to the negotiation was the desire of Lebanon and Syria to regain occupied territory and of the Palestinians to achieve independence from Israel, which was occupying their land. As the Arab parties' relationships with Israel were the focal point of the negotiation, the comparative strength of Israel in relation to that of its neighbours was a factor. Israel's predominance was such that any accommodation could only be on the basis of what Israel was prepared to concede. A *pax judaica*, negotiated within the framework of the Madrid conference, would serve the interests of the United States. By 2001, the United States had decided that no resolution of the dispute was possible that did not lead to the formation of a Palestinian state and subsequently secured Israel's concurrence in that proposition. The asymmetrical nature of the Israel–Palestinian contest was demonstrated when Israel moved unilaterally to contain the Palestinians within the Gaza Strip and part of the West Bank. The co-authors of the roadmap could do little other than claim Israeli action as transitional toward the declared two-state objective.

In reviewing the objective of the United States, it cannot be asserted that some course of action would have been more productive than the ones pursued by American presidents to 2006. Possible alternative directions at particular points have been postulated in earlier chapters. They were not tried, and there is no evidence that they were among the options considered.

CONSTRAINTS

There were a number of constraints, domestic and foreign, on the ability of the United States to effect a negotiated comprehensive settlement of the Arab–Israel dispute. The domestic constraints were either intrinsic to Clinton's and Bush II's approaches or political factors that one or other felt necessary to take into account.

Presidential predispositions toward Israel

The principal domestic constraint, common to both presidents, was their attachment to Israel. Clinton and his wife had visited the Holy Land in 1981 in the company of his pastor. The pastor had warned him that God would not forgive him if he ever forgot Israel,[3] an anecdote of sufficient significance to the president to warrant its retelling. His Administration 'was *not* about to do anything to cause an open crisis with Israel'.[4] There was a number of occasions during Clinton's presidency when chastisement of Israel, or coercion, might have pressured Israel into addressing critical issues. The president seemingly proscribed such measures; the application of the power of the United States was accordingly constrained.

Clinton's response to Israel's settlement policy provides an example of his propensity to accept a 'political' compromise rather than to uphold a principle. While opposed to the Har Homa project, Clinton was prepared to use Netanyahu's need to assure his position within his own cabinet as a means of extracting the prime minister's agreement to a further transfer of territory to the Palestinians. In return for Netanyahu's concession, the president acquiesced in the project.[5]

It was one thing for Clinton to pledge never to criticise Israel publicly, another for the United States to decline to uphold the provisions of an international agreement to which it was a signatory. Why did Clinton accord higher priority to backing Israel in the face of its clear breach of the provisions of the Fourth Geneva Convention than to upholding the Convention's normative value? Israel denies that the West Bank is occupied territory and consequently the applicability of the Convention to it, because Jordan relinquished its claim to the West Bank in 1988. There is, however, a responsible body of opinion, including UN Security Council Resolutions 242 and 338 on which the Madrid conference was based, that contests the Israeli position. This example is illustrative of choices that governments have to make when objectives collide. A frequently used diplomatic procedure is to reaffirm support for the principle in question, while refraining from naming any recalcitrant party. Clinton chose not to offer even this back-handed public rebuke. He may have feared that United States criticism would have given Netanyahu an excuse to jettison the peace process.

Bush II trusted Sharon and was disposed to leave matters in the prime minister's hands. It was only when he judged the IDF's actions to have gone too far that the United States associated with other members of the UN Security Council in demanding restraint. The president was also opposed to Israel's continued building of settlements in the West Bank. United States criticism of Israel was tempered: Bush II characterised the West Bank barrier as a temporary security measure, and neoconservatives within the Administration persuaded him to change his mind while Powell was on a mission to deliver a critical message to Israel and the Palestinians that he had authorised.

America's pro-Israel lobby

Extrinsic to the presidents was the need to retain the support of America's pro-Israel lobby. Political parties in the United States are, of course, attuned to the views and representations of special interest groups, and the pro-Israel lobby is an active and effective agent. The lobby derives from a congruence of support for Israel among America's Jewish community and that of fundamentalist Christianity, backed by defence industry interests, and uses America's democratic processes very effectively. The lobby is not monolithic: it is open to the competing claims of forces in support of, or opposition to, Israeli governments. Rabin had championed the creation of the Israel Policy Forum in an attempt to offset the influence of the American Israel Public Affairs Committee (AIPAC). In the final stages of the negotiation of 'Oslo II', Israel's Labor government had to exercise such influence as it could muster within the lobby to counter a campaign launched by its opposition to discourage the provision of US assistance for Palestinian economic and social development. Bush II had to confront the Christian 'right' with his two-state objective and refusal to acquiesce in further settlement building in the vicinity of East Jerusalem, which seemingly denied his fundamentalist supporters' dispensationalist belief.

Congressional constraints

Domestic constraints were imposed upon Clinton by the Congress. He failed domestically to sell an Arab–Israel peace as a strategic interest of the United States.[6] An inability to articulate a clear foreign policy objective, together with a decline in public interest in international affairs, left the field open to media-wise special interest groups, like AIPAC.[7] After the mid-term election of 1994, he faced a Republican-dominated Congress for the remainder of his presidency. Yet he was able to form temporary coalitions with centrist Democrats and Republicans to secure support for a number of his foreign policy objectives[8] and could have tried to forge a centrist coalition to strengthen his presentation of a United States position on the terms of any peace settlement. The president was able several times to secure congressional authority to extend inducements to Israel. Might not the inducements have been accompanied by forceful argument in favour of a preferred course of action? Might not Clinton have approached the Congress about assistance to Israel to overcome Israel's water shortage, thus addressing one of the concerns in relation to a settlement with Syria; or for additional funds to build housing settlements *within* Israel, thus attempting to deflect the Israeli government away from further demographic change in the West Bank? Such initiatives would have afforded the United States leverage in its dealings with the parties concerned.

US aid to Jordan, the Palestinians and Syria was either proscribed or restricted, limiting the ability of the United States to garner support through positive sanctions. Bush I recognised that Jordan's participation was essential to any comprehensive settlement and, against congressional opposition, provided food aid to that country as part of its process of re-establishing friendly relations after the 1991 Gulf War. The incorporation of Jordan into the negotiation framework was to be rewarded by the conclusion of a peace treaty between Israel and Jordan. Some American aid was channelled to the Palestinian Authority, although, respecting congressional constraints, project implementation was largely through American non-governmental agencies. Clinton largely circumvented this constraint by mobilising international assistance for the Palestinians, and the Europeans became the principal donor to the Authority. A casualty was the proposition that the United States might station a military observer force on the Golan Heights should Israel and Syria agree on the terms of a peace settlement and seek such help. A ruthless campaign within the Congress brought any thought of a US presence on the Golan Heights to an end.

Some congressional requirements that might have seemed proscriptive proved capable of being employed to strengthen United States leverage, especially in relation to the Palestinians. A legislative prohibition on dealing with the PLO was paraded to persuade the PLO to abjure terrorism and excise denial of Israel's right to exist from the Palestine National Charter as a precondition for United States recognition. After the passage of the Middle East Peace Facilitation Act, the demand for regular congressional reviews of Palestinian policies was used to encourage Arafat to conform to its prescriptions.

The Congress favoured the relocation of the Embassy of the United States from Tel Aviv to Jerusalem. Land had been allocated in Jerusalem for that purpose. Hillary Clinton supported the congressional view when campaigning for election to the Senate, leading her husband to distance himself from her position. He cited legislation that permitted members of the Congress, and those seeking election to it, to express their own opinions without constraining the authority of the executive branch, and set the matter aside.[9]

United States engagement elsewhere in south-west Asia and the continuing Israel–Palestinian conflict meant that the scope for initiatives relating to the two parties was circumscribed during Bush II's presidency and few congressional constraints were attached to his handling of the matter.

External constraints – terrorism

The principal external constraint to confront Clinton and Bush II was terrorist activity against Israel conducted by individuals and groups opposed to the peace process. At various times and in varying measure Israelis, Lebanese and Palestinians were either determined to derail the process or accorded higher priority to their immediate interests than to the prospect offered at some remove by a negotiated settlement. A need to prevent the process of negotiation from foundering became a major preoccupation of the two presidencies. As the process was designed to bring peace, this phenomenon is discussed in greater detail in the section below on unintended consequences.

External constraints – international differences

There were two other external constraints upon the United States's freedom of action. The United States and Israel had long shared the view that the intrusion of other states into a peace process could be unhelpful. The United States wished to keep the reins of the peace process in its own hands. The international conference at Madrid in 1991 was as far as either was prepared to go in accommodating internationalisation of the issue. The co-optation of European assistance by the United States was not without complication because the Europeans viewed the Arab–Israel dispute differently from the Americans.[10] The Europeans had taken the initiative in commissioning the World Bank to prepare an estimate of the needs of the Palestinian Authority, and they were interested in the prospect offered for regional economic development through the multilateral working group that they chaired. Clinton's convening of an international pledging conference predicated on the World Bank's estimates, without the Europeans' co-sponsorship, and his attempt to exclude the occupied territories from consideration within the working group chaired by the European Union on regional economic development, caused the Europeans to feel undervalued.

Britain and France and other Western members of the UN Security Council, co-sponsored a draft resolution critical of Israel's decision to build a settlement at Har Homa. In their view, settlements altered the facts on the ground and pre-empted the final status negotiations. Although the United States was to use this argument in private with Netanyahu a year later, it tried unsuccessfully to persuade the co-sponsors to employ language that would permit it to abstain when the matter was before the Council. In an all-too-evident difference of opinion within the Western alliance, the US vetoed the draft resolution.

Bush II was less proprietary in his approach to the Palestinian question. He needed the understanding of Arab states and the Islamic world for United States policies in Afghanistan and Iraq, and its contest against Iran on nuclear matters. The United States supported the UN Security Council's call for Israeli restraint in, and withdrawal from, Palestinian territory, and it joined Russia, the European Union and the UN Secretary-General in sponsorship of the roadmap.

The election of a Hamas-led government of the Palestinian Authority has exposed different appreciations of the situation. Bush II and the Europeans, the major financial benefactors of the Palestinian Authority, have called upon Hamas to cease violence and to negotiate with Israel. They have joined in proscribing financial assistance to the Palestinian Authority in order to coerce acquiescence. Russia invited Hamas representatives to visit Moscow for the purpose of urging the party to act responsibly and to keep the path open for mediation,[11] and France endorsed this move, distancing itself slightly from the European consensus.

In short, none of the three presidents enjoyed an unfettered ability to employ the power of the United States. There were domestic and international constraints upon them. The constraints were not comprehensive, however, and there remained sufficient flexibility to prosecute their objectives.

THE MEASURES EMPLOYED

These constraints provide some explanation for the presidents' reluctance to use all the instruments at the command of the United States. This section will analyse the effectiveness of those selected. Whether other instruments might have been effective is a hypothetical question: Clinton and Bush II were unwilling to employ them.

Positive sanctions

Positive sanctions may be offered either as an inducement to achieve an objective or as a reward for services rendered. The United States made extensive use of this instrument. Clinton persuaded Egypt to provide leadership on many occasions, knowing that Egypt had its own interest to serve in re-establishing its credentials among Arab states after having concluded a peace treaty with Israel in 1979, and that Egypt's economy was heavily dependent upon the annual $2 billion aid contribution from the United States. Clinton also co-opted the services of Jordan's King Hussein, who helped secure the Hebron agreement in 1997 and the conclusion of the Wye River memorandum in late 1998. Jordan became an annual recipient of United States aid after its conclusion of a peace treaty with Israel in 1994; its contribution in 1998 brought additional rewards, and a free trade agreement was concluded. Jordan, Morocco, Qatar and Tunisia received Israeli and other delegations at international economic conferences, enabling the United States to demonstrate that the peace process enjoyed regional support and to create an environment in which regional cooperation with Israel was practised and Israel's legitimacy as a neighbour was facilitated. Cairo was advanced as the location for a regional development bank, and Tunis became the headquarters of the Middle East–Mediterranean Travel and Tourism Association.

Clinton employed positive sanctions to try to induce Israel and the Palestinian Authority to reach an accommodation. At Camp David he held out the prospect of substantial United States aid, amounting to $35 billion, if the parties could conclude an agreement.[12] Even such an exceptional sum was insufficient to persuade the parties to depart from deeply held positions of principle.

Israel's sense of insecurity exposed a weakness that was susceptible of United States manipulation, and its continued cooperation with the peace process was induced a number of times by attempts to assuage its security concerns. The positive sanctions extended to the Palestinians had both a psychological and material dimension. United States aid was not voluminous, because of legislative constraints. Its value lay principally in its psychological dimension. Arafat attached great value to Clinton's participation in the peace process.[13] Bush II's espousal of a two-state solution was a signal contribution that he persuaded Israel to endorse. Although the international behaviour of the United States, especially in the UN, showed a clear bias toward Israel, its strategic partnership with Israel did not prevent either Clinton or Bush II from urging Israel to accept Palestinian positions that they held to be reasonable.

It is questionable whether the Oslo process would have lasted for as long as it did without the application of positive sanctions. Its contribution was mixed, however. Aid could underwrite agreements reached within the process and help build public support for compromises and conciliation, but it could also quickly dissipate, becoming 'life support' for recurrent policies and practices.[14] In that context, the threat of a cessation of aid could be more potent than the prospect of additional disbursements. The withdrawal of assistance to the Palestinian Authority could, however, affect agencies such as those concerned with public security that were needed by the United States and Israel to control violence and facilitate a return to negotiation.[15] Also, positive sanctions in the form of US security cooperation proved ineffective in restraining those Palestinian groups committed to violence against Israel.

Notwithstanding the volume of United States military and other assistance to Israel, Sharon was to conclude that it was either insufficient or inappropriate for addressing Israel's internal security concerns. He moved to remedy this by containing the Palestinians behind the West Bank barrier and within the Gaza Strip.

International norms

The strength of an international norm's influence in foreign relations depends upon the number of actors that share an expectation of patterns of behaviour, and how precisely the norm distinguishes between appropriate and inappropriate behaviour. Peer pressure may induce compliance where a state accords importance to its reputation, but reputation cannot guarantee observance where a state believes that some overriding interest would be compromised by doing so. In predicating a comprehensive settlement of the Arab–Israel dispute on UN Security Council Resolutions 242 and 338 and the principle of territory for peace, Bush I reaffirmed the United States's commitment to an international requirement that it had helped to shape. Not only do these resolutions command respect due to their provenance from the UN Security Council, they also fulfil the second requirement for normative behaviour in indicating that the only appropriate action would be Israel's withdrawal from territory occupied during the 1967 and 1973 wars. The demand for Israel's withdrawal from Lebanon is the subject of UN Security Council Resolution 425. An expectation of Israeli behaviour in relation to occupied territory is also expressed in the Fourth Geneva Convention. States hold that Israel is obligated by its subscription to the UN Charter and to the Convention to observe Security Council resolutions and the provisions of the Convention.

The international community adopted a series of progressively more insistent demands for the cessation of Israeli settlement activity based upon an almost universal understanding of the Fourth Geneva Convention. The intent was to shame the United States and Israel (and Micronesia) that alone stood in the way of universal acceptance of its normative value, and to embarrass the United States into pressuring Israel to acquiesce in its demand that settlement activity be stopped. Although Clinton urged Netanyahu to desist, the United States denied any role for the international community in determining an outcome in this matter, and used its veto in the UN Security Council to that effect. The United States also tried in 1994 to have all General Assembly resolution language referring to final status issues dropped.[16] Clinton's failure to endorse the application of the Convention to the occupied territories diminished the worth of a norm in international relations that the United States had helped to forge and that it might, conceivably, wish to uphold under other circumstances. In turn, the erosion of the norm weakened the strength of his argument that Israel desist from practices that were altering the bases of any final status agreement while the parties were proceeding toward its negotiation.

Again, the United States was prepared to forgo the moral force of an international regime as either the basis for, or as supplementary to, the projection of its power in relation to the Nuclear Non–proliferation Treaty (NPT). In closing down debate within the Arms Control and Regional Security (ACRS) working group, greater credence was given to shielding Israel from international pressure to subscribe to the NPT than to the universality of an international regime that the United States was championing.

Bush II was also to subordinate a normative requirement in order to satisfy Israel. Israel's construction of the West Bank barrier contravenes the essential requirement of UN Security Council Resolution 242 that it withdraw from occupied territory, and effectively demarks a border that has yet to be agreed. Both the International Court of Justice and the UN General Assembly have condemned its construction and an Israeli court has demanded alteration to some of its intended route. But the United States has not challenged the validity of the barrier.

Persuasion

The purpose of persuasion is to appeal to the national interest of the target state, which may involve encouraging the target state to change its perception of its national interest or to conform to international standards of behaviour. Persuasion may take different forms. Its moral element may be subsumed within normative behavioural expectations, while the application of a punitive or coercive element lies within the compass of negative sanctions. A political element was the measure most frequently employed by the United States in seeking to foster a settlement between Israel and its neighbours.

Many of the ideas advanced by the United States went to getting the parties – Israel and either Syria or the Palestinians – to remain at, or to return to, the negotiating table. It was invariably successful. It was less successful in persuading them to make the accommodations necessary for peace. Dialogue, a necessary intermediate objective, was attained, but the overall objective remained out of reach. Although preoccupied with the need to keep the dialogue going, and resigned about Syria's refusal to conclude an agreement with Israel and disappointed by the failure of the Camp David meeting, Clinton never lost faith in the need for an Israel–Palestinian settlement and even advanced ideas for its solution toward the end of his presidency.

The United States became hostage to its insistence on a cessation of violence as a necessary prerequisite for negotiation. Bush II's refusal to meet with Arafat showed the depth of his resolve, and while it sent a clear signal to the Palestinians, it closed off an important avenue of communication. The United States might have used that channel to explore measures whereby the Palestinian Authority could exercise the numerical superiority of its security forces to restrain the militant Palestinian elements. The inability of both Clinton and Bush II to persuade the array of belligerent Palestinian actors to subsume their individual agendas within a common path to a negotiated peace, or to restrain their extremist behaviour, is clear evidence of a limit of the power of the United States.

Bush II was on stronger ground when he urged reform of the Palestinian Authority. Although the United States cannot claim sole credit for the outcome, public identification with the requirement acquired significance and authority from United States espousal of the need.

The roadmap, too, gained considerably from the contribution of the United States, but neither Israel nor the Palestinians have found its framework persuasive. Had it been launched before September 2000, it might have had some bearing upon the subsequent course of events. By the time of its publiccation in April 2003, circumstances had changed, United States intervention in Iraq raised questions about the US's motivation in releasing it, and Sharon was able to circumvent it.

Public diplomacy

Public diplomacy is a diffuse measure that seeks to influence foreign audiences through the projection of the differing views of individuals, organisations and governments. It is qualitatively different from governmental public information programmes. It is a vehicle for the projection of Nye's 'soft power' in that it seeks 'to entice and attract'.[17] The United States might have done more through public diplomacy and non-governmental 'second track' channels to build a constituency for its desired outcome without necessarily transgressing norms of acceptable diplomatic behaviour. It was apparent that Israel, Syria and the Palestinians had done little to prepare their peoples for the transformations that would occur were peace settlements to be achieved. Mythologies that shaped perceptions, such as the right of Palestinian refugees to return to their original homes or that Israel's security could only be assured through a maximalist land grab,[18] had to be pricked. There was a real need for the promotion of people-to-people contact.[19] The United States might have encouraged informal debate within academic and other cultural communities, nationally and internationally, about issues that could affect the outcome, the accommodations that would have to be made to achieve it, and what the future might hold.

UNINTENDED CONSEQUENCES OF NEGOTIATIONS

The negotiation produced a number of unintended consequences. The most significant of these was the extreme to which some Israeli and Palestinian perpetrators were prepared to go to ensure that the Oslo accords foundered. Opposition to the Oslo accords may have been expected, but the United States could hardly have anticipated that it would assume so trenchant a form. Palestinian rejectionists saw the Oslo accords as offering too little, which encouraged them to engage in expressive behaviour. The rejectionists were never under Arafat's control, and some may have become encouraged by

Barak's withdrawal of the IDF from southern Lebanon to believe that sustained insurgency could work to the Palestinians' advantage. That Israel would react to Palestinian civil disturbance could be anticipated, but probably not the wholesale and prolonged shutdown of the borders affecting commercial intercourse between Israel and the Palestinian territories that caused a significant decline in the living standards of Palestinians and exacerbated the situation.

Clinton described the cycle of violence and retribution as the toughest issue he had to face.[20] The United States proscribed assistance to Hamas, and committed officials to work with Israelis and Palestinians to prevent the violence. Subsequent attempts by Bush II to halt the violence and bring the parties into dialogue failed and as the level of trust between the parties dissolved, Sharon concluded that Israel should assure its own security and initiated measures unilaterally to achieve that outcome. He was able to evade American criticism by eliding his measures with the war against terrorism and presenting them as consistent with the purposes of the roadmap.

The functionalist approach championed by the United States through the economic conferences was intended to foster regional development, incorporating Israel, and to produce a win-win result for the region's inhabitants. The United States could not have foreseen that an Israeli government would work against the country's longer-term economic interests. The approach was working well until it was jeopardised by the policies of Netanyahu's government, and an apprehension emerged in some Arab states that a comprehensive settlement would establish Israeli economic hegemony in the region. The proposal for a regional bank was intended to offset Israeli predominance by assisting in the development of Arab states, but it was set aside when the multilateral channel was abandoned.

POST HOC EVALUATION

Some of the instruments of power projection having been employed by the United States, and the US having shown flexibility in moving to counter unexpected obstacles, why was it unable to achieve its objective? Three reasons are adduced: the objective of the United States was imprecise; the negotiation process was predicated upon a false expectation; and the United States was unable to persuade other parties that accommodation was in their national interests.

Imprecision, but flexibility

America's objective was presented in broad terms. Imprecision in defining the objective and tactical means of attaining it in 1991 contributed to its inability to achieve a comprehensive settlement. This is not to argue for a prescriptive outcome: flexibility was essential. Nevertheless, the wisdom of embarking upon a journey without some idea of how to get to the destination might be questioned. The roadmap of 2003 was designed to remedy this deficiency.

Clinton found that leaving matters of substance to the contesting parties was not without cost or personal embarrassment. Lacking precise objectives of his own, natural curiosity might have led him to clarify the parties' intents with a view to assisting in securing particular outcomes. Clarification was not always easy. His Administration probed for Syria's bottom line; Ross found it difficult to extract position statements from Arafat, whose negotiating technique was to withhold decision making until the last possible minute;[21] Rabin was less than frank with Christopher about the negotiation at Oslo; and Barak deliberately concealed his intent from Clinton at Camp David. When it came to his turn, Bush II was to be confused by Sharon's presentation of his objectives in terms consistent with Bush's war on terrorism.

It is hard to understand why Clinton should have permitted the office of the President of the United States of America to be used as an emissary of Israel to both Assad and Arafat without having first arrived at some understanding of Israeli intentions. He had foreseen that a comprehensive settlement would entail considerable concessions on Israel's part, but failed to establish with the Israelis the implications of Israel's ceding territory on its northern, eastern and western frontiers. The absence of agreement on so fundamental an issue added to confusion between the preference of the United States for a resolution with Syria, and Israel's ambivalence about whether to proceed with the Palestinians or Syria.

In respect of Syria, Assad might be forgiven for thinking that the basis of a settlement was at hand, having received a message from Clinton saying that he had agreement on the 4 June 1967 line in his pocket. The United States had invested heavily in the Syrian negotiation, and had brought Israel very close to acceptance of Syria's basic territorial demand. It is surprising that Clinton did not press for its conclusion. Also, he appears not to have questioned Barak's decision unilaterally to withdraw from Lebanon. Had a peace agreement been concluded between Israel and Syria – even a 'cold peace' – Lebanese and Palestinian insurgents would have been deprived of Syrian support, and the way opened for the conclusion of an agreement with Lebanon.

An agreement with Syria would have left Israel unencumbered to focus wholly on the Palestinian question. The United States would have had to convince Assad that a Syria–first strategy was intended as a forerunner of a resolution of the question of Palestine. The United States ought to have presented it to Barak as a gamble worth taking provided that an agreement could be reached with Syria about the volume of water that might be withdrawn by both parties from the Sea of Galilee and that Israel could be assured of alternative water supply.

Clinton's Administration became engaged in detailed negotiation about Palestinian territory when it helped reformulate the Hebron agreement in 1996–97. The Wye River Plantation and Camp David discussions drew the United States further into the debate about area. Following the unproductive meeting at Camp David, Clinton suggested principles that might be pursued in allocating territory between Israel and the Palestinians, but refrained from being drawn into detail. Israel's bid was to secure at least 77 per cent of the 'total area of Israel and Palestine between the Jordan river and the sea'.[22] Israeli negotiators had in mind an eventual transfer to the Palestinians 'of slightly under 90 per cent of the area of the West Bank'[23] which, were it to be accepted, would see an expansion of the area controlled by the Palestinian Authority to 21 per cent of the area of the former British mandated territory. The Palestinian Authority under Fatah sought 22 per cent.[24] The issue for the United States, no less than for the Palestinian Authority, was whether the Palestinian people could be persuaded to endorse and honour a peace agreement that offered the prospect of sovereignty and independence over less than one-quarter of their historic homeland.

As the Israel–Palestinian negotiation progressed, as the United States increased its depth of understanding, and as the actions of Palestinian rejectionists became more insistent, the United States reappraised the position it had adopted in 1991. By the end of his term Clinton had decided that 'there could be no genuine resolution to the conflict without a sovereign, viable, Palestinian state that accommodated Israel's security requirements and the demographic realities'.[25] The US policy change in favour of a two-state solution was affirmed by Bush II in November 2001, and the United States persuaded Sharon publicly to endorse it in 2003.

The policy of the United States that Jerusalem remain undivided seemingly complicated any prospect of achieving an outcome on Jerusalem acceptable to both parties. Was it originally code for acquiescence in Israel's conquest of East Jerusalem in 1967, suggesting that sovereignty over the whole city be vested in Israel? Or did Clinton's subsequent proposition that a solution might be found on the basis that 'what is Arab should be Palestinian … what is Jewish should be Israeli'[26] offer the prospect of separate sovereign areas within an undivided city? From the negotiation in early 2001 it appears that 'undivided' might be interpreted as implying unity in a municipal sense, presumably embracing a city-wide provision of services. Ideas were advanced that would have recognised the attachment of various religions to sectors of the Old City of Jerusalem, but they were submitted too late in Clinton's term for him to broker an agreement. Israeli and Palestinian negotiators were later to express the view that during the negotiations at Taba in January 2001 they had arrived at common ground on Israeli sovereignty over the Jewish quarter of the Old City and parts of the Western Wall. Even if the negotiators were to be satisfied that an agreement could be reached broadly in conformity with Clinton's proposal, they could well face a difficult task in selling it to their own domestic and religious communities.

Although imprecision about the preferred terms of the United States for any settlement enabled it to accommodate the dynamic of the negotiation and to respond flexibly to changing circumstances, a broadly expressed objective did not present an operational target. Diffusion worked against the goal's attainment.

False expectations

The second reason for the failure of the United States to secure a comprehensive settlement was that the negotiation process was founded on three significant false expectations. The United States had assumed that confidence-building measures would create sufficient trust among the parties to permit the conclusion of peace agreements; that the demography of the West Bank and East Jerusalem would not be materially altered during the negotiation; and that countries of the Middle East would find peace an attractive 'public good'.

Lasting peace could not be achieved in the absence of trust, but there was no guarantee that sufficient trust could be built. The premise was not tested in relation to Jordan, and had not been sufficiently developed in relation to Syria before negotiation with that country was aborted. In relation to the Palestinians, the building of confidence in accordance with a three-phase process over five years proved to be too protracted. Neither Israelis nor Palestinians could see immediate positive returns from the peace process, and both harboured elements that worked to see the process fail.

An expectation that demographic change in occupied territory prior to any final status negotiation was unlikely to be significant was eroded by Israel's building of settlements between East Jerusalem and its Palestinian hinterland. The United States made clear its objection to any unilateral action that would predetermine an issue that had been reserved for final status negotiations. Had Clinton chosen to do so when witnessing signature of the Declaration of Principles in 1993, he could have expressed a general expectation that nothing should be done by either party to complicate a possible resolution of the matters that had been reserved for final status negotiations. That would have been consistent with the Declaration's statement that the integrity of the West Bank and the Gaza Strip 'will be preserved during the interim period'. The Administration could then have held any recalcitrant party to account.

The omission of such a proviso on an occasion when it would have seemed appropriate to have included one complicated the United States search for an accommodation. Israel's settlements policy became a major cause for the loss of Palestinian confidence in the peace process, and the Palestinians were able to build it into a *cause célèbre* in the United Nations that the United States was unable to contain.

The United States expected that peace would introduce a 'public good' that would be attractive to the peoples of the region and beyond, and lessen the prospect of further challenges to United States national interests in the Middle East. It was hoped that the medium- to longer-term benefit of an Israeli–Palestinian settlement would be such that any opposition to its terms would be confined to the Israeli and Palestinian parliamentary systems. Palestinian violence was a manifestation of deeper grievances deriving from dispossession of Palestinian lands and humiliation arising from 'foreign' domination.[27] Violence was not the sole cause of the periodic breakdown of negotiation because the parties' aspirations differed markedly, but it was a major factor. The situation worsened during the presidency of Bush II, degenerating into warfare between Israel and the Palestinians, and a contestation for supremacy within the Palestinian community. For so long as the principal protagonists were unable to stop their fighting, any expectation of peace ushering in a region-wide 'public good' was illusory.

Persuasion, but no coercion

The third explanation for the inability of the United States to effect peace settlements between Israel and Syria and the Palestinians is that it was necessarily obliged to work through authorities that had their own dynamics. It could appeal to legislators and the public through persuasion and inducements, but it could not command. Rejection of the terms of the Oslo Declaration of Principles by Palestinian groups, and their subsequent boycott of the election of the *ra'is* and the Legislative Council in 1996, meant that Arafat's ability to carry the Palestinian community was circumscribed. He was either reluctant or unable to rein in his critics; was vulnerable to their charge of accommodating the Israelis, accepting far too little in return for what he was prepared to give up; the Oslo accords were perceived by Palestinian refugees as detrimental to their legal, national and human rights, reinforcing their sense of dispossession and disenfranchisement;[28] and his secularist policies were contrary to the religious ambitions of his Islamist opposition.

Moreover, Arafat and his Tunis-based cohort represented a 'foreign' culture, grown apart from the indigenous liberation movement that flowered in the first *intifada* in 1987. Arafat hoped to earn the support of his critics and to realise his claim to speak for all Palestinians. He felt that he could not put too much pressure on his opponents, whose opposition he had unsuccessfully tried to channel into the Palestinian legislature. When inclined to do so, he was able to exert authority over dissident groups in the West Bank and Gaza through repressive means, but had no leverage over those working from abroad.

Israel's complex political system constrained its leadership. Notwithstanding the direct popular election of its prime minister, the premier's mandate was hampered by the need to form a coalition government and vulnerability to the special interests of the minority parties within it. Both Netanyahu and Barak saw advantage in concluding a comprehensive 'Palestinian' package that might pass through the Knesset, rather than having to present serially a collection of piecemeal agreements. Clinton showed understanding of the Israel leaders' political difficulties, and concurred in their 'package' approach. Sharon was bolder: he was prepared to reshape his government and to legitimise his plans by submitting them to the Knesset. He initiated and executed a partial withdrawal from occupied territory. Bush II, who had had little input into the plan's genesis, concurred in his action.

Prior to the presidency of Bush II the United States jealously preserved the Arab–Israel peace process as a matter for its direction. It showed a marked reluctance to employ coercion in its bilateral relationship in order to achieve its objectives. Positive sanctions were preferred to negative ones. Clinton may have concluded that the commitment of the parties to the peace process was too fragile to withstand negative sanctions. This was true of Netanyahu, but not generally of the other leaders: even Assad had been coaxed into negotiation. While a policy of working constructively with the various parties toward an outcome has its attraction, a respectable argument can be made for the application of pressure in circumstances where it is seen that cooperation is not likely to produce a desired result. Clinton could have exerted pressure on Netanyahu in relation to Israel's settlements policy. He need not have employed the 'money lever' as bluntly as Bush I because the US–Israel relationship is broad-ranging and deep. He could have supported the principle that the Fourth Geneva Convention applied to the occupied territories, or he could have sought a specific appropriation to be used for the housing of Jewish *émigrés* from the former Soviet Union within Israel's 'green line'.[29] He might also have urged states contributing financially to the Palestinian Authority to impress upon Arafat the need to make a wholehearted and sustained effort to halt Palestinian violence as a condition of their continued support.

Bush II was more pragmatic than Clinton and displayed a preparedness to apply diplomatic and bilateral pressure to Israel, including through the UN Security Council, when he believed it was justified.

Clinton's disposition to shy away from exerting pressure on Israel contrasts with his exceptional resort to the UN Security Council to impose conditions on other countries. Almost 40 per cent of all resolutions adopted by the Security Council in its history to January 2001 were passed during Clinton's presidency. There are advantages in the instrumental application of a multilateral consensus where unilateral action is likely to exacerbate bilateral relations and to provoke criticism of the wielder. But the use of the United Nations by the United States sent confused or contradictory signals: in its view it was acceptable to use the Security Council to impose sanctions on Iraq in 1990–91, but unacceptable for the Council to criticise Israel; it was desirable in most cases to demonstrate American hegemony through that UN institution, but undesirable that the United Nations should play a central role in the search for a Middle East peace settlement. The consistent thread in Clinton's approach was that no external force should be permitted to interfere in the United States-designed peace process; if any pressure were to be applied to Israel, it should be by the United States and in private. Such persuasion as Clinton sought to exercise over Israel in private was insufficient to attain his goal. Doubt must be entertained about the force of his representations.[30] While he was willing to wield a big stick in multilateral company, he was less inclined to do so bilaterally. Clinton was endowed with an extraordinary capacity to reach out to people and to convey empathy with them but, as a student of leadership has commented, he was seemingly averse to conflict.[31]

Three reasons have been adduced for the failure of the United States to achieve its objective to date. They intertwine and it is difficult to identify one strand as being of greater significance than the others. There is no doubt about the strength of Clinton's commitment to the attainment of the overall objective, or that he worked for its realisation. Clinton displayed flexibility in adjusting to changing circumstances, especially the cycle of violence and retribution among Palestinians and Israelis, but was clearly reluctant to authorise coercive measures that might have assisted in the attainment of his goal. Bush II was prepared to demand the IDF's withdrawal from territory that had been transferred to the Palestinian Authority. The strength of his stand was, however, complementary to the priority given to other elements of his Middle East policy and diffused by clear differences within his Administration between the agenda of its neoconservative members and those of his first secretary of state. Bush II's inclination toward Israel, and wish to disengage from the minutiae of the Israel–Palestinian dispute cleared the way for Sharon to pursue his own agenda. The Palestinians will not be so fortunate. The United States, in association with Israel and the European Union, has proscribed financial support for the Hamas-led Palestinian Authority, raising questions about its viability and future direction.[32]

CONCLUSION

The employment of power to produce a desired outcome is a function of the wielder's choice among available resources and the efficacy with which they are used. Clinton's intent to secure a settlement was clear, but fell short of preparedness to use effectively all measures available to him to achieve his objective. He used the UN Security Council to impose negative sanctions on other states, but preferred to extend positive sanctions to Middle Eastern actors to encourage them to move forward. He was not prepared to put the United States relationship with Israel under strain, or to press the boundaries of his own relationship with the pro-Israel domestic lobby on Middle Eastern issues. He was not disposed to maximise the support of his European partners on certain issues where it would have seemed appropriate to do so, nor was he willing to associate himself with a legal interpretation, which commanded almost universal support, about the responsibilities of an occupying power. He could have used the weight of the European Union or wider international community to strengthen the force of his own representations, but chose not to do so. And he was reluctant to advance ideas of his own until far too late in the process to be able to influence their acceptance. It was not until the Wye River meeting in late 1998 that he became intimately involved in the negotiation process. He was to do so again at Shepherdstown in early 2000, at Camp David in the middle of that year, and in the ensuing months. His direct engagement in detail thus occurred so late in his presidency that there was insufficient opportunity to bring appropriate United States pressure to bear. The opportunity to prosecute an outcome through the power of United States ideas earlier in his presidency was not effectively used.

The Clinton Administration's most significant achievement was in keeping the negotiation process alive for so long, despite obstructions and constraints. It did this principally through the efficacious employment of positive sanctions. The process was in danger of collapse in 1997. Had it done so, it would have been extremely difficult to persuade the parties to recommit to negotiation. It was difficult enough in 1998 to get Arafat and Netanyahu back to the table under the existing structure after a year's estrangement, without having (in all probability) to devise and obtain regional concurrence in a new structure. Criticism of the Administration's actions in the United Nations and in relation to the Fourth Geneva Convention needs to be tempered by acknowledgement of this. Events since September 2000 have validated Clinton's focus on keeping the process alive, because history has now shown that it could not be reactivated after the *al-Aqsa intifada* had begun.

Clinton's greatest failing was his inability to persuade the parties to reach the accommodations necessary for peace. This was partly because he eschewed coercion as a tool. Clinton did not apply that measure to the Israeli government or urge the European Union to coerce the Palestinian Authority, presumably fearing that negative sanctions, when applied to Israel in particular, might prove counterproductive. Positive sanctions had proven useful, but without the countervailing threat of negative sanctions the United States power of persuasion was circumscribed. The utility of positive or negative sanctions as instruments of power lies in the target state's uncertainty about their application. Clinton's consistent use of the one, without employing or threatening the use of the other, removed the element of unpredictability and diminished their combined force.

Constraints that bore upon the actions of the United States included Clinton's need to be sensitive to domestic opinion; an obligation to deal with foreign actors who held strongly to perceptions of their national interests; and a requirement to address the involvement of Iran and Syria which supported groups that rejected the Oslo accords. The United States was generally able either to circumvent legislative restrictions by co-opting the services of other states, or to use congressional restraints to maximise its leverage. External actors' perceptions of their national interests proved particularly difficult to overcome. Prime examples were Clinton's failure to dissuade Peres from his adventure in Lebanon, or Netanyahu from his settlement activity, and his failure to sustain regional economic cooperation in the context of Arab apprehension of Israel and displeasure with its practices.

In choosing jealously to direct the process, the United States cut itself off from a possible source of independent advice and assistance. Consultation and cooperation among allies might have led to a more careful examination of the negotiation process and identification of appropriate tactics. On some important matters relating to Israeli objectives, this may have exposed the need for clarification before Clinton embarked on certain courses of action at Israel's bidding.

This *post hoc* evaluation has identified reasons for the failure of the United States to achieve a comprehensive settlement of the Arab–Israel dispute. By the time Bush II had taken office, the opportunity for the United States to effect this had passed and the issue had contracted to its Palestinian core. His contribution was constrained by an initial disposition to disengage from the matter, due in no small measure to his appreciation that the raging conflict between militant Palestinians and Israel could not be halted. The United States only intervened under his direction when he judged that Israeli retaliation had gone too far, and in doing so challenged the inclination of his domestic constituency. Bush II engaged intermittently in the search for a resolution of the Israel–Palestinian dispute. The timing and thrust of his interventions were largely subordinate to the other ambitions of the United States in the Middle East. Nothing should be done in relation to Israel and the Palestinians that could jeopardise the cause of regime change in Iraq. Despite an apparent commonality of purpose among Palestinians, Israelis and Americans on a need for reform of the Palestinian Authority, Bush II's insistence on an improvement in its governance owed less to his professed interest in democratisation than to a desire to encourage the development of a competent and reliable institution with which Israel and the international community could treat. The missing element in the Palestinian equation was an instrumentality that would be prepared to impose its authority over extremist elements. Once remedial action was in train, Bush II produced the roadmap to a two-state resolution of the conflict. The timing of its release, after the invasion of Iraq, led many to doubt the sincerity of his purpose. Scepticism about the purposes of the United States, Israel's sidelining of the proposal while pursuing an independent agenda in the Gaza Strip, and the new Israeli government's desire to continue with Sharon's legacy of unilateral withdrawal from selected bits of occupied territory, have laid it to rest.

This evaluation has addressed significant issues on which the United States has sought to influence parties to the Arab–Israel dispute, the capabilities that American presidents chose to employ in pursuit of their objectives, and responses that were elicited. Power is not an absolute: its capacity to produce an outcome is a function of circumstances, the effective utilisation of available resources, and leadership. Its limits may be exposed by the effectiveness of the application of available resources under particular circumstances, but circumstances vary. Not even the most determined and effective utilisation of resources will produce a desired outcome in every case. A target state may be able to evade, directly or indirectly, the effect(s) of the wielder's power. The failure of the United States to achieve an objective does not necessarily, therefore, expose the limits of its power. What this study has shown is that the presidents failed to marshal and apply effectively all of the available resources at the disposal of the United States in order to persuade the parties principal to accommodate one another. There may be lessons that could be learned from this analysis about the effective projection of American power that could be susceptible of more general application. The Conclusion will suggest that this is the case.

NOTES

1 Holsti (1988) p.142.
2 Baker (1991b) p.149.
3 Clinton, W.J. *Public Papers, 1998*, p.2172.
4 Cobban (1999) p.47 cites her interview with the head of Policy Planning at the State Department. Original emphasis.
5 Ross (2004) p.467. Clinton said: 'We weren't going to stop him on Har Homa now, so I thought we should get what we could for it.'
6 Haass and Telhami (1999).

7 Haass (1997) p.116.
8 Ibid. p.116.
9 Clinton, W.J. *Public Papers, 1999*, pp.1410–11.
10 European Community (1980) which asserts the right of the Palestinian people to self-determination.
11 Danilova (2006).
12 Lasensky (2004) p.211.
13 Clinton (2004) p.929.
14 Lasensky (2004) p.230.
15 Ibid. p.229.
16 El-Fassad (2000).
17 Nye (2002).
18 Ross (2004) p.337*n*.
19 Ibid. p.770.
20 Clinton, W.J. *Public Papers, 1995*, p.468.
21 Interview with Dennis B. Ross in Washington DC on 20 April 2001.
22 MidEast Web (2003) p.1. Israel's exclusion of certain areas from the base figure from which calculations are made affects the calculation.
23 Ibid. p.3
24 Bennet (2003).
25 Clinton, W.J. *Public Papers, 2001*, p.33.
26 Ibid. p.33.
27 Pape (2003). Pape's study shows that 'the raw number of suicide attacks is climbing ... even while the rates of other types of terrorism actually declined' over the period 1980–2001, and that 'nearly all suicide terrorist campaigns have in common ... a specific secular and strategic goal: to compel liberal democracies to withdraw military forces from territory that the terrorists consider to be their homeland.'
28 Bowker (2003) p.160.
29 Government of Israel, Ministry of Immigrant Absorption (2006). While the number of immigrants into Israel steadily declined over the decade of the 1990s from its peak in 1990–91, the percentage of immigrants from the former Soviet Union remained at 74.4 per cent in Clinton's last year in office.
30 George and George (1998) p.247.
31 Ibid. p.247; Webster (1999).
32 Erlanger (2006).

9. Conclusion

When the United States articulated its vision of a global society of states it identified an 'enlargement of the world's free community of market democracies'[1] as its primary objective, which it would hope to realise through American leadership and international cooperation. Human rights would be advanced through the process of democratic enlargement. This view was broadly held in common by Presidents Bush I, Clinton and Bush II. The United States would capitalise on the demise of bipolarity, maximising the opportunity extended by the unipolar moment to realise this vision. An implicit thread in Clinton's foreign policy was a belief that states recognise certain interests and cooperate in their achievement. Such matters have been addressed by scholars in their studies of international relations. Clinton's practice reflected the views of academic 'Rationalists' such as Hedley Bull.[2] Like members of the 'Realist' school, Clinton asserted that power matters,[3] but vowed that the United States would not seek to extend its reach by force.[4] Rather, it pursued a syncretic approach somewhat akin to that envisaged by the British theoretician E.H. Carr when he looked to peaceful change in international relations effected 'on that uneasy compromise between power and morality which is the foundation of all political life'.[5] Albright was to confirm, on the basis of her service at the United Nations and in the State Department, that in the current era no president or secretary of state could manage events without combining Wilsonian idealism and geopolitical realism.[6] Her observation was as apposite to the presidency of Bush II as to that of Clinton. While both presidents sought an enlargement of the number of democratic states, Bush II has been prepared to use force to displace dictatorships in Afghanistan and Iraq before overseeing the installation of ostensibly democratic regimes. Differences of agendas and priorities have distinguished between Clinton and Bush II at the conceptual level, while emphases and means have provided contrasting approaches.

Bush I and his two successors saw a settlement of the Arab–Israel dispute as sitting within the global vision of the United States of a post-Cold War world order. Bush II was, however, to accord higher priority to other international issues. For Bush I and Clinton a peaceful resolution of the dispute would demonstrate that under US hegemony a new world order could bring benefit to the Middle East by diminishing the likelihood of another conflict developing between Israel and its neighbours that would adversely impact upon United

States interests and disturb the tenuous pattern of regional cooperation established during the 1991 Gulf War. Concern about a possible adverse regional impact also motivated Bush II. He needed to garner the support of Arab and Islamic states as he mounted his case for and prosecuted the removal of Saddam Hussain's autocratic regime in 2003. But by the time of his election in 2000, the grandiose vision of Bush I and Clinton of a peaceful and comprehensive settlement of the Arab–Israel dispute had contracted to its Israeli and Palestinian core and violence between the two parties was escalating into open warfare. Despite some reluctance to become involved, Bush II could not escape the need to advance ideas both to restrain the conflict and to produce a credible outcome. His projection of the power of the United States to shape the end product and to determine how to arrive at it ameliorated, to some limited extent, his inability to effect a cessation of hostilities.

The three presidents sought to effect change through the projection of the unrivalled power of the United States. Bush II did not hesitate to project power through physical means where he believed it necessary, but power is more commonly exercised though other means. The power of the United States has been used in the Middle East in the expectation of producing the presidents' desired outcomes. 'Costs' might have to be borne by both the United States and its targets. It is assumed that a state's power is projected in the expectation that it can affect others more than they can affect it. A publicly accountable government, such as that of the United States, might be presumed to embark upon such a course only after undertaking an analysis of costs and benefits, but the extent to which this informed United States action in Iraq under Bush II is questionable.

The United States employed instruments from among the range identified by David Baldwin[7] in pursuit of a settlement of the Arab–Israel dispute. It used some more effectively than others, but declined to use the full range at its disposal. That it was unable to achieve its goal would not surprise Kenneth Waltz, who has declared that 'powerful agents fail to impress their will on others in just the way they intend to',[8] or Herbert Simon, who has concluded that '[a]ttainment of objectives is *always* a matter of degree'.[9] But the authors might have expected that the United States, having decided on a course of action, would employ all reasonable means at its disposal to achieve its goal. It seems unlikely that in developing their theses they would have entertained the prospect of an agent prosecuting its objective with one hand behind its back, which is what happened when both Clinton and Bush II eschewed coercion and the threat or employment of negative sanctions in relation to a resolution of the Israel–Palestinian dispute.

Did Clinton's and Bush II's decisions not to use all appropriate instruments suggest a lack of commitment to the attainment of a peace settlement? Glib assumptions have been made about the United States only exerting sufficient authority over Israel to satisfy Arab oil producers that it was doing something to address Palestinian grievances, or that the United States was constrained by the influence of the pro-Israel domestic lobby. The *post hoc* evaluation does not support so cynical a view. Given the different ambitions of the two presidents and the different circumstances under which they were pursued, different answers must be expected in relation to each.

Clinton never gave up on his efforts to bring the parties back to the negotiating table. Even if his expectation that face-to-face encounters could produce results was overly optimistic, movement was impossible without it. And it is a matter of record that negotiation did produce some positive results. Attachment to Israel, aversion to conflict, and the need to husband domestic support in the event of impeachment provide some explanation for Clinton's hesitancy about imposing negative sanctions on Israel.

These reasons do not address his failure to promote alternative measures. Nor do they address America's reluctance, apparent from the outset of the negotiation in 1991, to postulate a possible solution. The United States properly declined to *impose* a settlement: it preferred to offer bridging proposals than to propose some particular outcome. Clinton was reluctant, however, to employ the ideational power of the United States to advance terms on which a comprehensive settlement might be reached until the eve of his departure from office.

The existence of these lacunae does not expose the limits of America's power, for power was never applied. The self-selected 'no-go areas' became *ipso facto* 'no-power areas'. If the argument advanced in Chapter 8 that a *pax judaica* concluded within the Madrid framework would suit American interests is correct, why did Clinton decline to press Israel harder for it? The partial unilateral withdrawal that was to be undertaken by Sharon after the Clinton presidency was qualitatively different from an 'Israeli peace'. Clinton was prepared to back Israel in relation to the Hebron agreement, and to use the United States veto in the UN Security Council to shield the peace process, but was seemingly unable to persuade Rabin, Peres, Netanyahu or Barak that certain courses of action offered the prospect of a solution favourable to the common longer-term interests of the United States and Israel. Conclusion of a settlement with Syria, refraining from attacking Lebanon, and deferring withdrawal from Lebanon until after reaching an agreement with Syria, are cases in point.

The answer seems to lie in Clinton's reliance upon a relatively small company of advisers who were engulfed in the minutiae of the negotiation process, preoccupied by a necessity to keep it alive and to get reluctant parties back to the table, and obsessed with a fear that a breakdown of the process would leave the United States looking 'impotent'.[10] A well-worn approach of aid, and yet more aid, was tried – especially to accommodate

Israel's insecurities – rather than explore an effective use of resources through careful targeting. The provision of fighter aircraft to Israel could have little direct bearing on the peace process; a diversion of settlement construction away from the West Bank, or investment in alternative water supply, could.

Clinton's personal commitment to Israel and his numerous interventions ostensibly to protect the peace process led to questioning of the credentials of the United States as an honest broker. Despite its initial profession of that role, the United States was never an honest broker. A state exercises its power to protect, or to advance, its national interests. There are many means by which it may do so, but moral considerations and pretence of judicial impartiality do not normally inform the projection of power. It was Secretary of State Baker who claimed that the United States would be an honest broker, but the framework that he instituted at Madrid formalised the disparity between Israel and the Palestinians. Although both Israeli and Palestinian negotiators understood that the US–Israel partnership was inviolate, they were to learn that Clinton, in particular, was deeply committed to a negotiated resolution of their differences, which he believed to be in the national interest of the United States. They saw that he could not be deflected from that objective and that he was prepared to employ some of the instruments at the disposal of the United States to that end. They were more receptive to his contribution – albeit a partial one – than many external observers and persons within their constituencies who hankered after a 'judicial' American fiat. The efficacy of Clinton's contribution must be read in that context, not Baker's questionable undertaking. Nor could there be any doubt among Palestinians about Bush II's predilection toward Israel: his characterisation of Sharon as a 'man of peace' ensured that. Moreover, although prepared to make senior officials available to facilitate a ceasefire and to advance ideas, Bush II has never aspired to honest brokerage as his detached and episodic contribution shows. There is a qualitative difference between Bush's authorisation of chastisement of Israel in the UN Security Council, and the application of negative sanctions to the Hamas government with the intent of effecting its recognition of and cooperation with Israel.

Bush I's vision of a comprehensive settlement of the Arab–Israel dispute had all but vanished by the time his son took office in 2001. All that was left of the vision were parameters devised by Clinton within which a possible resolution of the Palestinian question might be found, a reduction that was important nevertheless because it addressed the issue at the core of the dispute. Bush I had left several Middle East issues unresolved at the end of his presidency. The Arab–Israel dispute was one of them. Another, in the eyes of his son, was an apparent regional threat posed by Iraq. It was judged by Bush II to be of signal importance, especially after the attacks on the

American homeland in September 2001. The group that attacked the World Trade Center and the Pentagon was argued to have some linkage with Iraq. Bush II's focus on Iraq did not prevent the United States, however, from exercising its good offices to bring about a cessation of hostilities between Israel and the Palestinians, or to advance ideas about the shape of a realistic outcome and the means of getting there. But his practice of sporadic engagement left the field to Israel as the dominant party. Israel took advantage of this, skilfully pursuing its own objective within the framework of the United States war against terrorism, which commanded bipartisan support in America and transcended the pro-Israel coalition of American Jewry and the Christian 'right'.

It is unlikely that the United States vision of an enlargement of the community of democratic states could determine its course of action in the Middle East. Indeed, it is questionable whether this aspiration could offer a real direction for foreign policy because in too many situations democracy could not be given a central place.[11] Its application in the Middle East rested on an assumption that economic cooperation would fuel demand for political liberalisation within Arab states. That was a very long-term proposition, and a questionable one. The Middle East and North Africa Economic Conferences might facilitate development and regional cooperation, but it is debatable whether they could produce a regional contribution to an enlargement of the world's community of market democracies. Strong self-preservation instincts within autocratic Arab regimes would need to be overcome. In the end, the functionalist approach failed not because it could not realise United States expectations, but because of regional mistrust of the policies of the Israeli government and fear of Israel's probable predominance in a peaceful Middle East.

In the circumstances, Clinton had little choice but to conform to Tony Smith's 'selective liberal democratic internationalism'[12] in the Middle East. Albright concluded in her memoir that the United States 'should have had the vision to risk upsetting traditional friends in the Middle East by pressing for democratisation within the Arab world'.[13] That was never a realistic option. The one opportunity open to Clinton to inject an elected and accountable government into the region was presented by the creation of the Palestinian Authority. Some of the characteristics expected of a democracy were displayed during its formation, but neither the Palestinian Authority's European backers nor Clinton's Administration was ever able to encourage it to reject the authoritarian practices of its progenitor organisation, the PLO. A high premium was accorded to a strong central system likely to be able to rein in insurgents, and Clinton was prepared to overlook transgressions of human rights by both Israelis and Palestinians in his concentration on the peace process.

Bush II placed greater emphasis on the advancement of democracy than his predecessor. The United States engineered regime change in Afghanistan and Iraq, with authoritarian structures being replaced by governments ostensibly committed in varying measure to the rule of law, universal suffrage and electoral procedure. There was an expectation that the example of authoritarian displacement would command the attention of the Arab 'street' and lead to a burgeoning of democratic institutions and practices. The United States was determined that Arafat's authority over the conduct of the Palestinian Authority and its financial power should be constrained. Reform of the Authority was pressed, and promise of a further US contribution to a peaceful settlement in the form of the Quartet's roadmap withheld until after the appointment of a prime minister with executive power. In 2006, the Palestinians were to use the electoral process championed by the United States to effect a change of government, unexpectedly producing one whose philosophy was antipathetic to Israel and the United States. The United States has also urged Egypt to lead the region in democratisation. Its representations have not been successful: presidential and parliamentary elections in 2005 were marred; some 1500 Muslim Brothers were arrested during their currency; local elections were postponed; and judges who protested against vote rigging were pressured. The United States responded by suspending talks on a bilateral free-trade agreement, but it has resisted becoming too involved with the electoral prospects of Egypt's principal opposition party, the Muslim Brotherhood, whose offshoots Hamas and Palestinian Islamic Jihad have been a sword in Israel's flesh.[14] Despite the centrality accorded to democratic enlargement in his vision, Bush II has found that practicalities require that he too pursue the objective of democratic enlargement selectively.

United States diplomacy has pursued a resolution of the Arab–Israel dispute over the past 15 years, building upon lessons learned from previous endeavours. During that time the United States has occupied the focal point of a unipolar world, enjoyed for the most part a benign international environment, and commanded the sympathetic understanding and support of important regional actors and a wider international community. It sought to remedy the core issue of Palestinian grievance, while assuaging Israeli concerns about the country's security. Does the inability of the United States to attain a comprehensive settlement of the dispute have implications for the global unipolar inter-state structure? Can lessons be drawn from its failure that might be applied more generally to the projection of its power in a unipolar world?

Implications of the United States failure for the unipolar structure can be dismissed. The *post hoc* evaluation shows that Clinton and Bush II declined to maximise the potential of the instruments at their disposal, and a single study is unlikely to support so broad an extrapolation. There is at present no other state with the resources or capacity to challenge the predominance of the United

States, whether it succeeds or fails in discrete adventures. A succession of US failures to achieve objectives over time will lead to questioning of the wisdom of American Administrations, and might encourage other states to develop a countervailing capacity to that of the United States, but that rests in the realm of conjecture.

Of more direct concern is the implication for other US interests in the Middle East of its failure to resolve the Arab–Israel dispute. Linkages exist between them and the dispute. But before Clinton's failure had a chance to impact directly upon other United States regional interests, Bush II began his moves against Iraq. The United States led a 'coalition of the willing' in March 2003 that removed from power the one Arab state that had demonstrated a capability to attack Israel. Iraq had launched SCUD missiles against Israel during the 1991 Gulf War, and was believed to retain ability at some later date to target other actors with weapons of mass destruction. Syria did not pose a direct threat to Israel, despite its proximity: its forces had been convincingly trounced by Israel a number of times. But Syria remained host to extremist Palestinian groups, facilitated entry into Iraq of activists opposed to US purposes in that country, and was responsible for the assassination of a former prime minister of Lebanon. Negative sanctions were imposed on Syria by Bush II because it was not doing enough to restrain extremist elements.[15] Israel remains vulnerable to insurgency and terrorism supported by Iran, but was beyond the reach of an accurate Iranian attack at that time. The United States is concerned that Iran continues to develop a nuclear enrichment programme and to improve its missile capability.

The pre-emptive action of the United States against Iraq foreshadowed a changed geopolitical environment in the Middle East. All regional states are conscious of this reaffirmation of United States military predominance, and that it was demonstrated contrary to the views of a majority of the permanent members of the UN Security Council and of most other nation states. If Bush II were to behave in a comparable manner elsewhere in the Middle East, it could have far-reaching implications for member states of the region.[16] The latent threat is potent. Much depends, however, on the outcome of the intervention in Iraq, and the success of the United States in ensuring that Iran's nuclear programme is not used to develop nuclear weaponry. The adventure in Iraq has exposed deep-seated sectarian differences between the Shi'ite and Sunni communities and between them and the Kurds and other minorities. It has also acted as a magnet to Arab and Islamic extremists, Iraqi and foreign, to target American troops and international institutions within Iraq. The extremists' actions command, in varying degrees, the sympathy of less radical Muslims critical of United States intervention and the manner in which it seeks to manage the promotion of democracy in Iraq. The potency of the latent threat of American power to regional states has been diminished by the extent to which the extremists have been able to frustrate or delay the imposition of its fiat. But this cannot affect the central position of the United States within the global inter-state structure.

There are lessons that can be learned from the experience of the United States in prosecuting a settlement of the Arab–Israel dispute that are susceptible of application to the projection of United States power elsewhere. The touchstone is that peace is intended to be enduring, while force such as that applied in Iraq is a shorter-term phenomenon. The attainment of peace deserves to be planned and executed with at least as much skill and commitment as military intervention. Were an American Administration to proceed in accordance with this precept, the following tactical considerations would enter its calculus:

- the need to define the objective or objectives if a staged process is envisaged with precision. It is insufficient to leave the terms of any final outcome to others;
- the need to determine how the objective or objectives might be attained, including preparedness to advance ideas and to employ all appropriate measures;
- the need to consider whether the objective might reasonably be achieved within a certain timeframe. Where a staged process is envisaged, timelines should be established for each stage. Insistence on conclusion of a negotiation by a deadline imparts a sense of urgency to the process;
- the need to build a constituency for the desired outcome at home, and within the target state through public diplomacy;
- the need to maximise the assistance available, co-opting the assistance of other states, involving them in planning, and making effective use of them as partners, rather than agents;
- the need to apply pressure to the target state as well as offering inducements. Coordination with partners could be helpful in sending a consistent message; and
- the need to respond flexibly when unforeseeable circumstances arise, or the power wielder's efforts produce unintended consequences.

These considerations are not exceptional: most are standard practice in relation to the application of force. Why should they not be employed in more pacific circumstances? Bush II engaged in conflict in Afghanistan and Iraq, but in neither country has the United States been able easily and effectively to apply its power to post-conflict reconstruction and to withdraw. Evidence has now emerged of a lack of coordination on the question of how to tackle this question in Iraq, with early planning by the State Department superseded by an approach developed within the Pentagon.

There are other international issues to which the principles advanced in this conclusion may apply. They are being employed in relation to Iran's development of its nuclear capability. The United States has been working closely with Russia, which is one state that has supplied nuclear assistance to Iran in the past, to encourage Iran to cooperate fully with the IAEA. The intent of this cooperative endeavour is to contribute to the achievement of the long-standing non-proliferation objective of the United States. Counterterrorism measures also require international cooperation and resolve. If the United States is to protect its state and non-state interests in a porous global environment, it must demonstrate an ability effectively to deploy the resources at its command in order to maximise the assistance of other actors. The general applicability of these principles would need to be analysed against the projection of US power to attain particular objectives. That is beyond the scope of this work.

The approach advocated in relation to Israel and the Palestinians under the roadmap of April 2003 shows that some of the lessons of the ill-fated Madrid process have been absorbed. Those lessons include the benefits of operational planning and international cooperation. Having heard Bush II commit to a two-state solution, the Europeans gave thought to how to realise that objective,[17] producing a performance-based and goal-driven roadmap that the United States undertook to pursue. The new plan's authority derives from its quartet of sponsors – the United States (power), the European Union (economic assistance), the United Nations (legitimacy) and the Russian Federation (a co-sponsor of the Geneva and Madrid conferences). The roadmap defines the Palestinian objective with greater precision than that of the Madrid process, although it is silent on contentious matters like border delimitation, area, sovereignty over the holy sites and the future of Jerusalem.[18] William Quandt is critical of the Clinton Administration for not having possessed a serious strategy for attaining its goal.[19] To some extent the roadmap remedies this defect. Its gradualist approach may be 'Oslo under a different name'.[20] Opinion may vary about the relative imposition on the parties were they to proceed toward the target, and the fairness of the outcome[21] but its compressed timeframe imparts a greater sense of commitment to achieving the designated target than that of the earlier process, and the conditions obtaining at the time of its introduction were qualitatively different from those of 1991. It is probable, however, that Israel has side-stepped the roadmap and that it may never provide the direction that its authors intended.

The outlines of any final settlement are far from clear and the range of matters to be resolved is considerable. Informal Understandings concluded in October 1995 between Abbas and Yossi Beilin, a minister in Israel's former

Labor-led government, addressed the shape of a possible settlement.[22] Clinton's parameters of December 2000 remain in the consciousness of negotiators, as do the Geneva 'accords' of 2003, and their ideas may be drawn upon in negotiation on specific matters. Any negotiated compact might be expected to bring into effect the Arab Summit's offer of 2002 of recognition of Israel and an end to the Arab–Israel dispute. Both Clinton and Bush II accepted that any Palestinian entity in the West Bank would exclude areas heavily populated by Israeli settlers, but neither defined the areas involved, leaving the detail for resolution between Israel and the Palestinians.

Israel's security, especially if a porous sovereign Palestinian state were to be established on its border through which Palestinian militias could be resupplied or Arab forces could move or assemble, the future of Jerusalem, the problem of the return of Palestinian refugees, and assurance of adequate water supply to Israel and 'Palestine' are among the most intractable of the remaining issues. The Oslo process had left most of them to the end, hoping that confidence-building measures would establish sufficient trust to ease the pain of the decisions that would have to be taken on these matters.

The parties' negotiators were narrowing their differences on Israel's security concerns in late 2000. They addressed the building of early warning stations, joint and cooperative responses to terrorism, and a reconciliation of Israeli aviation needs with Palestinian airspace. Israel sought a demilitarised Palestinian state; the Palestinians had more of a problem with the symbolism of not having an army than with the practicality of limiting their forces and the weapons they could possess. Joint patrols along the Jordan River, and Israeli access routes in the West Bank in the event of a threat from the east, proved to be contentious matters that remained to be resolved. At issue are questions about a Palestinian government's ability to observe any agreement on such matters, and Israel's confidence in its doing so.

Jerusalem's Haram al-Sharif/Temple Mount is a site of fundamental religious significance to Muslims and Jews. Israel has recognised the importance of the Haram platform to Islam since 1967 and entrusted management of it to Muslims. Both sides want sovereignty over the holy sites. Clinton floated the concept of Palestinian sovereignty over the Haram and Israeli sovereignty over the Western Wall and the space sacred to Judaism of which it is part, with either a firm commitment by both sides not to excavate beneath the Haram or behind the Western Wall; alternatively, he proposed a requirement of mutual consent before any excavation took place in these areas. If accepted, this proposition would, in effect, extend a concept akin to strata title for some multi-storey buildings into international law. Olmert is committed to completing the security barrier to separate Israelis from Palestinians, which has implications for Jerusalem. When finished, it will cut through 'Palestinian' Jerusalem and the West Bank's central economic zone, severing the zone from its hinterland. Nevertheless, its route will still leave some Palestinians on the 'Israeli' side, and some land planned for future Israeli settlements on the 'Palestinian' side. The prime minister seems intent to proceed with this division of the city. A Kadima representative of Jerusalem in the Knesset has said that the bits Israel does not want can serve as the capital of an eventual Palestinian state.[23]

In many ways the Palestinian refugee community has been ignored, their interests having been deliberately set aside until the final status negotiation. No clear leader has emerged within the diaspora to champion their cause. Meanwhile, the mythology of a 'right of return' has been allowed to flourish unchecked notwithstanding the array of difficulties that would make its realisation impracticable. At post-Clinton talks at Taba in late January 2001, a document seems to have been drafted by the parties on this matter but it has not been made public, giving rise to speculation that concessions were made for which the parties would now prefer not to accept responsibility. The only issue that could generate such heat would be a Palestinian concession on the claimed right of return. There is an account that the Palestinian negotiators agreed to waive the right of return in exchange for an Israeli statement accepting at least partial responsibility for the departure of the Palestinians in 1948. The possibility that Palestinian negotiators might go further and moderate the right of return for concessions on Jerusalem cannot be discounted. The unofficial Geneva 'accord' of October 2003 has proposed specific measures for the determination of compensation to refugees by an international commission.

The continuing construction of Israeli settlements in the West Bank is eroding the total area that might one day become a Palestinian state. The security barrier, with its incursions into the West Bank, and a network of Israeli-only roads in the West Bank, seem likely to result in the division of the territory into three major Palestinian cantons, in effect 'Bantustans' that Palestinians could inhabit under Israeli suzerainty. Abbas has been closely involved in the development of the Palestinians' negotiating position since the 1970s. His commitment to a negotiated solution cannot be doubted. He has been unable to persuade the Palestinian Authority's Hamas government to acknowledge the reality of Israel's existence and to negotiate an accommodation with Israel on the area of occupied territory to be returned to the Palestinians. For so long as Hamas remains obdurate, the probability is that Israel will feel free to cede only such territory as it chooses. It remains to be seen whether the financial blockade of the Palestinian Authority and the Authority's inability to meet the salary payments of its agents will foster a more receptive attitude toward Israel, or lead to domestic disturbance between Abbas's Fatah supporters and the rejectionists. There is a history of contestation between Palestinian factions. Were this to descend into civil warfare, it would reaffirm Israel's predisposition to disengage from the Palestinians and to proceed unilaterally in demarking 'Palestine'. Such an entity, under Israeli suzerainty, would not satisfy the Palestinians or satisfy generally accepted requirements for recognition of statehood.

The problem of water supply is closely related to that of territory. Israel uses more water than it can produce: agriculture consumes two-thirds of the available supply. It draws extensively from the Sea of Galilee and aquifers in the West Bank. There are disputed claims to both from Syria and the Palestinians respectively. In the 1990s Israel drew some 80 per cent of the West Bank aquifer supply, leaving the balance for the Palestinians' use. This residual allocation imposed a system of water rationing on Palestinian villages, and 37 per cent of the Palestinian villages were without running water.[24] The situation was further compounded over the decade as Israel's per capita annual water usage increased at a rate faster than that of the Palestinians'. By the twenty-first century Israelis were using on average at least four times more water per person than Palestinians. The route of the security barrier has placed wells discharging some 4 million cubic metres per annum on the Israeli side, separated from the Palestinian villages that depend on them. The Palestinians' average water consumption now fails to meet minimum World Health Organization standards. The situation will be exacerbated by population growth. Demographic projections for the West Bank and East Jerusalem are already high and will be compounded if many of the 1.5 million people who claim Palestinian refugee status were to seek to settle there.

An objective of the Israeli government, at the outset of the United States-inspired search for a comprehensive settlement of the Arab–Israel dispute, was Palestinian self-government in territory that would remain under Israeli suzerainty. The attachment of different Israeli governments to that precept has varied: Sharon subscribed in 2003 to the two-state solution advanced by the United States in 2001, although his subsequent action leaves doubt about the strength of his endorsement. If, as Olmert has said, Israel will determine the agenda, Kadima's policy of select land transfers seems likely to proceed. 'Palestine' will consist of the Gaza Strip and such parts of the West Bank as Israel cedes. Israel has already made it clear that it will retain responsibility for security patrols along the land and sea borders of the entity and control of its air space. That policy will apply to the western bank of the Jordan River. 'Palestine' will thus be denied an international border with any third party, and be composed of a patchwork of territories with tenuous internal linkages. The powers that its government would exercise would be those conferred by Israel, possibly through negotiation if Hamas could be brought to the table, but probably by fiat. The resultant 'Palestine' would become at best an entity in a dependant or trucial relationship with Israel as its protecting power, or a partner in a confederation with Jordan. Apart from the inherent demographic and resource problems that association with such an entity would bring to Jordan, the absence of territorial contiguity would make its administration an untenable option. In all probability, Israel would be unable to shed its creation for so long as it retained border control. While such an eventuality would exhibit consistency in Israel's pursuit of the 'Palestinian self-government' option over the length of the Madrid/Oslo process, it would not resolve broader questions about the demographic homogeneity of Israel's population, or the contradiction to its democratic aspirations inherent in a distinction between the rights and opportunities of the Jewish and Palestinian peoples under its control.

The preoccupation of Bush II with matters to which he accorded higher priority explains in part his failure to recognise the implications of Sharon pursuing an independent agenda and to move to head him off. The opportunity to do so has largely passed, unless the United States is prepared to exercise its power to greater effect than hitherto and persuade Israel that an artificial 'Palestine', with authority confined to self-government over a prescribed agenda, will not be agreed by the Palestinians, or acceptable to the international community including the United States.

In any negotiation there must be a balance between what is preferable versus that which is practicable. Israel has used its undoubted supremacy to constrain Palestinian ambitions. Asymmetric conflict has proven costly to both sides in social and economic terms,[25] and has produced results that have satisfied neither community. It has frustrated and disillusioned those Palestinians who favour a negotiated settlement, fuelling a growing belief that suicide bombing is a justifiable means of national self-expression. It has failed to produce the peace and security desired by the majority of Israelis. Are Israel's ambitions realistic? Conversely, have Israeli governmental policies pushed the Palestinians too far into the corner? Will a Palestinian entity, formed of residual areas not claimed by Israel, be viable? Neither the West Bank nor the Gaza Strip is richly endowed with natural resources. The West Bank's water supply and agricultural land (as defined by the 1967 'green line') has substantially been commandeered for the use of Israeli settlers and will probably be annexed by Israel; the territories' population and unemployment growth rates are considerable; and the Palestinians' economic and social prosperity depends to a considerable extent upon access to workplaces in Israel to which entry has been denied for security reasons. If 'Palestine' is not viable, the presence of an economic and socially depressed entity under Israeli suzerainty will have continuing implications for Israel's security.

It is in Israel's interests to assure the probable viability of a Palestinian state. To date, Israel has insisted on a total cessation of violence as a precondition for change. This has proven to be an impossible objective. Israel has a right to insist that a resolution of differences with the Palestinians be contingent upon the Palestinian Authority making every effort to restrain Palestinian insurgents, but no state can exercise complete control over all its citizens. For negotiations to succeed, Israelis would have to accept that sporadic acts of terrorism and violence were inevitable. Its tolerance of continuing insurgency would thus become a function of degree and frequency.

As the stronger party, Israel has a number of options. The Kadima-led government could unilaterally cede such West Bank territory as it wished to the Palestinian Authority, but the Palestinians and the international community would not recognise this outcome as a fulfilment of Palestinian expectations. Hostilities between the two parties would continue for an indefinite period. Exhaustion by either side does not seem imminent. Or Israel could try to entice the Hamas government into negotiation, perhaps to be held in secret initially, but in order to do so it would have to be prepared to hold out the prospect of an outcome that would satisfy Palestinian territorial demands. This could mean being rather more generous toward the Palestinians in negotiations than some sectors of the Israeli public would wish.

For the new Palestinian leadership the options are either to persist with violence, which will attract reprisals, or to join much of the rest of the Arab world in acknowledging Israel's existence and negotiate an accommodation with it. Polls show that most Palestinians want the latter. The Palestinian Authority can only hope to command the confidence of its people if it offers sound and responsible governance and demonstrates that it is capable of securing tangible benefits in negotiations with Israel. The Palestinians voted for change of government in early 2006 on precisely those terms.

The United States cannot afford to be a bystander. Abrogation of its ability to influence the shape of the outcome can only play into the hands of Israel at the expense of the Palestinians and will not resolve the conflict. In any negotiation, both sides would have to be brought to consider adjustments to longstanding objectives that might previously have been judged unthinkable. It would not be necessary for a third party to insist upon a complete cessation of hostilities before entering into dialogue with each of the two parties; a go-between might prepare the ground for negotiation. A third party's contribution in exploring the belligerents' 'bottom lines' and facilitating discussion of such matters would be invaluable. The parameters that Clinton announced in December 2000 addressed most of the sensitive issues. His assessment that any resolution of the dispute would be found within those parameters may yet prove to be his most valuable contribution to the subject. Their resurrection could prove to be a useful starting point. The United States should not be afraid to project its ideational power. It should do so dispassionately, not as proxy for one or other of the parties, for its national interest is in a durable and peaceful settlement. Only an outcome satisfactory to the majority public opinion of both parties can provide that.

Questions inevitably arise about the extent to which the United States can expect to persuade a sovereign democratic state, whose policies enjoy considerable domestic support, that an alternative course is in its national interest. The people of either side of the conflict have passions and interests and the challenge for Bush II is to alter the balance between them.[26] This cannot be achieved overnight, or with a Palestinian Authority whose power has been severely circumscribed by Israel, but Israel can create the context in which Palestinians are more likely to pursue their interests than their passions. There is an instrument at the disposal of the Administration that could be used to encourage the Israelis to do so, and which could offset the cost of relocating settlers from the West Bank and Gaza to Israel.[27] Both relocation and the wall's construction are expensive, and the Israeli economy is in difficulty. The Administration is well placed to argue that some of the generous United States aid annual allocation of $3 billion be allocated to relocation rather than toward the building of the wall.[28] Bush *père* took affirmative action in relation to the settlements, while Clinton declined to do so. The way is open to Bush II to emulate his father. He has shown a capacity to endorse a two-state solution and to challenge Israel on its incursions into Palestinian controlled territory, notwithstanding objection from his own domestic constituency.

President Bush II made it clear at the outset of his presidency that he had no wish to become personally engaged in conflict resolution. Although this does not exempt him from critical analysis of the efficacy with which the power of the United States was projected, his deployment of a limited range of United States resources must be read in that context. It is clear, however, that the resources of the United States exceeded Clinton's and Bush II's inclinations to maximise their efficacy. There was scope for the advancement of initiatives that lay untapped and avenues of persuasion that were not explored. Bush II was largely constrained in their application by hostilities between the parties, but nevertheless employed the ideational power of the United States when motivated to do so. The extent to which the Clinton Administration might have employed these resources is unclear. The responsibility to employ them lay with the president. Clinton made much of the fact that there was no issue to which he had devoted more time than that of a resolution of the Arab–Israel dispute, and that he had undertaken to work on that matter until his term expired. He engaged personally in negotiation, and invested the office of the President of the United States in the search for a solution. He tried to produce a settlement, first between Israel and Syria, and later between Israel and the Palestinians. He was not unduly constrained, and he tried hard, but he could have tried harder. Under neither President Clinton nor President Bush II was the power of the United States fully extended. Its limits were empirically determined by the presidents' decisions on how far either was prepared to go to achieve United States objectives. In the hands of someone averse to conflict like Clinton, that was not far enough. Under Bush II, a preference for disengagement could only result in ceding ground to Israel as the stronger of the disputant parties.

The instruments of statecraft discussed in this book, and the way that they may be used in the projection of state power, provide a methodology for analysing the strength of a state's determination to attain declared external objectives in circumstances other than the application of military force. Politicians may identify certain aims or foreign policy goals, but the integrity of their commitment can only be properly assessed against the effective employment of appropriate instruments to attain their desired outcomes.

Henry Kissinger has written of the Middle East peace process that United States diplomacy 'cannot succeed if we seem to want peace more than the parties'.[29] The United States may legitimately desire a Middle East peace more than Israel and its Arab neighbours. Not only does it share interests in common with Israel and in some respects with Israel's Arab neighbours, its national interests are different from and arguably broader than those of the parties because of its position in the global inter-state structure. The presumption that after weighing probable costs and benefits the United States would wield its power in order to achieve its objectives seems incontestable. The outcome of any such exercise may not be precisely that envisaged at the outset, and success cannot be assured, but it would be a dereliction of duty for a President of the United States to avoid pursuit of his country's national interest. If, after effectively deploying the range of instruments at his disposal the president fails to achieve an outcome that even approximates the objective, the limits of United States power will have been exposed. In respect of the Middle East peace process, United States presidents have constrained themselves by declining to deploy instruments that might antagonise Israel and Israel's American supporters. This has not determined the limits of American power: it has only shown the limits to which Presidents of the United States have been prepared to go in pursuit of United States national interests.

NOTES

1. Lake (1993) p.659.
2. Bull (1977) p.13.
3. Morgenthau (1978) pp.3–15.
4. Lake (1993) p.660.
5. Carr (1948) p.220.
6. Albright (2003) p.505.
7. Baldwin (1985).
8. Waltz (1979) p.192.
9. Simon (1957) p.177.

10 Albright (2003) p.303.
11 Haass (2001).
12 Smith (1994) p.325.
13 Albright (2003) p.507.
14 *Economist* (2006a).
15 US Department of State (2005). Negative sanctions were imposed under the Syria Accountability and Lebanese Sovereignty Restoration Act of 2003.
16 Glass (2003). Iran has come under considerable pressure within the International Atomic Energy Agency and the UN Security Council to conform to IAEA safeguards and to forswear the enrichment of materials that could be used in nuclear weaponry. The United States has robustly championed the need for Iranian acquiescence.
17 Ma'oz (2003a).
18 Doran (2003).
19 Quandt (1999) p.429.
20 Agha and Malley (2003).
21 Said (2003) states that 'The road map, in fact, is not a plan for peace so much as a plan for pacification: it is about putting an end to Palestine as a problem'.
22 Beilin (2004) Appendix 1 pp.299–312.
23 *Economist* (2006b).
24 Cordesman (2005) p.67.
25 Ibid. p.326. Cordesman cites data showing that as at May 2004, 35 per cent of all Palestinians killed since September 2000 were non-combatants, while 77 per cent of all Israelis killed were non-combatants.
26 Friedman (2003).
27 Grunzweig (2003). More that 70 per cent of settlers, a significant increase from previous polls, would agree eventually to leave the West Bank and Gaza if they were compensated, while 29 per cent are ready to leave right away. Seventy-one per cent of them said they believed that a peace agreement that would require them to leave their settlements was inevitable.
28 *Sydney Morning Herald* (2003). The Administration is considering deducting $50 million from recently approved loan guarantees, 'and might make further deductions based on the amount Israel spent on roads being built to route Jewish settlers around Palestinian towns and villages'.
29 Kissinger (2000).

Select Bibliography

Abbas, M. (1995). *Through Secret Channels: The road to Oslo*. Reading UK, Garnet Publishing Limited.

Abraham, S. (2002). *Testimony*. Presented at: House Committee on International Relations, 20 June 2002. Washington DC, US Department of Energy.

Abu Amr, Z. (2002). Political Reform: Prospects and obstacles. *Reforming the Palestinian Authority: Requirements for change*. D. B. Ross. Washington DC, The Washington Institute for Near East Policy pp.14–19.

Agha, H. and R. Malley (2003). 'Three Men in a Boat'. *The New York Review of Books*, 14 August.

Al-Saud, HRH Crown Prince Fahd bin Abdulaziz (1981/1998). 'The Fahd Plan – August 1981'. *The Middle East and North Africa 1999*. London UK, Europa Publications Limited p.124.

Al-Saud, HRH Crown Prince Abdullah bin Abdulaziz (2002). *Speech*. Presented at: Fourteenth Arab Summit, Beirut, Lebanon, 27–28 March.

Albright, M. K. (1997). 'U.S. Efforts to Increase Regional Economic Cooperation, 16 November 1997'. *US Department of State Dispatch* (December 1997) pp.6–9.

Albright, M. K. (1998). *The Middle East Peace Process*, 12 May. US Department of State.

Albright, M. K. (2003). *Madam Secretary: A memoir*. Basingstoke UK, Macmillan.

Andoni, L. (1996). 'The Palestinian Elections: Moving toward democracy or one-party rule?' *Journal of Palestine Studies* Vol.XXV No.3 (Spring 1996) pp.5–16.

Arab American Institute (2004). *About AAI*. Washington DC, Arab American Institute. http://www.aaiusa.org, accessed 3 April 2004.

Arab American Institute (2006). *U.S. Census*. Washington DC, Arab American Institute. http://www.aaiusa.org/arab-americans/22/demograpics, accessed 29 November 2006.

Aronson, G. (ed.) (1991a). 'Documents and Source Material'. *Journal of Palestine Studies* Vol.XX No.3 (Spring 1991) pp.133–170.

Aronson, G. (ed.) (1991b). 'U.S.–Soviet Letter of Invitation to Peace Talks in Madrid, 18 October 1991'. *Journal of Palestine Studies* Vol.XXI No.2 (Winter 1992) pp.120–121.

Baker III, J. A. (1991a). 'Remarks at the Royal Palace, Madrid, 1 November 1991'. *US Department of State Dispatch* (4 November 1991) pp.807–809.

Baker III, J. A. (1991b). 'U.S. Secretary of State James Baker's Press Conference, Madrid, 3 November'. *Journal of Palestine Studies* Vol.XXI No.2 (Winter 1992) pp.147–149.
Baker III, J. A. (1992a). 'U.S. Letter of Assurances to Israel'. *Journal of Palestine Studies* Vol.XXI No.2 (Winter 1992) p.120.
Baker III, J. A. (1992b). 'U.S. Letter of Assurances to Lebanon'. *Journal of Palestine Studies* Vol.XXI No.2 (Winter 1992) p.120.
Baker III, J. A. (1992c). 'U.S. Letter of Assurances to the Palestinians'. *Journal of Palestine Studies* Vol.XXI No.2 (Winter 1992) pp.118–119.
Baker III, J. A. (1992d). 'U.S. Letter of Assurances to Syria'. *Journal of Palestine Studies* Vol.XXI No.2 (Winter 1992) pp.119–120.
Baker III, J. A. (1992e). 'A Summons to Leadership, 21 April'. *US Department of State Dispatch* (27 April 1992) pp.321–325.
Baker III, J. A. (1995). *The Politics of Diplomacy: Revolution, war and peace 1989–1992*. New York NY, G.P. Putnam's Sons.
Baldwin, D. A. (1985). *Economic Statecraft*. Princeton NJ, Princeton University Press.
Baldwin, D. A. (ed.) (1993). *Neorealism and Neoliberalism: The contemporary debate*. New York NY, Columbia University Press.
Bartholomew, R. (1990). 'Defense Equipment for Saudi Arabia, 4 October'. *US Department of State Dispatch* (8 October 1990) pp.68–169.
BBC News (2003). 'Sharon signals "occupation" end' 27 May. http://news.bbc.co.uk/1/hi/world/middle_east/2939552.stm, accessed 10 October 2006.
BBC News (2004). 'Submissions to World Court on Israeli barrier' 24 February. http://news.bbc.co.uk/ 1/hi/world/middle_east/3517587.stm, accessed 6 November 2006.
Beilin, Y. (1999 (trans. Philip Simpson)). *Touching Peace: From the Oslo Accord to a final agreement*. London UK, Weidenfeld and Nicolson.
Beilin, Y. (2004). *The Path to Geneva*. New York NY, RDV Books.
Benn, A. (2002). 'U.S. tells PM that Muqata Siege Undermining Plans for Iraq'. *Haaretz*, 29 September. http://www.haaretzdaily.com/hasen/pages/ShArt.jhtml?itemNo=213461, accessed 6 November 2006.
Bennet, J. (2003). 'Abbas Sums up Vision for a Palestinian State'. *The New York Times on the Web*, 20 July. www.nytimes.com/2003/07/20/international/middleeast/20MIDE.html?ex=1160625600&en=edd65f9b31efdea3&ei=5070, accessed 10 October 2006.
Bennis, P. (1995). 'Clinton Administration Working to Ease U.N. Out of Middle East Process'. *Washington Report on Middle East Affairs* (July/August) pp.30, 93.
Boekle, H., V. Rittberger, and W.Wagner (1999). *Norms and Foreign Policy: Constructivist foreign policy theory*. Tübingen Germany, University of Tübingen, Center for International Relations/Peace and Conflict Studies.
Bowker, R. (2003). *Palestinian Refugees: Mythology, identity, and the search for peace*. Boulder CO, Lynne Rienner Publishers.

Brackman, N. (2000). 'The Multilaterals: Status and prospects'. *Peace Watch* No.244 (28 January 2000). Washington DC, The Washington Institute for Near East Policy.

Brand, L. A. (1994). 'Economics and Shifting Alliances: Jordan's relations with Syria and Iraq, 1975–81'. *International Journal of Middle East Studies* Vol.26 No.3 (August 1994) pp.393–413.

Bregman, A. (2005). *Elusive Peace: How the Holy Land defeated America*. London UK, Penguin Books.

British Petroleum (2002). *BP Statistical Review of World Energy, June 2002*. London UK, British Petroleum.

Brynen, R. (1996). 'Buying Peace? A critical assessment of international aid to the West Bank and Gaza'. *Journal of Palestine Studies* Vol.XXV No.3 (Spring 1996) pp.79–92.

B'Tselem (2006). *Statistics – Fatalities: 29.9.2000 – 15.5.2006*. Jerusalem, B'Tselem. www.btselem.org/English/Statistics/Casualties.asp, accessed 11 October 2006.

Bull, H. (1977). *The Anarchical Society: A study of order in world politics*. Basingstoke UK, Macmillan.

Buruma, I. (2003). 'How to talk about Israel' 31 August. www.nytimes.com/2003/08/31ANTISEMITISM.html?ex=1377662400&en=7a8cfb612d5fffa2&ei=5007&partner=USERLAND, accessed 7 November 2006.

Bush, G. H. W. *Public Papers of the Presidents of the United States – President Bush, 1990–1993*. Washington DC, Office of the Federal Register.

Bush, G. W. *Public Papers of the Presidents of the United States – President Bush, 2001–2002.* Washington DC, Office of the Federal Register.

Bush, G. W. (2000). *Texas Gov. George W. Bush Speaks at AIPAC's 2000 Policy Conference*. The American Israel Public Affairs Committee, 22 May.

Bush, G. W. (2002). *President Bush Calls for New Palestinian Leadership*. Washington DC, The White House, Office of the Press Secretary. http://www.whiltehouse.gov/news/releases/2002/06/print/20020624-3.html – accessed 6 May 2003.

Bush, G. W. (2004). *President Bush Commends Israeli Prime Minister Sharon's Plan*, 14 April. Washington DC, The White House, Office of the Press Secretary. http://www.whitehouse.gov/news/releases/2004/04/print/20040414-4.html, accessed 18 January 2006.

Bush, G. W. (2006). *State of the Union Address by the President*, 31 January. Washington DC, The White House, Office of the Press Secretary.

Butler, L. (1997). 'Fresh Light on the Syrian–Israeli Peace Negotiations: An interview with Ambassador Walid Al-Moualem'. *Journal of Palestine Studies* Vol.XXVI No.2 (Winter 1997) pp.81–94.

Carr, E. H. (1948). *The Twenty Years' Crisis 1919–1939: An introduction to the study of international relations*. London UK, Macmillan & Co. Ltd.

Chayes, A. and A. H. Chayes (1995). *The New Sovereignty: Compliance with international regulatory agreements*. Cambridge MA, Harvard University Press.

Christopher, W. (1993). 'Resumption of Middle East Peace Negotiations, 10 March'. *US Department of State Dispatch* (15 March 1993) Vol.4 No.11 p.141.
Christopher, W. (1995a). 'America's Leadership, America's Opportunity'. *Foreign Policy* Iss.98 Spring 1995 pp.6–27.
Christopher, W. (1995b). 'A Common Strategy for Economic Growth in the West Bank and Gaza Strip, 29 September 1995'. *US Department of State Dispatch* Vol.6 No.41 pp.725–726.
Christopher, W. (1996). 'Opening Statement by Secretary Christopher at a Press Conference Following a Meeting with Syrian President Asad, Damascus, Syria, 12 January'. *US Department of State Dispatch* Vol.7 Nos 1–3 pp.2–3.
Clinton, H. R. (2003). *Living History*. New York NY, Simon & Schuster.
Clinton, W. J. *Public Papers of the Presidents of the United States – President Clinton, 1993–2001*. Washington DC, Office of the Federal Register.
Clinton, W. J. (1994). *Executive Order 12938 – Proliferation of Weapons of Mass Destruction*, 14 November. Washington DC, The White House.
Clinton, W. J. (1995). *Executive Order 12947 – Prohibiting Transactions with Terrorists who Threaten to Disrupt the Middle East Peace Process*, 24 January. Washington DC, The White House.
Clinton, W. J. (Bill) (2004). *My Life*. London UK, Hutchinson.
CNN.com (2004a). 'Arafat: Palestinians Won't Concede to Sharon's Plan' 15 April. www.cnn.com/2004/WORLD/meast/04/15/mideast.arafat/index.html, accessed 11 October 2006.
CNN.com (2004b). 'Israel Releases Details of Pullout Plan' 16 April. www.cnn.com/2004/WORLD/meast/04/16/sharon.plan/index.html, accessed 11 October 2006.
CNN.com (2004c). 'Blair Backs Israeli Pullout Plan' 16 April. www.cnn.com/2004/WORLD/meast/04/16/mideast.blair/index.html, accessed 19 October 2006.
CNN.com (2006). 'Hamas Leader sets Conditions for Truce' 29 January. www.cnn.com/2006/WORLD/meast/01/29/hamas.interview, accessed 11 October 2006.
Cobban, H. (1999). *The Israeli–Syrian Peace Talks: 1991–96 and beyond*. Washington DC, United States Institute of Peace Press.
Cordesman, A. H. (1999). *Iraq and the War of Sanctions: Conventional threats and weapons of mass destruction*. Westport CT, Praeger Publishers.
Cordesman, A. H. (2005). *The Israeli–Palestinian War: Escalating to nowhere*. Westport CT, Praeger Security International.
Council of Arab States (2002). The Arab Peace Initiative. www.al-bab.com/arab/docs/league/peace02.htm, accessed 11 October 2006.
Craig, G. A. and A. L. George (1995 (3rd edit.)). *Force and Statecraft: Diplmatic problems of our time*. New York NY, Oxford University Press, Inc.
D'Amato, J. V. (1991). 'How Regimes Profit by Curbing U.S. Television News'. *Orbis* Vol.35 No.3 (Summer 1991).

Danilova, M. (2006). 'Putin invites Hamas Leaders to Moscow' 9 February. http://abcnews.go.com/International/wireStory?id=1600036&CMP=OTC-RSSFeeds0312, accessed 11 October 2006.

Declaration of Principles on Interim Self-Government Arrangements, 13 September 1993. www.state.gov/p/nea/rls/22602.htm, accessed 11 October 2006.

Delaney, B. (1999). 'Syrian Expert: Assad ready to offer Israel peace for land' 16 June. www.cnn.com/WORLD/meast/9906/16/syria.israel, accessed 11 October 2006.

Diplomatic Conference of Geneva of 1949 (1949). *Convention (IV) Relative to the Protection of Civilian Persons in Time of War.* www.icrc.org/ihl.nsf/INTRO/380?OpenDocument, accessed 11 October 2006.

Djerejian, E. P. (1992). 'Statement before the Subcommittee on Europe and the Middle East of the House Foreign Affairs Committee, 17 March'. *US Department of State Dispatch* (23 March 1992) pp.218–220.

Djerejian, E. P. (1993a). 'Statement before the Subcommittee on Europe and the Middle East of the House Foreign Affairs Committee, 27 July'. *US Department of State Dispatch* Vol.4 No.32 pp.569–573.

Djerejian, E. P. (1993b). 'The Multilateral Talks in the Arab–Israeli Peace Process, 22 September'. *US Department of State Dispatch* Vol.4 No.41 pp.696–699.

Djerejian, E. P. (1993c). 'War and Peace: The problems and prospects of American diplomacy in the Middle East, 30 November'. *US Department of State Dispatch* Vol.4 No.51 pp.874–878.

Djerejian, E. P. (2003). *Changing Minds Winning Peace: A new strategic direction for U.S. public diplomacy in the Arab and Muslim world.* Presented at: House of Representatives, Committee on Appropriations. Washington DC, 1 October.

Doran, M. S. (2003). 'Q&A: Michael S. Doran on the Middle East road map' 1 August. www.nytimes.com/cfr/international/slot3_080103.html, accessed 11 October 2006.

Dougherty, J. E. and Robert L. Pfaltzgraff Jr (1990). *Contending Theories of International Relations: A comprehensive survey.* New York NY, Harper Collins Publishers.

Dunn, M. C. (ed.) (2004). 'Chronology July 16, 2003–October 15, 2003'. *The Middle East Journal* Vol.58 No.1 p.116.

The Economist (2006a). 'Who's Isolating Whom?' 23 February.

The Economist (2006b). 'The Last Conquest of Jerusalem' 12 April.

The Economist (2006c). 'A High-wire Act' 1 June.

El-Fassad, A. (2000). *Palestinians Defend Their Right to Return.* Protest.Net. http://www.protest.net/view.cgi?view=1935, accessed 24 July 2003.

Eldar, A. (2002). 'During the French Mandate, Shaba was Lebanese'. *Ha'aretz,* 27 June.

Enderline, C. (2002 (trans. Susan Fairfield)). *Shattered Dreams: The failure of the peace process in the Middle East.* New York NY, Other Press.

Erlanger, S. (1997). 'U.S. Shifts Stand on Mideast Talks, to Israeli Plan'. *The New York Times on the Web*, 7 August. http://select.nytimes.com/gst/abstract.html?res=F10C13FC3C580C748CDDA10894DF494D81&n=Top%2fReference%2fTimes%20Topics%2fPeople%2fR%2fRoss%2c%20Dennis, accessed 20 October, 2006.
Erlanger, S. (2006). 'US and Israel Determined to Force out Hamas'. *The Sydney Morning Herald*, 15 February.
Europa Publications (1998). 'The Framework for Peace in the Middle East, Camp David: 17 September 1978'. *The Middle East and North Africa 1999*. London UK, Europa Publications Limited.
European Community (1980). *Venice Declaration on the Middle East*, 12–13 June. http://ec.europa.eu/comm/external_relations/mepp/decl/#10, accessed 11 October 2006.
European Union (1998). United States–European Union Declaration on the Middle East Peace Process, 18 December. *Public Papers of the Presidents of the United States – President Clinton, 1998*. Washington DC, Office of the Federal Register p.2194.
Fisk, R. (2002). 'A Strange Kind of Freedom'. *The Independent*, 9 July.
Ford, G. R. (1975). *Letter from President Ford to Prime Minister Rabin*, 1 September. Washington DC, The Brookings Institution.
Foundation for Middle East Peace (2005a). *Israeli Settler Population in the West Bank 1972–2004*. Washington DC, Foundation for Middle East Peace.
Foundation for Middle East Peace (2005b). *Sources of Population Growth in the West Bank and Gaza Strip Settlements, 1999–2001*. Washington DC, Foundation for Middle East Peace.
Freeman, M. (1999). 'The Right to Self-determination in International Politics: Six theories in search of a policy'. *Review of International Studies* Vol.25 No.3 pp.355–370.
Friedman, T. L. (2003). 'Passions and Interests' 2 October. http://select.nytimes.com/gst/abstract.html?res=FB0E1FF63D580C718CDDA90994DB404482, accessed 11 October, 2006.
Gendzier, I. (1989). 'Memorandum Submitted to the Government of the United States of America by the Jaffa and Districts Inhabitants Council, Beirut, 11 April 1949'. *Journal of Palestine Studies* Vol.XVIII No.3 (Spring 1989) pp.96–109.
Geneva Accord, 2003. www.geneva-accord.org/Accord.aspx?FolderID=33&lang=en, accessed 11 October 2006.
George, A. L. and J. L. George (1998). *Presidential Personality and Performance*. Boulder CO, Westview Press.
Glass, C. (2003). 'Is Syria Next?' *London Review of Books*, 24 July.
Goldberg, J. J. (1996). Jewish Power: Inside the American Jewish establishment. Reading MA, Addison-Wesley.
Goodman, A. (1994). 'U.S. Wants U.N. Mideast Drafts to Aid Peace Process'. *Reuters News*, 21 September.

Government of Israel (2002). *IDF Spokesperson Announcements*, 1–2 March. www.israelemb.org/articles/2002/March/20020303.html, accessed 11 October 2006.
Government of Israel (2005). *Statement by PM Ariel Sharon at the Sharm el-Sheikh Summit*, 8 February. www.israel-mfa.gov.il/MFA/Government/Speeches+by+Israeli+leaders/ 2005/Statement+by+PM+Sharon+Sharm+el-Sheikh+Summit+8-Feb-2005.htm, accessed 11 October 2006.
Government of Israel, Ministry of Foreign Affairs (2001). Palestinian–Israeli Security Implementation Work Plan (Tenet ceasefire plan). *Ha'aretz*, 14 June.
Government of Israel, Ministry of Immigrant Absorption (2006). *Immigration from Former Soviet Union (F.S.U.) by Year of Immigration.* www.moia.gov.il/english/netunim/yachas.asp?KodTeur=1&KodShemDoch=4&ezor=0, accessed 11 October 2006.
Government of Switzerland (2001). *Conference of High Contracting Parties to the Fourth Geneva Convention:* declaration, 5 December. http://domino.un.org/UNISPAL.nsf/85255db800470aa485255d8b004e349a/8fc4f064b9be5bad85256c1400722951!OpenDocument, accessed 11 October 2006.
Group of Eight (1997). *Communique*. Denver Summit, 22 June.
Group of Eight (2004). *Statement: Gaza Withdrawal and the Road Ahead to Mideast Peace*, 10 June. Washington DC, The White House, Office of the Press Secretary.
Grunzweig, E. (2003). 'Settlers Positions Towards Withdrawal from Territories'. *Peace Now* (23 July).
The Guardian (2004). 'Israel's "security barrier" is Put on Trial' 18 February. www.guardian.co.uk/israel/Story/0,2763,1148932,00.html, accessed 11 October 2006.
Haass, R. N. (1997). 'Fatal Distraction: Bill Clinton's foreign policy'. *Foreign Policy* Iss.108 Fall 1997 pp.112–123.
Haass, R. N. (2001). *Assessing Bill Clinton's Legacy: How will history remember him?* Washington DC, The Brookings Institution, 9 January.
Haass, R. N. and S. Telhami (1999). *The Israel–Syria Talks: An assessment.* Washington DC, The Brookings Institution.
Hammami, R. (2002). 'Interregnum: Palestine after Operation Defensive Shield'. *Middle East Report* 223 (Summer 2002).
Hanieh, A. (2001). 'The Camp David Papers'. *Journal of Palestine Studies* Vol. XXX No.2 (Winter 2001) pp.75–97.
Hedges, C. (2001). 'The New Palestinian Revolt'. *Foreign Affairs* Vol.80 No.1 (January/February 2001) pp.124–138.
Heikal, M. (1996). *Secret Channels: The inside story of Arab–Israeli peace negotiations*. London UK, Harper Collins Publishers.
Held, D. and M. Koenig-Archibugi (2004). *American Power in the Twenty-First Century.* Cambridge UK, Polity Press.

Herman, E. S. and G. O'Sullivan (1989). *The 'Terrorism' Industry: The experts and institutions that shape our view of terror.* New York NY, Pantheon Books.
Hermann, M. G. and J. D. Hagan (1998). 'International Decision Making: Leadership matters'. *Foreign Policy* Iss.110 Spring 1998 pp.124–137.
Holsti, K. J. (1988). *International Politics: A framework for analysis.* Englewood Cliffs NJ, Prentice Hall.
Hudson, M. C. (1998 (3rd edit.)). The United States and the Middle East. *World Security: Challenges for a new century.* M. T. Klare and Y. Chandrani. New York NY, St Martin's Press pp.113–134.
Human Rights Watch (2004). *Israel, the Occupied West Bank and Gaza Strip, and Palestinian Authority Territories.* New York NY, Human Rights Watch.
International Court of Justice (1945). Statute of the International Court of Justice. www.icj-cij.org/icjwww/ibasicdocuments/ibasictext/ibasicstatute.htm, accessed 11 October 2006.
International Press Center (2006). *President Abbas In Morocco: Sanctions on the Palestinians bode interior explosions.* International Press Center, 13 April.
Israeli–Palestinian Interim Agreement on the West Bank and the Gaza Strip, 28 September 1995. www.israel-mfa.gov.il/MFA/Peace+Process/Guide+to+the+Peace+Process/THE+ISRAELI-PALESTINIAN+INTERIM+AGREEMENT.htm, accessed 11 October 2006.
Israeli Supreme Court (2004). Judgement Regarding the Security Fence, HCJ 2056/04, 24 June.
Jervis, R. (1970). *The Logic of Images in International Relations.* Princeton NJ, Princeton University Press.
Kadman, N. (1998). *1987–1997: A decade of human rights violations.* Jerusalem, B'Tselem.
Kay, D. (2003). *Testimony.* Presented at: House Permanent Select Committee on Intelligence, House Committee on Appropriations (Subcommittee on Defense), and Senate Select Committee on Intelligence. Washington DC, 2 October. http://www.cnn.com/2003/ALLPOLITICS/10/02/kay.report/, accessed 9 November 2006.
Keal, P. (2003). *European Conquest and the Rights of Indigenous Peoples: The moral backwardness of international society.* Cambridge UK, Cambridge University Press.
Keohane, R. O. (2002). *Power and Governance in a Partially Globalized World.* London UK, Routledge.
Keohane, R. O. and J. S. Nye Jr (1989 (2nd edit.)). *Power and Interdependence: World politics in transition.* Boston MA, Little, Brown & Co.
Kesler, G. (2006). 'Bush at Risk of Losing Closest Mideast Ally'. *The Washington Post,* 5 January.
Khalidi, R. I. (1996). 'Reflections on the Peace Process and a Durable Settlement: A roundup of views'. *Journal of Palestine Studies* Vol.XXVI No.1 (Autumn 1996) pp.5–26.

Khalidi, R. I. and L. Butler (eds) (2002). 'Documents and Source Material: World Bank, findings on corruption and anticompetitive practices in the West Bank and Gaza, May 2001'. *Journal of Palestine Studies* Vol.32 No.1 (Autumn 2002) pp.152–4.
Kissinger, H. (2000). 'Break With the Past in the Middle East'. *The Jerusalem Post*, 6 July.
Klare, M. T. and Y. Chandrani (eds) (1998 (3rd edit.)). *World Security: Challenges for a new century*. New York NY, St Martin's Press.
Klein, M. (2003). 'By Conviction, Not by Infliction: The internal debate over reforming the Palestinian Authority'. *The Middle East Journal* Vol.57 No.2 (Spring 2003) pp.194–212.
Knowlton, B. (2003). 'U.S. Inspector Sees Much to Pursue in Iraqi Weapons Search' 5 October. www.nytimes.com/2003/10/05/international/middleeast/05CND-WEAP.html, accessed 11 October 2006.
Krauthammer, C. (2002). 'The Unipolar Moment Revisited'. *The National Interest* No.70 Winter 2002 pp.5–17.
Lake, A. (1993). 'From Containment to Enlargement: 21 September'. *US Department of State Dispatch* Vol.4 No.39 pp.658–664.
Landau, E. (2001). *Egypt and Israel in ACRS: Bilateral concerns in a regional arms control process*. Tel Aviv Israel, Tel Aviv University, Jaffee Center for Strategic Studies.
Lasensky, S. (2004). 'Paying for Peace: The Oslo process and the limits of American foreign aid'. *The Middle East Journal* Vol.58 No.2 (Spring 2004) pp.210–234.
Laub, K. (2002). 'Palestinian Security Force in Ruins'. *The Washington Post*, 25 April.
Lesch, D. W. (ed.) (1999 (2nd edit.)). *The Middle East and the United States: A historical and political reassessment*. Boulder CO, Westview Press.
Likud Party Platform, 1996. Chevy Chase MD, Jewish Virtual Library. http://www.us-israel.org/jsource/Politics/likud.html, accessed 29 December 2003.
Lippman, T. W. (2000). *Madeleine Albright and the New American Diplomacy*. Boulder CO, Westview Press.
Luft, G. (2000). 'Israel's Security Zone in Lebanon: A tragedy?' *Middle East Quarterly* Vol.VII No.3 (September 2000) pp.13–20.
Makovsky, D. (2001). 'Middle East Peace Through Partition'. *Foreign Affairs* Vol.80 No.2 (Mar/Apr 2001) pp.28–45.
Makovsky, D. (2003). 'Taba Mythchief'. *The National Interest* No.71 Spring 2003 pp.119–129.
Malley, R. (2001a). 'The Logic of Historic Reconciliation will Prevail'. *Middle East Insight* Vol.XVI No.5 pp.57–84.
Malley, R. (2001b). 'Fictions About the Failure at Camp David' 8 July. www.library.cornell.edu/colldev/mideast/malley.htm, accessed 11 October 2006.
Malley, R. and H. Agha (2001). 'Camp David: The tragedy of errors'. *The New York Review of Books*, 9 August.

Malley, R. and H. Agha (2002). 'Camp David and After: An exchange: 2. A reply to Ehud Barak'. *The New York Review of Books,* 13 June.
Mansour, C. (1993). 'The Palestinian–Israeli Peace Negotiations: An overview and assessment'. *Journal of Palestine Studies* Vol.XXII No.3 (Spring 1993). pp.5–31.
Ma'oz, M. (1996). 'Reflections on the Peace Process and a Durable Settlement: A roundup of views'. *Journal of Palestine Studies* Vol.XXVI No.1 (Autumn 1996). pp.5–26.
Ma'oz, M. (2003a). *Policy Brief: Israeli options on the road map*. Washington DC, The Middle East Institute.
Ma'oz, M. (2003b). *Policy Brief: Israel and Syria: From water to peace*, Washington DC, The Middle East Institute.
Mark, C. R. (2002). *Lebanon*. Washington DC, Congressional Research Service, The Library of Congress.
Mark, C. R. (2003). *Palestinians and Middle East Peace: Issues for the United States*. Washington DC, Congressional Research Service, The Library of Congress.
Mark, C. R. (2006). *Israel: U.S. foreign assistance*. Washington DC, Congressional Research Service, The Library of Congress.
Mearsheimer, J. and S. Walt (2006). 'The Israel Lobby'. *London Review of Books*, 23 March.
Melman, Y. and D. Raviv (1994). *Friends in Deed: Inside the U.S.–Israel alliance*. New York NY, Hyperion.
MidEast Web (2003). The Israeli Camp David II Proposals for Final Palestine–Israel Peace Settlement, July 2000. www.mideastweb.org/ campdavid2.htm, accessed 11 October 2006.
Migdalovitz, C. (2002). *The Middle East Peace Talks*. Washington DC, Congressional Research Service, The Library of Congress.
Morgenthau, H. J. (1978 (5th edit., rev.)). *Politics Among Nations: The struggle for power and peace*. New York NY, Alfred A. Knopf.
Morris, B. (2001). Righteous Victims: A history of the Zionist–Arab conflict, 1881–2001. New York NY, Vintage Books.
Morriss, P. (1987). *Power: A philosophical analysis*. Manchester UK, Manchester University Press.
Muslih, M. (1990). 'Towards Coexistence: An analysis of the resolutions of the Palestine National Council'. *Journal of Palestine Studies* Vol. XIX No.4 (Summer 1990) pp.3–39.
Muslih, M. (1994). 'Dateline Damascus: Asad is ready'. *Foreign Policy* Iss.96 Fall 1994 pp.145–163.
The New York Times on the Web (2003). 'New Tries for Mideast Peace' 31 October. www.nytimes.com/2003/10/31/opinion/31FRI1.html?ex=1382936400&en=d03afd4da95643ea&ei=5007&partner=USERLAND, accessed 11 October 2006.
Noyes, J. H. (1997). 'Does Washington Really Support Israel?' *Foreign Policy* Iss.106 Spring 1997 pp.144–160.

Nye Jr, J. S. (2002). The Paradox of American Power: Why the world's only superpower can't go it alone. New York NY, Oxford University Press.
Ozga, D. A. (1994). 'A Chronology of the Missile Technology Control Regime'. *The Nonproliferation Review* Vol.1 No.2 (Winter 1994) pp.66–93.
Palestine Facts (2003). Current Events: Road Map for Peace. www.palestinefacts.org/pf_current_roadmap.php, accessed 6 November 2006.
Palestine Facts (2006). Israel 1991 to present: Mitchell Commission. http://www.palestinefacts.org/pf_1991to_now_alaqsa_sharmelsheikh 2000. php, accessed 5 May 2006.
Palestinian National Authority (2003). *Q & A: The Palestinian Prime Minister*, 10 March.
Palestinian Negotiating Team (2001). *Remarks and Questions from the Palestinian Negotiating Team Regarding the United States Proposal*, 1 January. Washington DC, The Brookings Institution.
Pape, R. A. (2003). 'Dying to Kill Us'. *The New York Times*, 22 September.
Parsons, A. (1996). 'Reflections on the Peace Process and a Durable Settlement: A roundup of views'. *Journal of Palestine Studies* Vol. XXVI No.1 (Autumn 1996) pp.5–26.
Pelletreau Jr, R. H. (1994). 'The Growing Role of Economics in the Middle East Peace Mosaic, 17 November'. *US Department of State Dispatch* Vol.5 No.48 pp.791–795.
Pelletreau Jr, R. H. (1996). 'Statement Before the House International Relations Committee, 12 June'. *US Department of State Dispatch* Vol.7 No.26 pp.336–341.
Peres, S. (1993). *The New Middle East*. New York NY, Henry Holt and Company, Inc.
A Performance-based Roadmap to a Permanent Two-State Solution to the Israeli-Palestinian Conflict, 2003. www.un.org/media/main.roadmap 122002.html, accessed 10 October 2006.
Perl, R. (2003). *Terrorism, the Future, and U.S. Foreign Policy*. Washington DC, Congressional Research Service, The Library of Congress.
Perl, R. (2004). *The Department of State's Patterns of Global Terrorism Report: Trends, state sponsors, and related issues*. Washington DC, Congressional Research Service, The Library of Congress.
Perlez, J. (2000). 'U.S. Draft of Israel–Syria Treaty Reported in Israeli Newspaper' 13 January. http://partners.nytimes.com/library/world/ mideast/011300israel-syria.html, accessed 11 October 2006.
Peters, J. (1994). *Building Bridges: The Arab–Israeli multilateral talks*. London UK, The Royal Institute of International Affairs.
Powell, C. L. (2001). *United States Position on Terrorists and Peace in the Middle East*, 19 November. Washington DC, US Department of State.
Prados, A. B. (2001). *Jordan: U.S. relations and bilateral issues*. Washington DC, Congressional Research Service, The Library of Congress.
Prados, A. B. (2002). *Syria: U.S. relations and bilateral issues*. Washington DC, Congressional Research Service, The Library of Congress.

Project for the New American Century (2001). *Letter to President Bush*, 20 September.

Project for the New American Century (2002). *Letter to President Bush*, 3 April.

Quandt, W. (1999 (2nd edit.)). New U.S. Policies for a New Middle East? *The Middle East and the United States: A historical and political reassessment*. D. W. Lesch. Boulder CO, Westview Press. pp.426–432.

Quandt, W. (2001 (rev. edit.)). *Peace Process: American diplomacy and the Arab–Israeli conflict since 1967*. Washington DC, Brookings Institution Press and University of California Press.

Rabil, R. (2001). 'The Ineffective Role of the US in the US–Israeli–Syrian Relationship'. *The Middle East Journal* Vol.55 No.3 (Summer 2001) pp.415–438.

Rabinovich, I. (1998). *The Brink of Peace: The Israeli–Syrian negotiations*. Princeton NJ, Princeton University Press.

Reagan, R. W. (1982/1998). 'The Reagan Plan – 1 September 1982'. *The Middle East and North Africa 1999*. London UK, Europa Publications Limited p.124.

Reich, B. (2002). 'Israel's Quest for Peace'. *Mediterranean Quarterly* Vol.13 No.2 pp.67–95.

Reinhart, T. (2002). *Israel/Palestine: How to end the war of 1948*. Crows Nest NSW, Allen & Unwin.

Report of the Sharm el-Sheikh Fact-Finding Committee (Mitchell Report), 30 April 2001. http://www.state.gov/p/nea/rls/rpt/3060.htm, accessed 6 November 2006.

Republican National Convention (2000). *Party Platform: Foreign Policy – The Middle East and Persian Gulf*. http://www.cnn.com/ELECTION/2000/conventions/republican/features/platform.00/#53, accessed 9 November 2006.

Reus-Smit, C. (2003). 'The Misleading Mystique of America's Material Power'. *Australian Journal of International Affairs* Vol.57 No.3 pp.423–430.

Rodman, P. W. (2000). *Uneasy Giant: The challenges to American predominance*. Washington DC, The Nixon Center.

Rosenau, J. N. (1968). 'Comparative Foreign Policy: Fad, fantasy, or field?' *International Studies Quarterly* Vol.12 No.3 September 1968 pp.296–329.

Ross, D. B. (1999). The Middle East Peace Process in the Wake of Ehud Barak's Victory. Presented at: *The Barak Victory: Implications for Israel, the peace process, and US policy*. Soref Symposium 17–18 June 1999. Washington DC, The Washington Institute for Near East Policy.

Ross, D. B. (ed.) (2002a). *Reforming the Palestinian Authority: Requirements for change*. Washington DC, The Washington Institute for Near East Policy.

Ross, D. B. (2002b). 'Yasir Arafat'. *Foreign Policy* Iss.131 Jul/Aug 2002 pp.18–23.

Ross, D. B. (2004). *The Missing Peace: The inside story of the fight for Middle East peace*. New York NY, Farrar, Straus and Giroux.

Ross, D. B. and G. Grinstein (2001). 'Camp David: An exchange'. *The New York Review of Books*, 20 September.

Roy, S. (1998). *The Palestinian Economy and the Oslo Process: Decline and fragmentation.* Abu Dhabi UAE, The Emirates Center for Strategic Studies and Research.

Rubenberg, C. A. (2001). 'The Clinton Years: U.S. policy toward Israel and Palestine, Part One'. *Information Brief* No.61 (19 January 2001). Washington DC, Center for Policy Analysis on Palestine.

Said, E. W. (2003). 'A Road Map to Where?' *London Review of Books*, 19 June.

Savir, U. (1998). *The Process: 1,100 days that changed the Middle East.* New York NY, Random House.

Schanzer, J. (2003). 'The Challenge of Hamas to Fatah'. *The Middle East Quarterly* Vol.X No.2 (Spring 2003).

Schelling, T. C. (1991). 'What purposes can "international terrorism" serve?' *Violence, terrorism and justice.* R. G. Frey and C. W. Morris. New York NY, Cambridge University Press pp.18–32.

Schenker, D. (2000). *Palestinian Democracy and Governance: An appraisal of the Legislative Council.* Washington DC, The Washington Institute for Near East Policy.

Sciolino, E. and Tyler, P. E. (2001). 'Saudi Charges Bush with Failure to Broker Mideast Peace'. *The New York Times*, 9 November.

Seale, P. and L. Butler (1996). 'Asad's Regional Strategy and the Challenge from Netanyahu'. *Journal of Palestine Studies* Vol.XXVI No.1 (Autumn 1996). pp.27–41.

Segev, S. (1998). *Crossing the Jordan: Israel's hard road to peace.* New York NY, St Martin's Press.

Sharabi, H. (1998). *The Palestinians: Fifty years later.* Washington DC, The Center for Policy Analysis on Palestine.

Sheehan, E. R. F. (2003). 'The Map and the Fence'. *The New York Review of Books*, 3 July.

Shikaki, K. (1996). 'The Palestinian Elections: An assessment'. *Journal of Palestine Studies* Vol.XXV No.3 (Spring 1996) pp.17–22.

Shlaim, A. (2000). *The Iron Wall: Israel and the Arab world.* London UK, Penguin Books.

Shultz, G. P. (1988/1998). 'The Shultz Plan – February 1988' *The Middle East and North Africa 1999.* London UK, Europa Publications Limited p.125.

Sid-Ahmed, M. (1999). '2000: The year of settlement'. Letter from Cairo No.359. *Al Ahram Weekly,* 19–22 December.

Silver, M. L. *Functionalist Theory*. Hempstead NY, Hofstra University. http://people.hofstra.edu/faculty/Marc_L_Silver/S%20185/Functionlisttheory.htm, accessed 22 January 2003.

Simon, H. A. (1957 (2nd edit.)). *Administrative Behaviour: A study of decision-making processes in administrative organization.* New York NY, The Macmillan Company.

Slater, J. (2001). 'What Went Wrong? The collapse of the Israeli–Palestinian peace process'. *Political Science Quarterly* Vol.116 No.2 pp.171–199.
Slater, J. (2002). 'Lost Opportunities for Peace in the Arab–Israeli Conflict: Israel and Syria, 1948–2001'. *International Security* Vol.27 No.1 pp.79–106.
Smith, T. (1994). *America's Mission: The United States and the worldwide struggle for democracy in the twentieth century*. Princeton NJ, Princeton University Press.
Sontag, D. (2000a). 'Rabin Vowed to Pull Back from Golan, Barak Says' 28 February. http://partners.nytimes.com/library/world/mideast/022800israel-syria.html, accessed 16 October 2006.
Sontag, D. (2000b). 'Israeli Bill May Hobble Barak Efforts with Syria' 2 March. http//select.nytimes.com/gst/abstract.html?res=F7071EFF355D0C718CDDAA0894D8404482&n=Top%2fReference%2fTimes%20Topics%2fPeople%2fS%2fSontag%2c%20Deborah, accessed 16 October 2006.
Sontag, D. (2001). 'Quest for Middle East Peace: How and why it failed'. *Journal of Palestine Studies* Vol.XXXI No.1 (Autumn 2001) pp.75–85.
Stein, J. G. (1989). *Getting to the Table: The processes of international prenegotiation*. Baltimore MD, The Johns Hopkins University Press.
Strindberg, A. (2003). 'Syria's Palestinians under Fire'. *Middle East International* No.707 (22 August) pp.27–29.
Suskind, R. (2004). *The Price of Loyalty: George W. Bush, the White House, and the education of Paul O'Neill.* New York NY, Simon & Schuster.
Swisher, C. E. (2004). *The Truth About Camp David: The untold story about the collapse of the Middle East peace process.* New York NY, Nation Books.
The Sydney Morning Herald (2003). 'It's the Security Fence or Loans, US tells Israel' 6 August.
Tessler, M. (1994). *A History of the Israeli-Palestinian Conflict*. Bloomington IN, Indiana University Press.
United Nations. *Yearbook of the United Nations 1990–1997*, Vols 44–51. United Nations NY.
United Nations (1997). *Draft Resolution in the United Nations Security Council.* Document S/1997/199.
United Nations (2002). *Report of the Secretary-General Prepared Pursuant to General Assembly Resolution ES-10/10.*
United Nations (2003a). *New Wall Projections*. United Nations NY, UN Office for the Coordination of Humanitarian Affairs.
United Nations (2003b). *Question of the Violation of Human Rights in the Occupied Arab Territories, Including Palestine.* Document E/CN.4/2004/6.
United Nations (2004a). 'Security Council Fails to Adopt Resolution Condemning Killing of Hamas Leader'. *Press Release* SC/8039.
United Nations (2004b). General Assembly Emergency Session Overwhelming Demands Israel's Compliance with International Court of Justice Advisory Opinion. *Press Release* GA/10248.

United Nations (2006). *Statement by the President of the Security Council*, 29 March. Document S/PRST/2006/15.

United States Department of State (1978). Israeli Settlements in the Occupied Territories. *Digest of United States Practice in International Law*. Washington DC, US Department of State, Office of the Legal Adviser.

United States Department of State (1999). *The Sharm el-Sheikh Memorandum on Implementation Timeline of Outstanding Commitments of Agreements Signed and the Resumption of Permanent Status Negotiations*, 4 September. Washington DC, US Department of State. www.state.gov/p/nea/rls/22696.htm, accessed 11 October 2006.

United States Department of State (2001). *Daily Press Briefing*, 17 April. Washington DC, US Department of State.

United States Department of State (2002). *U.S. National Security Strategy: Overview of America's international strategy*. Washington DC, US Department of State.

United States Department of State (2003). *Patterns of Global Terrorism 2002*. Washington DC, US Department of State.

United States Department of State (2005). *Background Note: Syria*. Washington DC, US Department of State, Bureau of Near Eastern Affairs.

United States Information Agency (2002). *What is Public Diplomacy?* Washington DC, US Information Agency.

Usher, G. (1996). 'The Politics of Internal Security: The PA's new intelligence services'. *Journal of Palestine Studies* Vol.XXV No.2 (Winter 1996) pp.21–34.

Waage, H. H. (2002). 'Explaining the Oslo Backchannel: Norway's political past in the Middle East'. *The Middle East Journal* Vol.56 No.4 (Autumn 2002) pp.597–615.

Wagner, D. E. (2001). *Dying in the Land of Promise: Palestine and Palestinian Christianity from Pentecost to 2000*. London UK, Melisende.

Walker, T. and A. Gowers (2003 (rev. edit.)). *Arafat: The biography*. London UK, Virgin Books.

Waltz, K. N. (1979). *Theory of International Politics*. New York NY, Random House.

Waltz, K. N. (2002). The Continuity of International Politics. *Worlds in Collision: Terror and the future of global order*. K. Booth and T. Dunne. Basingstoke UK, Palgrave Macmillan pp.348–353.

Washington File (2003). *U.S. Expects Israeli Government to Accept Road Map*, 23 May. www.globalsecurity.org/military/library/news/2003/05/mil-030523-usia04.htm, accessed 11 October 2006.

Watson, A. (1982). *Diplomacy: The dialogue between states*. London UK, Eyre Methuen Ltd.

Webster, S. (1999). *President Bill Clinton's Foreign Policy: A critical assessment*, 7 May. College Park MD, University of Maryland, The James MacGregor Burns Academy of Leadership.

Wye River Memorandum, 23 October 1998. www.arabicnews.com/ansub/ Daily/ Day/981024/1998102453.html, accessed 11 October 2006.

Zartman, I. W. (1989). Prenegotiation: Phases and functions. *Getting to the Table: The processes of international prenegotiation*. J. G. Stein. Baltimore MD, The Johns Hopkins University Press. pp.1–17.
Zogby, J. A. (2004). *The Arab American Vote in the November 2000 Election*. Washington DC, Arab American Institute.
Zunes, S. (2000). 'Israeli Occupation of Lebanon and the Formation of Hezbollah'. *Information Brief* No.46 (1 September 2000). Washington DC, Center for Policy Analysis on Palestine.

Index